Ernest R. (Ernest Richard) Suffling

The Land of the Broads

A Pratical and Illustrated Guide to the Extensive but Little-known District...

Ernest R. (Ernest Richard) Suffling

The Land of the Broads
A Pratical and Illustrated Guide to the Extensive but Little-known District...

ISBN/EAN: 9783744777995

Printed in Europe, USA, Canada, Australia, Japan

Cover: Foto ©Andreas Hilbeck / pixelio.de

More available books at **www.hansebooks.com**

THE
LAND OF THE BROADS.

, *A Practical and Illustrated Guide to the*
Extensive but little-known District of the Broads of
Norfolk and Suffolk.

Written for the use of all who take an interest in one of the Quaintest and
most Old-World parts of England, either from an Archæological,
Historical, Picturesque, or Sporting point of view.

BY

ERNEST R. SUFFLING.

ILLUSTRATED EDITION.
WITH LARGE COLOURED MAP.

LONDON :
L. UPCOTT GILL, 170, STRAND, W.C.
1887.

LONDON:
PRINTED BY A. BRADLEY, 170, STRAND, W.C.

PREFACE TO FIRST EDITION.

WHILE inditing the following pages, I have borne in mind the well-known quotation from our great poet:—

> To gild refinèd gold, to paint the lily,
> To throw a perfume on the violet, ...
> Is wasteful and ridiculous excess.
> —KING JOHN;

which I consider a most appropriate motto to remember while writing upon the Rivers and Broads of Norfolk: The glorious summer sun does all the gilding, and Nature all the painting and, perfuming that is requisite, without any aid from my pen. I have, therefore, simply shown the Broads as they really are, without any endeavour to extol their varied beauties, or to add charms of imagination, when they may be discovered in reality by a brief visit.

It has been my endeavour to take the reader over the principal navigable portions of the " Three Rivers "—the Bure, the Waveney, and the Yare—

and upon all the Broads of any extent or importance; and, *en passant*, I have glanced at the various objects of importance on each bank. Pains have been taken to point out the chief ecclesiastical features, as in this respect Norfolk is peculiarly endowed. Having aimed solely at producing a plain, unvarnished guide, I trust that my effort may prove successful.

Inaccuracies will occasionally creep in, despite one's utmost care, and should my readers discover any, I shall esteem it a favour if they will point them out to me.

ERNEST R. SUFFLING.

Blomfield Lodge, Portsdown Road,
London, W.,
July, 1885.

PREFACE TO SECOND EDITION.

THE rapid sale of the First and Unillustrated Edition has encouraged me to devote more time to the compilation of this Second, and Illustrated, Edition of the "Land of the Broads." It now appears more than trebled in size, and, I trust, in interest, as I have aimed at keeping up its character of a practical guide. The whole work has been re-written, and a larger tour of the district taken, embracing some fifty miles more of rivers, and many more villages.

The Illustrations are truthful representations of places and things seen in the Broad District, as they were, with a few exceptions, either ˙ sketched or photographed on the spot. Chapters have been added on the City of Norwich ; others describing the Fish and their mode of capture ; the Dialect and Characteristics of the Natives; the Broads at various Seasons, and a great deal more—all of a practical nature. By letting my pen run free with anecdotes, songs of the fens, local tales, and traditions, I might have made the present volume a very substantial tome, but have refrained from doing so, as these things, although extremely interesting, are not, perhaps, what my worthy publisher desires—"a practical guide only."

The Map may be thoroughly relied upon. Small parties who, dispensing with the aid of a man, are desirous of themselves navigating the 300 miles of navigable rivers in the district, will find it indispensable, every village, bridge, stream, Broad, or spot worth mention, being clearly shown upon it.

As in the First Edition, I will ask readers who may find any inaccuracies to be kind enough to point them out to me, as it is only by these little blunders being noticed that a perfectly accurate guide can be obtained. Although a Norfolk man, and a native of the Broad district, it is impossible to be infallible in everything appertaining to this large tract of country. Only one or two errors have been pointed out in the First Edition, and these have now been corrected.

ERNEST R. SUFFLING.

Blomfield Lodge, Portsdown Road,
London, W.,
May, 1887.

CONTENTS.

CHAP.   PAGE

I. INTRODUCTORY   1

II. PREPARATIONS FOR THE TRIP . . . 11

III. YARMOUTH TO LOWESTOFT . . . 24

IV. LOWESTOFT TO NORWICH .   49

V. A RAMBLE THROUGH NORWICH .   69

VI. NORWICH TO YARMOUTH .   97

VII. UP THE BURE TO ACLE BRIDGE. .   112

VIII. ACLE TO AYLSHAM 120

IX. UP THE ANT, TO BARTON AND STALHAM BROADS 150

X. THE ANT, TO NORTH WALSHAM AND CROMER . 177

XI. THURNE MOUTH, TO HICKLING, MARTHAM, &c. 193

XII. COMMISSARIAT DEPÔTS. . . 205

XIII. THE BROAD DISTRICT IN SPRING . . . 209

XIV. THE BROAD DISTRICT IN SUMMER . . 218

XV. THE BROAD DISTRICT IN AUTUMN 225

XVI. THE BROAD DISTRICT IN WINTER . . 231

XVII. THE CHARACTERISTICS AND DIALECT OF EAST NORFOLK NATIVES . . . 240

CHAP. PAGE

XVIII. THE FISH OF THE BROADS, AND HOW TO
CATCH THEM 278

XIX. TABLE OF DISTANCES FROM YARMOUTH BRIDGE 310

XX. TABLE OF TIDES, &c. . . . 314

XXI. TABLE OF CARRIERS FROM YARMOUTH . 315

THE LAND OF THE BROADS.

CHAPTER I.

INTRODUCTORY.

TRIANGLE, having the coast for its base (Lowestoft at the left, and Palling at the right angle), with Norwich at its apex, will contain nearly the whole of the Broad district, with its 5000 acres of lakes and Broads, and 200 miles of navigable river. In these, say, 250 square miles, may be found, during a holiday trip, delightful occupation for seekers of "fresh scenes and pastures new." For the angler, such sport awaits him as he cannot obtain elsewhere, as the takes of fish, at certain times and places, are simply extraordinary, especially of the coarser kinds of fish, such as bream, pike, &c. He may choose for his fishing-ground water either deep or fleet, running or still, clear or obscured, with the assurance that he will not go away either empty-handed or disappointed.

B

For the yachtsman—Where in England can he find greater scope for his hobby than on these splendid stretches of water? He may take his choice from almost every rig conceivable—cutter, yawl, lugger, Bermudan, schooner, or lateen ; and for sailing-masters the wherry-men cannot be excelled—so that, for those who wish to learn to sail a boat, a capital opportunity offers. For a study of quaintness, both in language and ideas, and also in manners, the wherryman may be interviewed with profit.

The artist may find anywhere, everywhere, pictures ready for his canvas, of scenery that is peculiar to Norfolk. There is no need to go to Holland for a sketching-ground, for here it is within four hours of London. Here are the flat, green plains, with the river simply kept within bounds by its banks, and being in many places 2ft. above the field through which it winds. Here are the windmills and wherries, the red and white cattle, and picturesque peasantry, simply waiting to be transferred to canvas. Where out of Holland can a more Flemish scene be found than the tree-planted Quay at Yarmouth?

To the archæologist and searcher into things ecclesiastic, there are no end of churches, priories, castles, halls, and old buildings, which will afford him a vast fund of delightful research. The architect should not, therefore, neglect to bring his sketch-book with him, for he may take it back full of odd fancies and curiosities of ages long gone by.

To the entomologist, ornithologist, and botanist, I

would say, "By all means take your holiday here, for you may bring back with you specimens wherewith to beguile many a long winter's evening with your favourite pursuit. For butterflies, birds, and plants, this is a perfect El Dorado."

To the poet, this is a land of——. But there! I will leave him to see for himself. The beautiful, secluded scenery will supply him with themes galore for his fanciful imagination.

For the robust man, the Broad district is a paradise ; and to the weakly, here is a physician in the balmy and pure atmosphere, by which he may become in a short time quite strong again, and return home, at the conclusion of his holiday, with such increased vigour as to make his butcher and baker rejoice at the abnormal increase in his appetite.

The general tourist, who is nothing in particular, may while away the longest summer day in perfect happiness, and at small cost, for very little money can be spent by the most extravagant, as many of the villages possess only a single shop, which, however, seems to contain everything, from a pickaxe to a rasher of rusty bacon.

Now, after this long flight, let us descend to a few dry, tangible facts regarding the district.

The climate of Norfolk is exceedingly dry ; in fact, the rainfall per annum does not exceed 24in., whereas the average for the whole of England is about 36in. In Cumberland and Westmoreland the annual fall exceeds 70in. On the score of dryness overhead, therefore, the tourist has nothing to fear ; for, although all is water beneath, very little moisture comes from the clouds above, in comparison to other holiday resorts in Great Britain. This is, I believe, partly on account of the flatness of the county, and partly by reason of its extreme eastern position, many of the rain-clouds having exhausted themselves while travelling from the West of England, before reaching Norfolk. Storms and tempests occur rather oftener than in less level districts, and are very violent, but usually of short duration.

The rabbit is an object of considerable importance here, as, from their great numbers on the warrens, there is a large trade done with the London market. Some of these warrens are of large extent, and teeming with these pretty but destructive little animals. The principal warrens in the district are at Horsey and Winterton on the coast. Among the birds, several rare and curious species are to be found. The long-winged owl, the most destructive of his tribe, and that singular species of the sandpiper, *Tringa pugnax*, are still to be seen ; the male birds are called ruffs, and the females reeves.

The churches of this county are worthy of especial attention, many of them being exceedingly old, dating as far back as the twelfth century. To the student of the various styles of architecture there is an ample field for exploration, as the different churches will take him from the twelfth, through the thirteenth, fourteenth, and fifteenth centuries—just the period when ecclesiastical architecture was at its best. Some fine sculptured tombs with recumbent figures will be found, as also many splendid examples of wood-carving, numbers of churches still retaining their ancient oak chancel-screens and stalls of intricate carved work. Relics of all kinds may be met with— curious coffins, weapons that have been dug up, hour-glasses, ancient books, wall paintings, keys, &c. It is also remarkable that many of the registers, still in a good state of preservation, date as far back as A.D. 1500, or nearly 400 years.

I would particularly call attention to the Round Towers to be found in several parishes, and which are ascribed to the Saxon or Danish period: many of them were, after the Norman Conquest, sur-mounted by an octagonal upper storey. Most of the Norfolk churches are constructed of flint, as very little building stone is found in the county, except in the western division.

Many brasses will be found in the churches, to which access may be obtained, and a rubbing taken. All that is required in the shape of materials is a large sheet of rather thin white paper and a piece of heel-ball, which may be purchased at any bootmaker's shop. Simply fasten the paper over the brass, with pins, which should be stuck in the crack between the edge of the plate and the stone surrounding; then rub the heel-ball gently over the surface, when the impression will appear in black and white on the paper. A roll of "lining paper," 12yds. long

and 22in. wide, may be purchased at any paper-
hanger's shop in town, for about eightpence, and is of
just the required thickness for taking perfect rubbings.
Persons fond of epitaph-hunting will be amply repaid by a stroll through some of the churchyards, and
will meet with many exceedingly queer and quaint
verses. A good plan is to inquire of the sexton
or his wife—who usually reside very close to the
churches under their care—what of note is to be
seen in the church or its burial-ground. The sexton
of Martham Church has some printed cards with the
inscription from the grave of a person buried there,
which I believe is the record of a sad event which
took place many years since through the accidental
marriage of very close relations—mother and son. It
reads as follows :—

Here Lyeth yᵉ Body of
Christopher Burrancy
Who departed this life
yᵉ 18 day of October
Anno Domini 1730
Aged 59 years

And thus lyes Alice
Who by her life
Was my sister, my mistress
My mother & my wife
Died
Febr yᵉ 12. 1729.

The son was sent to Australia when very young ;
came back to Yarmouth, and, hearing that a man
was required to work on a farm at Martham, obtained
the situation, and, after a few years, married the lady

proprietor. Years after, a birthmark was the means of discovering the relationship. The mother died raving mad, and was quickly followed by her son.*

Prehistoric remains are continually coming to light, especially along the coast, and these either go to enrich the collections of private persons, or are added to the already large store of them at the public museum, Norwich. Of animal remains, may be noted, bones of those gigantic mammals, the mastodon (*Arvancusis*), *Elephas meridionalis*, and *Elephas antiquus*; as also of the rhinoceros, hippopotamus, red and roe deer, stag, wild ox, and even of the beaver. In nearly every part of the county, discoveries have been made connected with the Stone Age. The earlier portion of that age, called the Palæolithic period, is represented by instruments of chipped stone of various shapes and sizes, usually of an oval or pointed form. These implements bear no sign of polishing, or other attempt at smoothness of surface. Those of a later period, called the Neolithic Stone Age, show evident signs of rubbing and polishing in order to give them more symmetry and keenness.

A favourable time for relic-hunting is immediately after a strong north-west gale. When the wind is in that quarter, with a heavy sea on, masses of the cliff are undermined, and huge pieces, falling upon the beach, are swept away by the surf. This fall of the face of the cliff frequently leaves relics of various

---

* I find the stone has been removed to the tower, and is covered by the organ.

kinds exposed to view; and persons of keen eyesight and great perseverance have occasionally made very valuable discoveries in consequence.

Barrows and tumuli are to be seen near Attleborough, Weeting, Sporle, Pentney, North Walsham, and other places. A barrow at a place called "Grimes' Graves," Weeting, was opened by Canon Greenwell in 1870, and some ancient tools, made of deerhorn, discovered. The Canon says : " It was a most impressive sight, and one never to be forgotten, to look, it may be after a lapse of 3000 years, upon a piece of work yet unfinished, with the tools of the workmen still lying as they had been left many centuries before." Some of these implements — picks, &c. — still retained upon their chalky incrustation the exact impressions of the fingers of these Ancient Britons.

When trawling along the coast, the fishermen frequently bring up in their nets the fossilised remains of large mammals; of these, the late Rev. Jas. Layton formed a very fine collection, which may be seen at the British Museum.

The villages will be found very much scattered, and only here and there will a fair-sized town be found. I think that, excepting Norwich, Yarmouth, and King's Lynn, no other town of 5000 inhabitants is to be met with in the whole county. Indeed, the towns containing 3000 inhabitants may be counted on the fingers of the two hands. The county, in 1881, contained 444,749 persons, spread over 1,356,173 acres, giving just three acres to each individual—a very sparse population indeed. Contrast this with Lancashire and its 1,208,154 acres and 3,454,541 inhabitants, or three persons to each acre. On the score of quietness the tourist may, therefore, make his mind easy, as he will be "far from the madding crowd."

I would like to point out to the etymologist that, if he keeps his ears open when talking with the country people, he will hear many pure Saxon words used, which are quite obsolete among town folk or educated persons. Thus, a gift is a "largesse," a housecloth a "dwile," to raise a thing is to "hain" it, a lane is a "loke," an unmarried girl is a "mawther," and a "dickey," although it has a melodious voice, is not a bird—it is a donkey.

The "natives" are a fine race, usually with the flaxen or tawny beards, fair skin, straight noses, and blue eyes characteristic of the Norse or Danish type. They are noted for their hardihood and endurance, most of them leading a life that compels them to be in the pure, bracing air a great part of their time, as they are mostly either agricultural or seafaring men. A walk along the quay or fish-market in Yarmouth will show what a number of tall, powerful men are to be found among the East Anglian fishermen—all bone and muscle, with shoulders as broad as those of Hercules. The ports of Yarmouth and Lowestoft are used by upwards of 10,000 fishermen, most of them hardy Norfolk men, the greater proportion of whom could be, in time of war, turned into men-o'-war's men at very short notice. These men have, times without number, performed such heroic and daring deeds that, like Marshal Ney, they have earned for themselves the distinction of being known as " the bravest of the brave." Not a winter passes but some startling deed of "derring do" is performed by these men during the gales.

Having taken a brief glance at the characteristics of the county, its climate, and its inhabitants, we will now make a closer acquaintance with the purport of our pilgrimage—the Broads.

CHAPTER II.

PREPARATIONS FOR THE TRIP.

A grassy mead, with leafy shade—
Our bark rocks near the brink.
Hampers ashore, and cloth arrayed ;
Come, sit, and feast, and drink.
Pass each platter,
'Mid much clatter,
Joke and banter,
Noise and chatter,
Singing, laughter gay and hearty :
Won't you join our Water Party ?

E will now proceed to business, which with us is synonymous with pleasure, and see how we are to set about enjoying our holiday.

In the first place, we will suppose we have arrived at Yarmouth from London, Birmingham, or some other large city, and, as our time is limited, wish to commence our journey without delay. The Broads cannot well be visited in less than a fortnight, and it would be as well to make our holiday of that duration ; but those who can spare a longer period will find quite enough wherewith to occupy themselves.

Our first care will be to select a craft of suitable
size for the number of our party. If the company
is composed of four gentlemen, a sailing boat of
about 25ft. in length and 8ft. beam, with cabin
amidships, will be found most comfortable. If a
larger party, of, say, a dozen (including several
ladies), can be made up, then a wherry would

A NORFOLK WHERRY.

be the most suitable craft. This is a local production, built somewhat like a sailing barge, carrying one immense sail, and usually managed by a
man and a boy. The wherry took the place, early
in the century, of the old-fashioned "keel," whose
mast was stepped nearly amidships, unlike the

wherry's mast, which is placed within a few feet of the bows. Beware of getting in the way of these immense winged leviathans, for, as they come roaring along with a good wind on the quarters, they would annihilate any small craft that came in their way. A wherry is divided into three compartments —viz., bedroom, saloon, and kitchen. The bedroom and saloon are under one roof, and occupy nearly two-thirds of the length of the vessel. The fore-part, or bows, is left clear as a promenade deck; then comes the ladies' bedroom, occupying the whole width of the craft (some 10ft.), and about 10ft. of its length; next this is the saloon, 20ft. long, nicely carpeted and painted, &c., with a large dining-table in the centre, and, at the after end, the crowning glory—a piano. After dark, with the lamps lighted, and the merry party gathered around this instrument, many a happy hour is passed away; and, as the Licensing Act does not hold sway here, I am afraid that the small hours often arrive ere the saloon is closed, and "sleep, Nature's sweet restorer," brings silence and rest to the *voyageurs* "rocked in the cradle of the deep." I might add, that the pianoforte is not always by Broadwood or Cramer, but is still a very acceptable, and often very fair, instrument.

Next the saloon, with a serving-door leading into it, is the kitchen, fitted with a neat American range, which is presided over by the skipper, who, besides being sailing-master, is also cook and steward.

The dirty work is performed by the "crew"—a lad of sixteen or seventeen years of age. All washing-up, potato-peeling, fish-cleaning, &c., falls to his lot.

For parties of two or three there are plenty of smaller boats; but I would recommend at least four to go together, as, besides being more economical, everything is then more enjoyable than when there are too few.

Ladies on small yachts I consider out of place. Pardon me, fair readers, and allow me to explain. In the first place, the sleeping accommodation is very limited—so limited, indeed, that one cabin has to accommodate, say, four persons; therefore, unless the party consists entirely of ladies, they are better absent altogether. On the large wherries, a special cabin is partitioned off for the use of ladies, so that they secure both privacy and comfort, without which the holiday would be most unenjoyable. Again, the amount of "roughing it"—to men a source of great delight—would, to ladies unused to it, prove intolerably uncomfortable.

The sleeping accommodation is very comfortable, but of course the luxuries of town life must not be looked for. A flock mattress (which in the daytime forms a kind of locker-couch), a bolster, and two blankets, are provided for each person, and nothing further during summer time, is really required. Sleep usually falls upon one directly the lamp is extinguished (after the first night), thanks to the fatigues of a long, enjoyable day. The first night is usually very strange to those unaccustomed to sleep in a yacht—the continuous plash of the water against the sides of the vessel, the soughing of the wind among the reeds, the cry of different birds, the assorted snores of friends, and other unique sounds, together with the novelty of sleeping in a berth, tend to keep one awake wondering for a long period.

"What is the cost?" you ask. Well, for a boat to accommodate two persons, without a man, the cost would be about 30s. per week, including crockery, cooking apparatus, and bedding. A decked cutter to accommodate four or five, with a man, and every convenience for cooking and sleeping, could be procured for about £4 per week. A wherry to carry a dozen, with crew, &c., would cost from £12 to £14 per week, or, say, from 20s. to 25s. per head per week. This will be found much more economical than occupying even ordinary apartments at a fashionable watering-place. The following is a list of prices per week for typical yachts and their crews. The names are fanciful ones:—

Name.	Size.	Accommo- dation.	Charge per Week.	Crew.
*Tower of Babel	30 Tons	12 Persons	£10 to £12	£2 10 0—2 men
Empress	14 ,,	8 ,,	£ 10 0	2 5 0—1 man and lad
Happy Medium	12 ,,	6 .,	4 10 0	2 0 0—1 ,, and boy
My Delight ..	8 ,,	4 ,,	4 0 0	1 5 0—1 ,,
Jack o' Lantern	4 ,,	2 ,,	2 5 0	1 5 0—1 ,,

* A wherry.

Perhaps, as many of my readers are strangers to the Broads, I had better mention the places where boats may be most easily procured. Mutford, Yarmouth, Brundall, Norwich, and Wroxham, on the navigable waters, are all likely places ; while, for the land-locked Broads of Ormsby, Rollesby, and Filby, boats may be had at the Eel's Foot, Ormsby, and at other places, which will readily be pointed out to the visitor inquiring for them. Visitors to Fritton Decoy will find boats at their service at Fritton Hall, one mile from St. Olave's Station. Both rowing and sailing boats may be obtained. They are the ordinary open boats, as there is no means of getting large yachts there by water.

When hiring a yacht, it is well to have a written agreement, in order to avoid any subsequent misunderstanding. These agreements are usually in the following form* :—

MEMORANDUM OF AGREEMENT for the Hire of Yacht [*Hirondelle*] between [*Henry Imer Fenman*], owner, of the one part, and [*Adolphus Caller Steward*], hirer, of the other part. The said Owner agrees to let, and the said hirer agrees to take, the Yacht [*Hirondelle*] from the [*27th July*, 1886], for [*three weeks*], at the rate [*of Five Pounds per week*], which includes one man (namely, the navigator's wages). The hirer finds all consumable stores, and agrees to Insure Yacht against any damage done, up to [*Ten Pounds*], paying [*Five Shillings per week*] for the same [*or Seven Shillings and Sixpence per week for damage up to Twenty Pounds*]. The said Yacht [*Hirondelle*] to be delivered back in good condition as when received to [*The Cherry Inn, Calthorpe Broad*], including Cabin inventory (fair wear and tear

---

* The words printed in brackets represent the portion to be filled in by individual *hirers*, according to terms procurable.

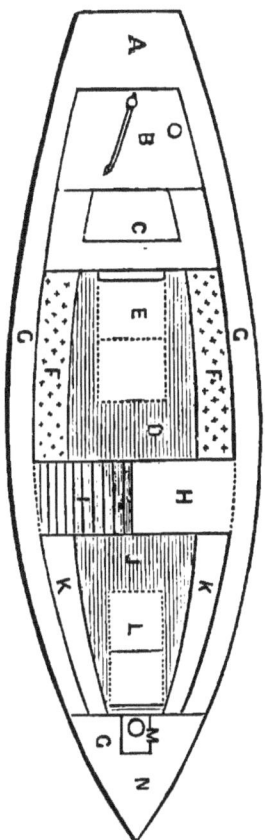

PLAN.

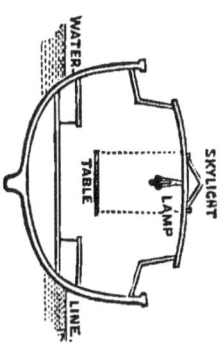

SECTION THROUGH AFTER CABIN.

NORFOLK BROAD CRUISING YACHT.

I here give an illustration of the type of craft in use for pleasure parties on the Broads. Scale, ⅜in. to 1ft.: 32ft. long, 9½ft. beam. For hire at £6 per week, including man. Will carry six persons (two ladies and four gentlemen). Is one of the most comfortable boats in Norfolk, and can go anywhere, as her draft aft is only 2ft. 3in.

A, Counter. B, Stern Sheets, used for cooking in calm weather. C, Man's Cabin, and used for Kitchen in windy or wet weather; Man sleeps athwart ship. D, Chief Cabin; spring seats, lockers under and at side; table folds to after bulkhead. E, Table extended for dining. F, Spring Seats, for Beds at night; they extend under Deck G, and are 2ft. wide. G, Deck. H, Lavatory, with water laid on, and W.C. I, Companion Stairs to deck. J, Fore Cabin for gentlemen; will sleep four. K, Locker Seats, with extra hinged flap for sleeping accommodation. L, Folding Table, to button against forward bulkhead. M, Mast and Tabernacle. N, Fore Peak, for stores and spare gear.

excepted). If not returned as above Agreement, the Hirer to pay any loss
sustained by Owner.

Half hire money paid as deposit, when engaging the Yacht; balance
before sailing.

> *Witness to the Signature* [JACOB DEADEYE,]
>   [*Navigator of Hirondelle.*]

Instead of paying the balance of hire before sailing,
it will be best to keep it in hand until the agreement
has been properly fulfilled on the part of the owner,
or his representative waterman, and the trip is concluded. By so doing, you retain the power of compelling the man to do your bidding, and insure the
contract being carried out according to your wishes.
If the man behaves well—and, as a rule, these men
are very obliging and pleasant—it is usual to give
him a present at parting ; indeed, some of these men
are so poorly paid by the owners that they rely upon
donations from the parties engaging them to make
up their salaries.

The idea of insurance is quite a new feature, and
is only adopted by a few of the owners. It is, however, a capital plan to thus insure, as, for the small
sum of 5s. per week, you are free from liability connected with any accidents which may take place aboard,
or to the yacht, up to the amount of £10. Frequently,
with amateurs, oars are broken, glass skylights demolished, gear lost overboard, crockery broken or left
behind, &c., the expenses of which mishaps may be
covered by this insurance plan. At the same time, it
would be very wrong to be careless of the yacht and
its belongings merely because of this exemption from

C

payment; and it is as well to know that culpable and deliberate negligence is punished by compelling the delinquent to make good the damage in full.

Victualling next claims our attention. "What provisions shall we take?" is always asked before commencing a trip, and I will endeavour to answer this question fully, as a great deal of the enjoyment of a cruise depends upon the commissariat.

Foremost on the list comes bread; this can usually be procured at the villages on the route, say, every second day; but as at times it is not procurable, a supply of biscuits should be taken. Biscuits suggest jam and marmalade.

As these trips are mostly undertaken during the summer months, tinned food is consumed to a large extent, as fresh meat and other perishable articles soon become tainted in the confined and hot lockers. It may be as well to point out that a good supply of ice may be procured at Yarmouth from the Icehouse on the Quay (where it is sold for preserving the fresh fish), and, although more out of the direct line of sailing, at Lowestoft.

The supply of fresh meat cannot be relied upon, as few of the villages can boast of a butcher's shop; and in those that do, no animal is killed until enough orders have been given to insure the sale of the whole carcase. Tinned meats are always handy, and, being already cooked, can be warmed at a few minutes' notice; a few onions and potatoes added make a capital stew. Curried rabbit, ox-cheek, tongue, spiced beef, boiled and roast mutton, kidneys, hare-soup, lobster, salmon, &c., are all nice, and a selection, according to taste, may be taken. If you can obtain a piece of boiled salt beef at starting, it will last several days, if kept in a cool place, and form a *pièce de résistance.* Tinned mutton, stewed with rice, makes an excellent dish, and one that is quickly and easily cooked.

Butter should be kept in a wide-mouthed jar. Cheese, according to taste; but remember that Norfolk is noted for bad cheese, so beware! A good supply of onions and potatoes should be taken; of the latter, about 1lb. per day per head. A bottle of anchovy sauce, for eating with the fresh-water fish captured, will be necessary; also, if procurable, a bunch of sweet herbs and some parsley. A jar of pickles; sugar, salt, and pepper, all in bottles. To these may be added any little delicacies which the *voyageur* may care for. Fruit, either fresh or preserved, is a nice relish. Try a tinned pineapple, and you will, probably, like it as well as the article *au naturel.* I have merely mentioned the necessary articles, but each individual must vary the list according to his taste.

Don't forget the matches! and a candle or two; also a pound or two of soap. Tobacco and cigars must also be taken; the tobacco may be procured at the village shops, but only those who are used to strong kinds will esteem it. Cigars which are smokable are not to be had at all.

Cooking utensils are always provided, as also crockery, knives, forks, towels, &c., so no thought need be given to these.

What shall we drink? Here I would advise the reader to supply himself according to his own taste, as opinions on the drink question vary so widely. Tea tightly corked in a bottle, and coffee and cocoa in tins, are generally necessary. Tinned milk may be taken, and fresh milk may be obtained at most, but not at all, villages ; when a supply is procured, bottle some of it for future use. If spirits are needed, it is best to take a supply, as the quality of those obtained at the inns is of a "fiery, untamed" order, with the exception of Hollands, which at some places is very fair. Beer, of the peculiar sweet flavour in vogue in Norfolk, but, nevertheless, pure and wholesome, may be had anywhere. Some of the inns keep an old ale in stock, called "Old Tom." It is exceedingly intoxicating, and costs one shilling per quart. A bottle of Rose's Lime Juice Cordial may be added to the cellar, also syrups of any kind, especially raspberry, and lemonade and ginger-beer. The water for cooking is usually taken from the river, when it is clear, and that for drinking purposes is procured from the cottage wells on the route.

For gentlemen's dress, there is nothing like white flannel, with polo or straw hats. A thin macintosh, for wet weather, is very handy ; also a good warm overcoat for night work, as, even in the height of summer, the nights are often chilly. A pair of easy shoes, and a pair of watertight boots, will be required for fishing from the bank in boggy places. For ladies' dress (I will say little here, or I shall get out of my latitude), nothing can compare with navy serge made up in a very plain manner, so as to present as few folds as possible for boughs of trees, oars, &c., to catch in. A little bright colour in the trimming, if you please, ladies! and be sure and wear strong, watertight boots in place of dainty, fancy, French shoes.

For the impedimenta in the way of fishing-tackle, &c., I will not advise the reader here. A good book on angling, or his own experience, will probably serve him as well as I can on the subject. Most of the fishing requisites are mentioned in the following ancient verse from Izaak Walton's book :—

> My rod and my line, my float and my lead,
>   My hook and my plummet, my whetstone and knife,
> My basket, my baits both living and dead,
>   My net, and my meat (for that is the chief) :
> Then I must have thread, and hairs green and small,
>   With mine angling purse—and so you have all.

A gun will be found useful, as the shooting on all the rivers, and some of the Broads, is free. Plenty of sport may be had in the early morning and at dusk among the dabchicks, coot, waterhens, pewits, snipe, &c.

I found a cricket-bat of service, as there are some tremendous matches played between the rival villages, which take weeks to arrange, and are played with as much determination as if a battle were being fought.

A stranger who can play fairly well is eagerly enrolled in the team of some belligerent village, and his services are heartily appreciated. A tennis-set is handy, as there are many opportunities afforded for those who indulge in this popular pastime ; plenty of level meadows will be found, where the boats may be moored to the bank and a tennis-court improvised. After being in a boat for a time, exercise on shore will be found very beneficial. A pack of cards and a few books may be taken as a preventive of *ennui* on a wet day, or for use after dark. As we want to see all that can be seen, a pair of field or powerful opera-glasses will be found very useful.

I will add a few lines here on behalf of the farmers and landowners, who are, most of them, very friendly and sociable, and will readily allow those persons constituting water-parties to wander about their meadows and lands, so long as they are content to enjoy themselves in a becoming manner, not detrimental to the land, crops, or cattle. I am sorry to say, however, that of late years numerous complaints have been made as to saplings being pulled up by the roots, and of fences and gates being broken down, for the purpose of making camp fires ; but surely there are plenty of sticks and twigs to be got without damaging private property. Another annoyance is the breaking of bottles over the fields. The bottles, when empty, are set up for " cock-shies," and the *débris* is left strewn around ; the cattle or horses then step on pieces and cripple themselves, or lie on them, and are severely wounded. I would suggest that the oldest person in each party should take upon himself the *rôle* of constable, and so put a stop to these foolish proceedings.

CHAPTER III.

YARMOUTH TO LOWESTOFT.

Oh, the gallant fisher's life,
    It is the best of any!
'Tis full of pleasure, void of strife,
    And 'tis beloved by many :
        Other joys
        Are but toys;
        Only this
        Lawful is ;
        For our skill
        Breeds no ill,
    But content and pleasure.—Izaak Walton.

AVING given some idea of the boats and outfit required, I will ask the reader to accompany me upon a trip in which I shall endeavour to take him to all the principal Broads and places of interest. It matters little from what town the start is made, whether Yarmouth, Norwich, Wroxham, or Lowestoft, each having its partisans.

On this occasion we will start from Yarmouth, principally because I think it the most convenient place from which to reach any given point quickly,

YARMOUTH, LOOKING SOUTH-EAST.

and also because our little steam yacht happens to be moored in Breydon Water, near the Ale Stores, Bure Mouth. Here she is, the "Lily"—somewhat like a launch in hull, but broader in the beam in proportion to her length. She is 30ft. long and 7ft. 6in. beam. Forward in the peak is a small American cooking-stove; so that the man who drives the engine, which comes next, can keep one eye on the dinner which is preparing, and the other on the machinery. A cabin amidships makes a snug dining and bedroom combined, 9ft. long, 7ft. wide, and 5ft. 9in. high. It contains innumerable lockers for the thousand-and-one articles to be used on the voyage. Long seat-lockers fold down at night, forming ample sleeping accommodation for four persons. Large stern-sheets, with lockers all round, forming seats, fill up the space between the cabin and the stern.

I would point out to my readers, ere we start, that although we are about to undertake the trip in a steam yacht, the journey may be made with equal ease in a sailing vessel. Indeed, most persons would prefer being under sail, so as to obviate the incessant vibration caused by the throbbing of the propeller, and also the unpleasantness of the smoke. Our chief motive for taking the voyage by steam is its quickness. We have but a limited period at our disposal, and shall not, therefore, loiter for any length of time at any particular spot, either to fish or sketch, but merely long enough to note the points of interest.

Those who wish to learn to sail a boat will have

a splendid opportunity of doing so here, as the flaws
of wind may be seen ruffling the water or bending
the reeds before striking the sails, and the amateur
yachtsman will soon learn to make the most of these
" puffs " when a steady breeze is not available. The
various reaches in the rivers will teach him the
science of tacking, which is one of the first and chief
things to be learned on narrow waters. He will like-
wise learn the rules of the river, how to pass other
craft, to know the indications which surely proclaim
a shoal, and the many points of observation and
practice necessary to success as a yachtsman.

To return to our steamer. Catching the first of
the flood, we cast off for a run across Breydon, down
the Waveney to Lowestoft. Being a fine day, with a
nice breeze, the water is alive with yachts of all rigs,
shapes, and sizes, from the tiny lug skiff to the
queenly twenty-ton racing yacht. This is the great
regatta and match-sailing course for the East Coast.
The course is marked by a line of stakes from the
Swing Bridge to the Berney Arms, a distance of four-
and-a-half miles. The quantity of canvas carried by
racing craft is simply enormous, and will at once
attract the notice of our Midland or town friends.
The shooting is free, and sometimes, in severe
weather, capital duck-shooting may be had on these
waters. The area is about 1300 acres, and any part
of it may be traversed, in search of wildfowl, by
using a flat-bottomed punt, which may be hired for a
shilling per day ; this punt is necessary, as the water

is in some parts very fleet, and, as the tide ebbs, large
banks covered with mud are left exposed. Those who
venture upon these banks must first don the mud-
pattens, usually to be found in the boat, and which are
simply flat pieces of board, strapped upon the feet to
prevent the wearer from sinking into the slimy mud.
They are very awkward things at first, and more
care is usually necessary to look after one's self than
the wildfowl; a little practice, however, soon teaches
one to flounder about capitally.

Having gained the western extremity, we find the
mouths of two rivers right ahead; that to the right
is the Yare, from which Yarmouth derives its name,
and leads to Norwich, &c.; that to the left, up
which our way lies, is the Waveney. At the juncture
you may see the skeletons of two or three yachts
which have met with sudden ends by missing stays,
&c., and drifting upon the dreaded Burgh Flats. On
our immediate left, but a short distance inland, are the
remains of the ancient Burgh Castle, which should
not be passed without a visit. The Roman walls of
this castle—for it is at least 1500 years old—are in a
remarkably perfect state. They inclose five-and-a-half
acres of ground, and are of red bricks (which are even
now as hard as when first baked), laid in alternate
layers with the usual flintwork. Being so close to
Yarmouth, it is a great resort for picnic parties.

After viewing these interesting ruins, we again
embark, and, after a run of six or seven miles, arrive
at St. Olave's Bridge, where we again land for a

walk to Fritton Decoy, to my mind one of the finest, if not the most delightful, of the Broads. Walking half-a-mile, we arrive at the junction of two roads ; take the right, and another half-mile brings us to Fritton Old Hall, a most picturesque old manor-house, delightfully situated, and with a very fine garden. Here boats (which, however, are the roughest and most ramshackle things of the kind I ever saw offered for hire) may be procured, from the middle of March to the end of September. During the remaining months the Broad is kept private, so that the decoying of wild ducks may be uninterrupted.

A decoy is a very simple contrivance, made by erecting a series of semicircular hoops, gradually diminishing in size, for some 70yds. or 80yds. The mouth hoop would be perhaps 5yds. across, the next a trifle smaller, and so on, till those at the farther end would be only about 2ft. across. These hoops are covered with wire netting, so that, when the fowl are once in the mouth, they cannot again get out. Under the arches is dug a canal, or channel, also gradually diminishing as the hoops get less; and at the far end is attached a movable tail, or " cod-piece," from which the fowler may take the birds as they are scared to their doom.

It is necessary that the decoy be erected in a secluded spot, as ducks and other aquatic fowl are extremely shy. Fowl come to these waters for two purposes—for retirement, and to seek for food ; after satisfying their hunger, they have a habit of selecting a grassy bank, upon which they congregate and plume their feathers. It is usual, therefore, to provide a nice green bank, near the mouth of the "pipe," as the entrance to the decoy is called, where they fraternise with the decoy ducks belonging there. Presently, when all is quiet, a dog is seen approaching, and, although only a little fox terrier, he is large enough to inspire the fowl with alarm; so they betake themselves to the water, where they feel safer. The decoy ducks, when once in the water, make for the mouth of the pipe, as in the decoy they have been fed daily; but our little friend the terrier takes to the water also, and swims after them until they enter the mouth of. the pipe. When fairly entered, the decoy man, in his boat, suddenly appears from behind a rush screen, where he has been anxiously awaiting the time when he can suddenly dart forth and scare his prey. Directly he appears in the entrance, the wild fowl naturally take wing, and fly in an opposite direction to their persecutor; but this only takes them farther and farther into the toils, till at length they have no room to spread their wings for flight, and are then driven into the tail of the net, whence they are withdrawn by the fowler—the "decoys" to be returned to their grassy patch, and the strangers to receive the "garotte," and repose in the fowler's basket. As many as fifty brace of birds have occasionally thus been caught at one "push," as the drive is technically termed.

The following extract, relating to Fritton Decoy,

from a book printed at the end of the last century,
may be interesting: "Fowl and fish are very plentiful here, the pike and eels being very large. The
duck, mallard, and teal, are in such plenty as is scarce
to be conceived. They are taken in prodigious flocks
at a time, in the decoys. They send these fowl to
London twice a week, on horseback, from Michaelmas
to Lady Day, and one decoy will furnish twenty dozen
or more, twice a week, for the whole season. Two
teal are usually reckoned equal to one duck, and five
duck and twelve teal are accounted a dozen of wild
fowl. The usual market price is about 9s. for such
a dozen."

Fritton Decoy is about two-and-a-half miles long,
and is very deep (in some places 18ft. or 20ft.), and
contains about 200 square acres. It is beautifully
surrounded by woods. Some of the trees are grand
old specimens of gnarled English forest trees, whose
roots stand out of the water like some huge Hydra.
Here is sketching-ground for the artist, indeed, and
the water is fairly teeming with fish for the angler,
as, being private property, it is not so much netted
as some of the Broads have unfortunately been.
Indeed, some twelve or fourteen years since the
Broads were so netted by gangs of poachers that,
had not certain gentlemen of authority put a stop
to it by obtaining an Act of Parliament to prevent
netting and liggering, the water stood in a fair way
of becoming exhausted of fish. The poachers have
at times brought in and sent by train as much as

seven or eight tons of fish, without any attempt at concealment. When the price offered would not pay for carriage, the fish were simply used for manure. It is pleasant to hear that some of the true lovers of angling have hit upon a plan to stop drag-net poaching in the rivers. They watch, and, having discovered who the poacher is, take measures to stop his unlawful proceedings without setting the law's majesty in motion, by taking the law into their own hands, thus: They procure an old barrel, which they stud thickly all over with tenter nails; this is then carried to the river at the spot where the poaching takes place. It is then loaded with stones or brickbats, and dropped into the river-bed. The next time the poacher drags, his net is irredeemably tangled in the "devil," and rendered useless. The heavy expenses incurred in the preservation of the Broads and rivers are defrayed by the voluntary subscriptions of anglers and others; and I would earnestly request all gentlemen who may visit these waters to collect a small amount among themselves, and send it to the Hon. Secretary to the Board of Conservators, Norwich. The Act just mentioned had the effect of breaking up these gangs of poachers, and the stock of fish has again become plentiful. However, even now strict watch requires to be kept, and more funds will give the committee power to exercise greater vigilance.

The fish at Fritton are pike, perch, silver bream, roach, rudd, pope, and eels; the last two named are a perfect pest to the angler, as they spoil the bait, and are worthless when caught.

Visitors to Fritton will do well to take their own provisions, as there is no means of obtaining refreshment there; the nearest inn is about a mile distant.

The church, near the west end of the Decoy, and which is passed by visitors along the road from the river or railway station, contains an old oak screen, besides other things of interest. The register dates from A.D. 1559. The building is very small and unpretentious.

On re-embarking at St. Olave's Bridge, we again shape our course southward, through marsh and meadow-land, containing great numbers of cattle. The wooded Herringfleet Hills are on our left, covered with beautiful heather, and a stroll over them, and the view to be obtained from them, will be found most delightful. Five miles from St. Olave's Bridge we leave the Waveney, and enter Oulton Dyke.

Somerleyton Hall and grounds, the seat of Sir Saville Crossley, are, in the summer months, thrown open to the public, and many Yarmouth and Lowestoft visitors avail themselves of the opportunity of viewing this fine mansion. It is on our left before coming to Oulton Broad. The grounds are noted both for their natural beauty and for the skill devoted to them by a little army of gardeners.

Excursion tickets are issued, during the summer months, to Somerleyton from Yarmouth; but, instead of taking a return ticket, the walk back should be enjoyed, over the heather-covered Herringfleet hills, the home of the pewit, and past Fritton and Belton, to Gorleston, whence a couple of miles on the tram brings you to Yarmouth Bridge.

Oulton Dyke is one-and-a-half miles long, and nearly as wide as the river, so there is ample room for sailing. The part of the dyke past the Horse-shoe bend is called, for a reason I cannot fathom, Fisher's Row. Oulton Broad is a fine, clear expanse of deep water, with good fishing; it is about a mile long, and contains upwards of 100 acres. Upon entering the Broad, a lone house will be noticed on the left. It is built of stone and brick, and is sur-rounded by a belt of fir trees. It was the home of George Borrow, the celebrated "Romany Rye," who wrote so many books upon gipsies, and their manners and customs. His best-known work, "The Bible in Spain," is a book interesting to everyone. He died only five or six years since. There is a station at Oulton, at the lower end of the Broad, from which it is only five minutes' journey to Lowestoft, and twenty to Yarmouth. Boats, bait, and light refresh-ments, or substantial meals, may be obtained at the Wherry Inn, adjoining the Broad, and close to the station. The bar-parlour of the Wherry is quite a museum, and contains curiosities from all parts of the world; but to the local productions the principal interest is attached. One case contains four perch, averaging 2½lb., forming part of a take of twenty-

D

seven fish captured in the space of an hour. Another
has a large otter (18lb., I believe) which was caught
here a year or two ago. On the day of my last
visit (March, 1887) to this cheerful hostelry, a 15lb.
otter was caught in the Waveney, making the fifth
since Christmas. Although not so numerous as
formerly, they are far from being extinct in these
waters, as some persons suppose. The bittern—two
specimens of which are to be seen—is, I am afraid,
now extinct in the county. An hour may profitably
be spent in this parlour museum, and a lot of information gathered from the practical host.

The Backwater, or whatever the small arm of the
Broad is called, forms a harbour in winter for laying-
up yachts, as it lies in a snug corner, at the back
of the village. The tall building overlooking this
part of the Broad is an ice-house, from which parties
starting on a summer trip may obtain a supply of
ice to keep the various eatables and drinkables cold—
a great desideratum in July and August. Travellers
from London who take a fortnightly return ticket
to Lowestoft should alight at Carlton Colville if they
wish to visit Oulton Broad. A walk of five minutes,
over Mutford Bridge, will bring them to the starting-
place of the yachts.

Passing under the Bridge and through the Lock, we
enter Lake Lothing, a large sheet of water lying between two hills, two miles in length, and deep; at
times large shoals of mullet and smelt enter the lake,
and good takes are sometimes to be had with a net.

At the eastern end, communication with the sea may be obtained by passing through the locks into Lowestoft Harbour, which has now nearly been completed by the Great Eastern Railway Company, at a cost of over half-a-million sterling. Being more accessible in all weathers to fishing vessels than Yarmouth, it is expected that the fishing industry at this most interesting port will be largely and remuneratively increased. Lowestoft is by many visitors preferred to Yarmouth, being very picturesquely situated on the brow of a hill overlooking the sea, while Yarmouth is excessively flat. It is also much quieter, and not so much overrun by cheap trippers. Relics of various kinds are often dug out of the cliffs in the neighbourhood, many of which may be seen in the Museum at Norwich. Lowestoft should be visited by all means, if only for an hour or two; but, as we have little to do with the towns, I must leave it to the reader to inquire for the places of interest in Lowestoft itself. I may, *en passant,* note that the town contains one long main street, with numerous short ones diverging from it on either side; its ground plan is, in fact, like the backbone of a fish, just as the map of Yarmouth was likened by Dickens to a huge gridiron. These, I think, are most appropriate plans for fishing towns. Lowestoft has two lighthouses, which are greatly needed on this most dangerous coast: one stands high on the cliff, and the other, a short, skeleton tower, is on the beach, not far above high water mark. The pier, which has a reading-room at the extreme end, is about 400yds. in length, and is usually crowded at the time the band is appointed to play in the evening. St. Margaret's Church is a splendid building, which stands some distance from the town, and should not be missed. There are some glorious country walks around Lowestoft, and the drive to Yarmouth (ten miles) is very delightful. Now that we are near the

BURGH ST. PETER CHURCH.

sea, we will take a stroll on the beach, and have a dip, while our man in the fore-peak prepares our meal, which we hope to eat with enhanced appetite after our sea-bath.

If it be wished to lengthen the trip on the Waveney, that river can be ascended for many miles, as it is navigable for large vessels as far as Beccles (eight miles), and, for moderate-sized yachts, even to Bungay (fifteen miles). To visit these places from Lowestoft, we must retrace our course through Lothing and Oulton Broads, and Oulton Dyke, until we arrive at the junction of the Waveney. Through the dyke we have been steering due north; but when we arrive at the Waveney we alter our head to southwest, and run past the village of Burgh St. Peter, which is on our right. The ancient church, dedicated to St. Mary, is a small, thatched edifice, with a brick and stone tower, containing a solitary bell.

The tower, which is unique in construction, appears to have been built at different periods, as the base, or lower storey, is of brick and stone, worked into geometrical patterns, the second and third of brick, the fourth of stone and brick, and the fifth of brick. The capstone, which, at a very

FINIAL OF BURGH ST. PETER CHURCH.

recent period, was perched above a short wooden spire, now lies in the churchyard. It is of freestone, with a wooden finial. This was the crowning effort of the genius who built the curious five-storeyed tower. The interior of the church presents a curious appearance, being more like a corridor or cloister than the nave of a parish church; this is on account of the extreme narrowness in comparison with the length. It is about 110ft. long, and only a little over 14ft.

wide. The number of candles and crosses in the
chancel are in strong contrast to the usual Low
Church proclivities of the Norfolk people. The
vicar, the Rev. — Boycatt, is brother to Captain
Boycott, against whom originated the "boycotting"
system in Ireland. I was told an a-mews-ing tale concerning the discrepancy in the spelling of their names,
but do not think it worth while printing. Notice also
the octagonal font, the rood staircase, sedilia, and
other equally interesting features. From a distance
the tower looks like a huge telescope set on end, as
each successive storey is much smaller than the one
beneath it.

Our progress along the river is through seemingly
illimitable marsh or fen land, with a patch of cultivated land at intervals, and we see no other village
till we reach Beccles, on the left bank, although
we pass within three-quarters of a mile of the considerable village of Aldeby. If we wish to pay this
place a visit, we must moor to the right bank just
before we come to the railway bridge, and walk.
The only thing worth seeing, however, is the fine
old church of St. Mary, the tower of which (containing
four bells) springs, a solid, square mass, from the
junction of the nave and chancel.

Archæologists may find instructive examples upon
which to comment in several parts of the church,
especially the doorway, of old Norman masonry, situate
at the west end. While passing through this hoary
portal, which is said to be as old as the time of

William II., we are confronted by a venerable font, which, by the style of the carving, appears to be of the fourteenth century, or perhaps a little earlier. There may also be seen a piscina and two sedilia, while the register is also extant, dating from the year 1541. Many other noticeable features will not be passed over by those who are versed in architecture of an ecclesiastic kind. To prove its antiquity, there is still in existence a charter, by which, in the reign of Henry I. (1100 to 1135 A.D.), the church was given to the Cathedral Monastery of Norwich, by Agnes de Belfo, wife of Robert de Kia. The Bishop of Norwich then founded a small priory here for the maintenance of a prior and three black monks, the remains of which are still to be seen, as they form part of the Priory Farm, and may, by the permission of the occupier, Mr. William Blyth, be visited.

Yachts can pass the swing bridge at all times when the flag is down; but when it is elevated to the top of the pole, this is a signal that a train is due, and until it has passed those in charge will not open the bridge; so that, for those in a hurry, there is no way but to lower the mast. This proceeding, instead of saving time, often loses it.

Beccles, on the left bank, is one of the largest and busiest towns in Suffolk, containing upwards of 6,000 inhabitants. It is agreeably situated on rising ground, and, besides a town hall and theatre, boasts of a capital race-course (half a mile east of the town), upon which racing takes place in the Spring and

Autumn. There is a free school for boys, founded, in the year 1631, by Sir John Seman, who also endowed it with 100 acres of land. The grand old church, with its huge *detached* steeple, or rather tower—for it is a most massive, square structure—must be visited and its carved stone decorations inspected. It may be doubted if any church in the county can boast of such a grand entrance-porch as the one belonging to this cathedral-like church. The building was erected in 1369, just the period when ecclesiastic architecture was at its zenith. Beccles does a large trade in corn, coal, malt, and other heavy goods, which, since the deepening of the Waveney in 1832, have been transported principally by water; in fact, although thirteen miles from the sea *viâ*

ENTRANCE-PORCH OF BECCLES CHURCH.

Lowestoft, it might almost claim the privileges of a seaport, so broad and deep is the channel for the admission of vessels quite up to the town. Saturday is market day, when a very good show of all kinds of provisions and the usual household stores is displayed. There are also plenty of shops, at which, on other days, the ordinary visitor may replenish his wasting stores. Delicious butter

may be had at a reasonable rate, sold by the intel-
ligible pound instead of the "pint" which was
formerly in vogue in all the Eastern Counties. The
"pint" contained twenty ounces, and was a cylin-
drical mass in the shape of the ordinary upright
hand churn or large milk-can so familiar to travellers
on the railway. Perhaps a dice-box will give a
better idea of the shape,
but instead of the waist
being in the centre, it was
about one-third of the way
from the small end. Speaking of butter, it may be
noted that until quite recently it was sold in Cam-
bridgeshire by the yard.

Having spent a few hours
at the old town of Bec-
cles, and made one or
two small purchases, we
again embark, and proceed
on our journey to Bungay,

CLOCHER OF BECCLES CHURCH,
APART FROM NAVE.

eight miles higher up the river. The aspect of
Beccles from the river—that is, after passing it some
distance—is extremely striking, and it will be difficult
to find a more picturesque town on these waters,
unless it be Wroxham, with its giant trees and
church-crowned hill. As the draught of the "Lily"
is but slight, we can travel very comfortably where
a large sailing vessel would be constantly coming

to grief on the bottom in tacking. For this reason
ordinary sea-going yachts are totally unfitted for river
work, and especially the comparatively shallow rivers
outside a radius of, say, fifteen to twenty miles from
Yarmouth.

Leaving Beccles, the district becomes much more
cultivated and less monotonous, and the marshes
fewer. While steaming steadily onward, there is
time to mention the subject of fogs, which, in these
fenny districts, rise without any warning; their ghost-
like presence alone making you notice that they are
there. They sometimes come in the form of rolling,
white clouds, bowling along the river's course at a
smart pace, so that one minute you may be in a
beautiful, clear atmosphere, while the next your craft
is veiled in a thick winding-sheet of white mist.
When it is very dense, the best plan is to lay-to
and moor to the bank till the fog has passed. It
generally departs as quickly as it came, and is seldom
met with except in early morn and at evening.
Sometimes, it will hang on the river and adjoining
country in a bank, or, if I may so term it, a carpet,
about two feet thick, while all above is quite clear.
At these times, the cattle grazing on the marshes
appear without legs or support of any kind, so that
their bodies seem to be floating in the dense atmosphere. If they bend to eat, off go their heads, so
that the whole herd present a curious appearance.
Trees grow apparently without trunks, and men
come gliding along the river, seated on a fogbank,

for their boat is invisible. Then the fog will at times hover in the air, cutting off the branches of trees, tops of cottages, &c. These peculiar fogs are experienced in Holland, and, I believe, in all flat, low-lying localities, in just the same manner. Spring and Autumn are the principal times of their visitation, although they are occasionally seen late in the evening or early of a morning in the summer; but they are very transitory, the morning mist melting with the first warmth of the glittering sun, who looks upon the fog as a treasonable and dangerous rival, and banishes him accordingly.

Gillingham lies on the opposite bank to Beccles, a good mile from the river, and is worth a visit, if only to see a genuine piece of Norman architecture, the Church of St. Mary, whose register dates from 1540. This church was built about A.D. 1120, and is unique, inasmuch as it has a galille, or women's porch. In the good old times when this edifice was constructed, women were so little honoured that they were not allowed to enter the body of the church on certain occasions, but were only permitted to hear the service from the porch.

I am not sure, but I believe this is the only instance of a galille in the county.

The finest specimen of a galille in England is in Durham Cathedral, and this is so large that it is used as a chapel for the undergraduates of Durham University. To show the manner in which women were tabooed from the sacred fanes of mediæval times,

visitors to Durham Cathedral are shown a large, black
stone cross, let into the floor of the nave, close to the
chancel, beyond which no woman was allowed to
pass, upon pain of all sorts of dreadful penalties and
punishments being meted out to her.

We will, however, come back to Gillingham. The
Hall, which stands in its own lovely grounds, is upwards of 200 years old, having been built in the reign
of James I. It is the seat of Admiral Eden, J.P., who
is also lord of the manor. As we progress up the
river, we notice a hill covered with fir trees, which
come quite down to the river, and look very rustic
and pretty. This is Dunburgh Hill, a well-known
angling spot.

The next village is Geldeston, a mile from the
river, also on the right bank. There is very little to
see to repay a visit. The church was restored, twenty
years since, at a cost of £1200, and is therefore practically a new church, but with a very old history, for
its register dates back to the year 1600. The Hall is
a modern brick building, erected at the beginning of
the present century, and stands in a well-wooded
park. There is a station here (Beccles and Bungay
line), which is half a mile from the river.

On the left bank, a mile inland, is Barsham, noted
as the birthplace of Dr. Laurence Eachard, the his-
torian and divine. On the same side, but within half
a mile of the river, is Shipmeadow, noted for nothing
in particular except its rural quietness. Here we are
stopped by a lock, and pay toll; the payment of this

one sum also takes us through two other locks before reaching Bungay. The locks, and their distances from Beccles, are as follow: first, Shipmeadow Lock, four miles; then, three miles farther, is Ellingham Lock; two miles more brings us to Wangford Lock; and another mile lands us at Bungay Staithe.

Farther along on the right bank, and adjoining the river, is Ellingham, which boasts of a railway station, five minutes' walk from the landing-place. It is but a small village, supporting, perhaps, 400 inhabitants, but still a thriving little place.

The church (St. Mary) is an ancient building, with a square tower containing five bells. In the chancel are a piscina and a large wall painting. The latter represents the angel appearing to St. Peter in prison, who is about to be liberated therefrom. Several of the windows are filled with memorials of stained glass, none of which are very grand specimens of nineteenth century work. It may be noted that the modern revival of stained glass has been taken up with such enthusiasm by the various artists in this beautiful work, that the old glass has not only, by some of them, been equalled, but actually surpassed. This has only come to pass during the last decade, as some of the work executed at the commencement of the revival is not only absolutely hideous in colour, but the drawing partakes of the grotesque or caricature order; while the designs are beneath criticism. The painting, too, is such as the merest novice in the profession would be ashamed of. This revival only took place about thirty years since; but now, during the past few years, notice the beautiful metamorphosis. Men who have since raised themselves to the head of their profession as artists, several of whom now write R.A. after their names, took the matter in hand, and gave the world such cartoons as it had never seen before for this special purpose. Clever chemists set to work and analysed the component parts of the old glass, and very soon produced such lovely colours and tints as the old monkish glass-painters never dreamed of. Then clever painters were sought for and found, and, with equally clever cutters and glaziers, windows have been produced during these last few years which have never been surpassed since stained glass has been used as a church decoration. Although perhaps a hundred glass-painters may now be found in Great Britain, the real masters of the art might be counted on the fingers of the two hands. So much for this subject, which was brought on the *tapis* by gazing on the pictorial windows of Ellingham Church. The register carries us back to the days of Bluff King Hal, for it was commenced in 1538.

After passing a large island in the river, we are in sight of that scarcely euphoniously named town, Bungay. It is of considerable importance, and musters between 3000 and 4000 inhabitants; but although a railway depôt, it has not kept pace with the times, as Beccles has done. Forty years since, before the advent of railways, the populations of Beccles and Bungay were nearly indentical, namely, 4098 and 4109 ; at the 1881 census, they were 5721 and 3579 respectively. The water carriage with Yarmouth, Lowestoft, and other places, greatly favours Beccles, and thus, by securing it greater commercial privileges, at the same time advances its population and prosperity.

There is very little of interest to see in the town, which is divided into two parishes, St. Mary and Holy Trinity. The parish church of the latter is an ancient little building, with a round, flint tower ; while that of St. Mary is a much larger structure, and of some architectural importance. There is a capital free grammar school, of ancient but uncertain foundation, which annually sends four scholars to Emanuel College, Cambridge. The market day is Thursday ; but the market cannot compare with that of the sister town, Beccles. The situation of the town is pleasant, and the streets well laid out.

The Waveney, after passing, at the east end of the town, the bridge uniting the counties of Norfolk and Suffolk, describes a most eccentric course, and, after flowing a distance of three-and-a-half or four miles, again passes the town at the south-east bridge, which is only about 500 or 600 yards from that first mentioned. From Bungay the river is only navigable for small boats, which may ascend for several miles ; flowing past Harleston and Diss, it takes its rise at the little hamlet of Lopham, in Norfolk, in a swampy land, and at a distance of a

stone's throw from the source of the Little Ouse,
which river, east and north, completes the boundary
of the counties of Norfolk and Suffolk. So close
are the sources of these two rivers, that a man with
a spade might, in a few days, make the county an
island !

From Bungay, Norwich may be reached in an hour
and a quarter ; so that, if you take a man from
Lowestoft with you, to take back the boat, you need
not retrace your steps (figurative ones) along the
Waveney.

The epithet, "Silly Suffolk," as it is generally
written and pronounced, is incorrect, and a libel on
the industrious and sharp people of that county.
The word "silly" is a corruption of the Saxon
"selli," which means happy, not foolish, as some
would have us believe.

We must, after a good night's rest, return early
in the morning, along the Waveney, to the entrance
to the New Cut, as we purpose paying a short visit
to the extremely ancient and interesting city of
Norwich. The whole of the river Waveney, from
Bungay to the New Cut, is a noted pike ground,
and on good authority I have it that, during
February of this year (1887), nearly 300 pike and
jack were taken by members of the angling clubs.

LOWESTOFT HARBOUR.

CHAPTER IV.

LOWESTOFT TO NORWICH.

O, Life is a river, and man is the boat
That over its surface is destined to float ;
While joy is a cargo so easily stored,
That he is a fool who takes sorrow aboard.
—JEFFREYS.

THE Yare, from which Yarmouth derives its name, takes its rise at Shiphdam, near East Dereham, flows eastward thirty miles to the junction of the Wensum, continues in a tortuous line twenty miles farther to its union with the Waveney, and expands into a large lake, called Breydon Water, at the east end of which it receives the Bure, whence it continues its course to the sea, a total distance of about sixty miles.

The Waveney has its source at Lopham, only a few yards from where the Little Ouse rises, and after running a course of fifty miles, falls into the west end of Breydon Water.

The Bure rises at Melton Constable, and flows in a south-east direction past Blickling, Aylsham, and

E

Wroxham, until it reaches St. Benet's Abbey, where it receives the waters of the River Ant, and, a little farther on, the inconsiderable stream of the Thurne ; thence it runs past Acle, and finally flows into Breydon, after a journey of fifty miles.

By going through the New Cut, three miles long, which connects the Waveney with the Yare, instead of going *viá* Breydon, we save twelve miles on our way to Norwich. A toll of 1*s.* is demanded for each yacht passing through, which is collected at Haddiscoe Lift Bridge, by a man who hands a bag to you fixed to the top of a long pole. As the banks are firm all along, many anglers prefer a roving commission on them to a fixed tenure in a boat.

On emerging at the other end of the Cut, we find the village of Reedham before us. This place is noted as having been the seat of the East Anglian kings, and it was here that Lothbrock the Dane was murdered. As few persons know who this personage was, perhaps it will not be out of place here if I give the story in a very brief manner: Lothbrock, or Lodrobrog, was a Danish chief ; and one day, while hawking for birds among the islands on the coast of Denmark, he was surprised by a sudden storm, driven across the North Sea, and found himself at the mouth of the Yare, which he entered, and landed at Reedham, where the Court of Edmund, King of the East Angles, was at that time held. He was received into Royal favour, and, in hunting, was frequently attended by the king's huntsman, Bern, whom he soon excelled in his own profession. Bern became jealous, and at length murdered Lothbrock in the woods; but the murder came to light through the affection of Lothbrock's dog. Bern was tried, and condemned to be cast away in a boat. Strangely enough, he drifted to the coast of Denmark, where, being tortured on the rack, to learn what he knew of Lothbrock's death, he concealed his own guilt, and attributed the assassination to King Edmund. The consequence was that 20,000 Danes, under the leadership of Hinguar and Hubba, invaded East Anglia, burned and slaughtered indiscriminately as they went, overcame Edmund, took him prisoner, and, after a mock trial, beheaded him. This put an end to the Saxon dynasty in East Anglia, about the year 870 A.D.

Yachts, unless very small, will have to wait at Reedham for the swing railway bridge to be opened before they can pass. I would call the attention of my readers to this bridge, which is supported in the centre by a huge column rising from the river; and upon this column it swings, on a pivot, parallel to the course of the river, to allow vessels to pass. The church (St. John the Baptist) contains a handsome marble monument, with effigies of Thomas Guybon, his wife and children. Most of the tablets here are memorials of the Berney family, one of whom built the Hall, in 1557. Dwellers in towns will be surprised at the extent of the marshes, and the number of cattle in these parts. Hundreds of oxen

E 2

stare at us listlessly as we pass, chewing their cud in
perfect contentment and undisturbed peace, or standing
knee-deep in the cool water, putting one in mind of
some of the cattle pictures by the old Dutch painters.
On the left, at the mouth of a small stream, the
Chet, stands Hardley Cross, marking the boundary of the jurisdiction of Norwich. The Chet, or
Ket, as it is commonly called, is a river, or rivulet,
taking its rise at the village of Poringland; its entire
course is not more than twelve or fourteen miles.
There are only two or three small villages on its
banks (none of any note), and the one considerable
town of Loddon, five miles from its mouth. The importance of Loddon may be estimated from the fact
that it is actually lighted with gas! It must not be
inferred that this has caused the town to become
inflated, for, according to the last census, its population was under 1,200. Nevertheless, it is a thriving
little town, and does a good trade with both Yarmouth and Norwich. It stands on an eminence overlooking the river, and consists of one long High
Street, with the usual little "backbone-like," short
turnings, branching therefrom. A conspicuous object
is the Church of the Holy Trinity, built, in the reign
of Henry VIII., by Sir James Hobart, a curious portrait of whom, and his wife, may be seen in the
church. In the same painting are representations of
the church and the town bridge (St. Olave's), which
latter was built, by Lady Hobart, at the same time
as the church. In the north aisle of the church is a

marble altar-tomb, with a recumbent effigy of Lady Williamson, dated 1684. The register dates from 1556. The east window is filled with a poor specimen of early-modern stained glass, which was placed in position about fifty years since, at a cost of £160. There is a Town Hall and fire-engine house also in this little self-reliant town.

The Chet, or Ket, is navigable for wherries quite up to Loddon, and for small boats some distance higher. Chedgrave is a small village on the right bank, and within a few minutes' walk of Loddon; its church is worthy of a visit, to inspect the old Norman doorway and stained-glass windows. Heckingham, on the left bank, is worth landing at, to see the church, which is quite 700 years old, or even more; it is principally of the Norman style of architecture. It is a small, thatched building, with a round tower, containing two bells. This is to avoid the monotony of a single tone; and so, on a Sunday morning, when tired of ringing "ding-dong," the ringers can produce a pleasant variety by ringing "dong-ding." Several, in fact many, of the churches hereabout, have thus recklessly secured the same number of bells, so that the inhabitants may practise that very simple and easily-learnt pastime of change-ringing. Mundham St. Peter, on the left bank, about two miles past Loddon, has a church of ancient origin, many portions of it being Norman work; it is dedicated to St. Peter. The remains of another church, dedicated to St. Ethelbert, may also be seen.

The Chet is excessively quiet, and nobody seems to dream of leaving the broad bosom of the Yare for this little arm, which is well worthy of a visit. With a fair wind, a small sailing boat could, by catching the first of the flood tide, reach Loddon in four or five hours; a sight of the Loddon lions could be enjoyed, lunch despatched, and, by catching the ebb, Yarmouth again reached the same evening. The distance from Yarmouth to Loddon is from fourteen to fifteen miles.

We resume our journey up the Yare: three miles past Hardley Cross, on the right, we come to Cantley. The " Red House " here is a noted fishing resort, being close to the railway station, and only a half-hour's ride from Norwich. The church is dedicated to St. Margaret; it is built in the Norman and Perpendicular styles, and has a register dating from A.D. 1559.

On the left, half a mile inland, is Langley Abbey, or Priory, built, in 1198, by Roger Fitzroger, for an abbot and sixteen canons of the Præmonstratensian order. The ample endowment of the founder was confirmed by King John, who granted to the parish a market and fair, with sac, soc, and other privileges. A stone cross, upon which are four statues, formerly stood close by, but has been removed to Langley Park, a splendid estate of 800 acres, and the seat of Sir Reginald Beauchamp. The hall is a veritable treasure-house of art, being filled with busts, paintings, and statues. The fine church of St. Michael contains several handsome stained-glass windows, memorials of the Beauchamp family, which are alone worth a visit.

On the left bank, opposite Cantley, is Claxton, which is a nice walk from the river. The church (St. Andrew) contains tablets to the Gawdy, Bushby, Rouse, and other families. The manor house, of which the remains still exist, belonged, in the reign of Edward III., to the Kerdiston family. This monarch gave them the right to castellate and fortify their mansion.

A dyke on the right, a mile or so past Langley, leads to Buckenham Broad (of inconsiderable size) ; while a little further on is Buckenham Ferry, where we will step ashore and sit under the cool, shady trees of the inn garden, which abuts on the river, and refresh ourselves. Plenty of fish are to be caught here, and large ones too, as the river is, in most places, some 12ft. or 14ft. deep. A walk of a hundred yards from the inn will give the visitor a good view of a fen, both for extent and flatness. Water-dykes are seen on every side, and care should be taken in walking, if a stroll is desired, that you do not get into a boggy spot, where you will be up to your knees in black peat mud in a moment.

The church (St. Nicholas) is an ancient edifice, and contains a font of the fifteenth century, which, on being restored, brought to light a number of emblematic carvings. The east window represents St. Nicholas and the four Evangelists. The knightly

family of Godsalve were lords of the manor till the
reign of Queen Mary, and their arms may still be
seen in the carved wainscot of the Hall, which building is now let out in cottages.

A mile further up, on the left, we come to the
only navigable dyke of the five leading to Rockland
Broad. As this is greatly overgrown with weeds,
we will take the jolly boat, as we shall not stay there
long. The pull up is very pretty, as we are hemmed
in on both sides by rushes, reeds, and all kinds of
aquatic plants and flowers. We find the Broad, upon
which we suddenly emerge, a very wild-looking place,
choked with weeds and reeds. Eels literally swarm
among these reeds. A man in a boat at a distance
is catching them, so we will endeavour to find our
way to him along the sinuous channels, and watch
him. He proceeds with his business thus: He has a
square-mouthed net, about 3ft. across, and only about
1ft. deep, the mouth of which is kept extended by a
strong iron rim, which is fixed in a short handle·
This net he thrusts down among the weeds, and
brings it up as full of them as he can lift; he carefully sorts these over, and throws them away, the eels
remaining behind at the bottom of the net. They
are then transferred to a trunk pierced with holes,
and if this be kept in water, the eels will remain
alive until wanted for market. We purchase half a
stone of him for 3s., and thread our way back to the
entrance of the dyke (locally pronounced "deek").
By the way, speaking of eels, is it not generally

thought that they have no scales, but simply a slimy skin ? This is certainly an error, as they have minute scales, which are, curiously enough, under the skin, instead of outside, as in other fishes. I would also point out that there are three species of eels, which may be easily distinguished: they are the

SHARP-NOSED EEL.

sharp-nosed eel, the broad-nosed eel, and the grig. The two former have dark, olive green skins, while the latter has a pale green, or celadon-coloured skin, and is not reckoned of so fine a flavour as its darker brethren. The natives

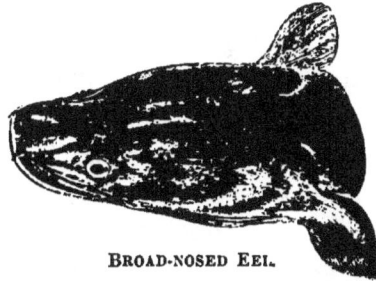

BROAD-NOSED EEL.

esteem the part from the vent to the tail as the best part of the fish. The back piece, immediately behind the head, is looked upon as a *bonne bouche.* Rockland Broad does

ORIG.

not exhibit its full size, by reason of the great reed-beds which are dispersed all over it ; but there cannot be much less than 120 acres. Rockland St. Mary's Church is a small, ancient Gothic structure, situated on an eminence commanding an extensive view. The churchyard contains the ivy-

covered ruins of the still older church of St. Margaret.
I think there are very few instances of two churches
in one churchyard. The register dates from A.D. 1558,
and for the first fifty years was kept in Latin.

Still bearing north by east for a couple of miles,
we come to Coldham Hall, on the left bank; this is
another favourite "angler's delight." In the season,
many fishing matches take place at staked swims
at this spot. The weighing-in, in the evening, is a
sight worth seeing, as not only are the takes great,
but there are also some fine specimens of the finny
tribes among them. Bream of extraordinary size are
taken, weighing up to 5lbs. and even 6lbs. The nearest
station is Brundall, three-quarters of a mile off, on
the opposite side of the Yare.

Midway between Buckenham and Brundall is the
village of Strumpshaw, standing on very high ground;
indeed, the windmill is supposed to stand on the
highest hill in the county, and from it may be
obtained one of the finest views. On a clear day
Norwich and Yarmouth are plainly visible, while to
the N.N.E. may be seen the two white towers of
Happisburgh Lighthouses.* To the south, the view
extends to the borders of Suffolk. This lofty eminence
would appear to have been cast up by the sea at some
remote period, as 100ft. below the surface of the
summit, boulder stones are found similar to those on
the coast adjoining Yarmouth.

From Buckenham Ferry to Norwich, a distance of

* The Low Light was demolished in 1886.

about ten miles, scores of "brethren of the angle"
may be seen, on any fine evening in summer, plying
their peaceful avocation; and yet there is room for
many more, and fish enough for all and to spare,
so long as fair angling only is practised and nets
are not used. Speaking of the angle, is it generally
known that angling is mentioned in the Bible in
one or two places, notably in Amos iv. 2 (B.C. 787);
Isaiah xix. 8 (B.C. 714); and again in Habakkuk
i. 15 (B.C. 625)? I cannot say if these are the only
references made to angling in the Bible, or other
authentic book, or whether they are the earliest.
Angling appears to have been pursued by the
Egyptians and Romans, much in the same way as
in our own day. Figures of persons angling occur
frequently in paintings from the Egyptian tombs,
and also on the walls of the buried city of Hercu-
láneum. In a painting from Beni-Hassan, the rod,
much shorter than the modern ones, is shown in one
piece, and no float is represented on the line, which
appears to be a very coarse one. Most of the
ancient lines were, I believe, like some of the modern
ones, made of horse-hair.

Coldham Hall stands close to Surlingham Broad,
which is nearly a mile long, and about a quarter of
a mile wide. This Broad is also much grown up with
weeds. Being particularly well watched, this lake
acts as a kind of harbour of refuge for young fish,
nets being strictly tabooed—as they should be, but
are not, on all the other Broads. Surlingham Broad

has an outlet into the river both at the east and west ends, so that many persons, while the yacht keeps to the river, take the jolly boat and pull across it, exploring its beauties on the way, and meeting the yacht at the other entrance.

The village contains two churches, St. Mary's and St. Saviour's; of the latter little more than the name remains, as the church was in ruins in Queen Elizabeth's reign.

From Brundall to Norwich is, without doubt, the finest part of the Yare, as the banks are well wooded, and the general aspect exceedingly varied and pleasant. The Wood's End hostelry, at Bramerton, should on no account be passed without a visit, as its grounds, covering nearly seven acres, are very tastefully laid out. The natural beauty of the hilly ground has been so helped by artificial means and good gardening, that these well-known pleasure gardens are now justly celebrated for their rustic elegance. Mount the winding path, to the highest part of the garden, and take in at a glance the tortuous course of the Yare and the surrounding country, and it will be confessed that the view is a lovely one.

Bramerton village lies a mile back from the river, at the rear of the hills, but is not remarkable for anything out of the common. The church, dedicated to St. Peter, is built in the Early English style, though not during that period of architecture, as it was not erected till the year 1462, whereas the Early English style of building died out about A.D. 1300, when its place was taken by the Perpendicular style. The reaches about Bramerton are noted pike haunts. An angler, on one Sunday during January of this year (1887), took seventeen pike, of an aggregate weight of 93lb., the largest being a long fish, in poor condition, weighing 13lb.

Continuing our course, we soon reach Postwick Grove, which consists of a long, red sand hill, covered with gorse and wild plants, and crowned with patriarchal oak and elm trees. As you will observe, this Grove must have been planted by the riverside for the purpose of providing a picnic ground for the populous city of Norwich. In fact, nothing could be better for the purpose, and the surroundings are such as to frame the picture formed by the picnic party and their craft. After passing the Grove, and making several windings, we see on the right the immense block of buildings called Thorpe Asylum; it usually contains about 600 poor imbeciles and lunatics, and is the asylum for the county. The part built of white brick was erected about 1814, while that of red brick is quite a recent addition.

On the left bank an object will be noticed which usually causes the sketch-book to make its appearance, and a halt to be called. This is the " Monkey House," a cottage built in the days of Good Queen Bess, and of a very picturesque appearance. It is so infirm from old age, that it has to be propped up to prevent it from committing suicide by tumbling headlong into the river. It stands in solitary decay, a conspicuous object, with its stunted fir trees, cabbage patch, and fen surroundings—a fit subject for the sketch-block.

Half a mile more brings us to Whitlingham, with its tree-covered hills, and conspicuously and romantically situated church, which forms a fine ivy-clad ruin. This church is planted right upon the edge of a precipitous, wooded hill, from which a good view of the surrounding district is obtained. The circular tower is nearly intact, but the church itself is roofless, and the interior contains a congregation of trees, in flourishing condition. The tower is surmounted by four figures, symbolical of the four Evangelists. These stone figures, according to local tradition, walk round the edge of the tower at midnight, meet, shake hands, and then resume their positions. This sight cannot be seen by married persons!

EARLY ENGLISH WINDOW IN TOWER OF WHITLINGHAM CHURCH.

After passing Whitlingham Church a few hundred yards, we come to a broad, river-like cutting, right in front of us, and which looks a very inviting piece of water, and loses itself in leafy shade in the distance. As there is a boom across the mouth, however, it is obvious that it is private property. This is the waterway to the estate of Mr. J. Colman, the "Mustard King," whose immense works at Carrow employ nearly 1000 men. We turn sharp to the right, pass beneath the wooden arches of the railway bridge, and find ourselves at the Thorpe Tea Gardens, which are so much frequented by the Norwich young men and maidens in the summer months. The correct thing seems to be for the young people, who leave off business early on Thursday afternoons, to walk to Thorpe, distance two miles, partake of some light refreshment, and then go for a long row or sail until dusk, when they return, and enjoy the stroll home again to Norwich. As we glide past the village of Thorpe, we cannot help being struck by the beauty of its situation. There it is, nestling on the declivity of a well-wooded hill, from which the suburban red houses of the Norwich magnates peep out, and look down upon the Yare which, a little higher up, turns off to the left, and our course is thence along the Wensum, which runs quite through the heart of Norwich. It always appeared to me, that the river along which we have come so far, and which runs straight ahead through Norwich, should be still called the Yare, instead of the Wensum. It appears to me, that the river which comes in so abruptly from the left (the Yare) should be styled the Wensum. Probably, time has given them such right to their names, bestowed some centuries since, that they will not alter them to agree with my fancy.

Thorpe is certainly a lovely little hamlet during the summer months, and its flowers, in every conceivable colour, its woody hills, its glittering, sun-kissed waters, would tempt a hermit from his cave,

especially if his said cave were in one of those awful
back slums of Norwich yclept a "yard." The church
is a new structure; but an idea of the diminutive
proportions of the old edifice may be obtained by
landing and viewing its ruins; its tower forms a
lych-gate to the new structure. One wall (the south)
still stands, and shows the length of the building. It
was, with one exception, the smallest church in England, that exception being St. Lawrence, in the
Isle of Wight. Thorpe Old Church and the *porch* of
Yarmouth Parish Church were identical in size.

A few minutes now suffices to bring us to Carrow
Bridge, in juxtaposition with which stands the immense factory of Messrs. Colman. An order to inspect
this firm's premises may be obtained at the office.

Immediately after passing Carrow Bridge, we notice
the ruins of two venerable circular flint towers, one
on either side of the river. These are the Boom or
Toll Towers, which, with the city walls, have been
allowed gradually to decay, as their functions have
long since passed away. Formerly no vessel was
allowed to pass these towers (which mark the city
boundary) without having first paid certain dues
towards maintaining the dredging of the river, the
repair of its banks, &c. These towers also formed a
military post in war time, and were strongly fortified.
On the hills, near the left bank of the river, will be
noticed the remains of other towers, which were
occupied, when necessary, by a company of soldiers,
to support their comrades on the river. All is now

brick and mortar on our left, and the broad tow-path and flats on our right. The next bridge is the new Foundry Bridge, erected in 1885, to take the place of the narrow and inconvenient iron structure which had for years spanned the river, and congested the traffic at this point. The large building on the right is the new railway station of the Great Eastern Railway, which is as perfect in its arrangements, and as handsome in structure, as the old one (now the goods station) was inadequate and ugly. A hundred yards brings us to Pull's Ferry, which was, at some remote period, the water-gate of the cathedral. The road beyond the ancient structure leads direct to the cathedral, of which more anon. Here we will land, and pay a visit to the lions of the most ancient and quaint city of Norwich.

The trip from Lowestoft is about thirty miles, parts of which are certainly somewhat tame; but the last six miles of varying landscape have amply repaid us for making the excursion. From Brundall to Norwich the scenery is very sylvan: green, undulating meadows; peaceful and picturesquely-disposed groups of parti-coloured cattle, quietly browsing; tree-crowned hills, with here and there the grey, ivy-covered, flint tower of an ancient church peeping out; or passing glimpses of red sand hills, covered with gorse and its yellow blossom; the bright and balmy air, the singing of birds, the hum of bees, and the fragrant perfume of flowers—all serve to make this part of the river supremely enchanting.

F

The Wensum, from Pull's Ferry, winds about, in a most eccentric manner, quite through the heart of the city, and its fringe of tumble-down, overhanging houses and warehouses, form endless themes for the pencil and brush of the artist. Some of the river-side houses, with their old, open timberwork sides and gables, make capital water-colour subjects, and are being continually sketched by both visitors and local artists. I would advise strangers not to pass beyond Pull's Ferry with their yacht, but to visit this waterway in the dinghy, or a boat hired for the purpose, as some of the bridges are very narrow and awkward. Bishop's Bridge dates from the thirteenth century, and, with Pull's Ferry, has been photographed, sketched, and painted far more than the most famous society beauty.

Before closing this chapter, we will just glance briefly at the chief characteristics of the Norfolk churches, which are far more numerous than those of any other county, not even excepting gigantic York-shire. The total number of churches in the county is upwards of 760. Many of them are not only ancient edifices, but are very fine specimens of the periods in which they were built. They are remarkable for their carved oak chancel screens, some of which cannot be surpassed in the delicacy of their tracery, and the skill shown in their intricate carving. Some of them are quite unique, having no peer in England. That in Worstead Church is a double one, of splendid work-manship, with paintings of various saints, and is the only one of its kind in England; while that of Ranworth is considered the ideal of a painted screen of the fifteenth century.

The stone and wood carver will find plenty to admire and study, and may quickly fill his sketchbook with curious gargoyles, corbels, finials, old fonts, and many other specimens of genuine thirteenth and fourteenth century carving.

Vandalism has, in some churches, run riot. Wall paintings have been plastered or whitewashed over, carved panels cemented up, and brasses taken from the walls for old metal, to the disgust of the modern æsthete.

The high-backed pews, which are fast disappearing, are not of such antiquity as many persons suppose. They are not older than the time of Queen Mary, and their use came about in this way. Bishop Burnet complained to Her Majesty that he could not fix the attention of the Court ladies, who took more interest in their own and others' finery than in his discourse, and desired the queen to have the pews made much higher. She consented, and the high-backed, head-topping pew was the result. So successful and snug were they, that they were soon imitated in other churches, and quickly became general all over the country. Now, after a century and a half, they are rapidly dying out, and will soon become a thing of the past. I am certainly glad I am not a boy now; for I should not be able to enjoy a juicy apple, some sweets, or a half-hour's nap, as I used to do when a little fellow, thirty years ago, in the cosy corner of the pew; that is, when I was not hauled out and seated on the pulpit stairs, by the sexton, for persistent talking, and asking irrelevant questions aloud. But, apart from the apple-eating seclusiveness of the high-backed pews, I think they had little else to recommend them.

In many instances, fonts have been restored, and from shapeless masses of cement or plaster, have become, by careful restoration, beautiful specimens of fourteenth and fifteenth-century stonework.

It is worth one's while to ascend one of the grand old flint towers, and gaze around at the country, spread for miles at one's feet, like a huge map. You can trace the courses of the various streams, meandering away as far as the eye can reach, till they are lost in the blue distance. It is curious to note the number of feet and hands cut on the leads of these church towers, most of them with initials and dates added.

It will be remarked that the boots, at the end of the last century, nearly came to a point at the toe, instead of being almost square, as at the present day.

As Norwich is such an interesting place, we will make it the subject-matter of an entire chapter.

CHAPTER V.

A RAMBLE THROUGH NORWICH.

NORWICH, in point of quaintness and antiquity, will vie with any English city, not even the old city of Chester excepted. Although it stands somewhat lower than the adjacent country, it has the appearance, to a person walking in its streets, of being built upon a hill, the apex of which is crowned by the Castle. It is built totally regardless of any pretension to preconceived ground plan, its streets meandering about in all kinds of eccentric curves and irregular turnings. There is no such thing as a level street in the city: those which do not go up, go down, but never for a hundred yards keep a decent level. They are also very narrow (except one, the Prince of Wales Road); and as the old houses, in many places, greatly overhang the yard-wide pavement, it is anything but pleasant to walk through one of them in wet weather, as there is a constant drip of water off the eaves of the houses. The side walks being so very narrow necessitates many pilgrimages along the gutter when one of the fair sex claims right of way.

Norwich is so old that the date of its birth has been forgotten by its mother—England. Many absurd legends are extant as to the foundation of the city, some of them making Julius Cæsar its builder. Although Cæsar was, undoubtedly, dead long before Norwich was thought of, it is very probable that the town had a Roman origin, or, rather, the Romans were indirectly instrumental in its being built. Thus, when the Romans quitted Britain, A.D. 426, they vacated the town of Venta Icenorum, upon which the present Caister now stands, three miles south of Norwich. Forsaken by its founders, the fortified town soon fell into decay; and twenty years later we find that the inhabitants migrated to higher ground, and there settled, gradually building a walled town, which was the foundation of the present city. Norwich may therefore claim a pedigree of fourteen-and-a-half centuries, dating, as it does, from A.D. 446.

The following couplet would appear from this to have much truth in it:—

> Caister was a city when Norwich was none,
> And Norwich was built with Caister stone.

To Uffa, first King of East Anglia, A.D. 575, we are indebted for the commencement of the Castle, which was in those days merely an enormous entrenchment of earth and defensive ramparts, three times circling the stronghold. Northwic, as it was anciently called, was, at the commencement of the seventh century, more strongly guarded by a Castle, erected by

another Anglian king—Anna—who gave it, and the
adjoining lands, to his daughter Ethelfreda, on her
marriage with Tombert, chief of the Gyrvii, or Fenmen. From this period till the time of Alfred the
Great, the Castle was constantly changing hands,
being taken and retaken by both Saxons and Danes.
Alfred, in 870, took the Castle, and, finding its
defences weak, had the walls and principal parts
built of stronger and more durable material. This
Castle lasted many years, but, at the advent of the
Conqueror, was in such a dilapidated condition, from
the frequency of its sieges, that one of William's
earls, Roger Bigod, rebuilt it entirely. In the reign
of Edward II. it was greatly beautified and repaired
by Thomas de Brotherton. It is calculated that
more men have been slaughtered in the defence of
this Castle than of any other place in England. Its
history is exceedingly interesting, and is inseparably
associated with the history of England in the Dark
Ages. The Castle, as known in modern times, consists simply of the keep and outer vallum. The
keep is in perfect condition; it is an oblong building,
110ft. by 93ft., and rises to the height of 110ft. It
is at present the county gaol, and may be viewed on
certain days by a magistrate's order; but during the
current year (1887) it is to be transformed into a
county museum, in commemoration of the fiftieth
year of the reign of Queen Victoria.

The Cathedral, whose lofty spire (second to but one
in the kingdom—that of Salisbury) serves as a land-

mark for many miles, was commenced in 1096, by Herbert de Losigna, who was afterwards its first bishop. His successor, Eborard, nearly completed the fabric; but it was not fitted and finished till 1171, in which year it was greatly damaged by fire, but was restored by Bishop Oxford in 1197. In 1272 it was partially destroyed by fire, and many of the monks slain by the incensed citizens, as a punishment for the disorderly conduct by which they had long disgraced their religion. Like a phœnix, from its ashes it rose again in 1278. The cloisters, said to be the finest in England, were commenced in 1297, and were not finished till 1430.

In 1798, a sailor-boy obtained admission to the tower, and ascended the interior till he reached the top window, but this not being high enough for his liking, he got out of the window, and ascended quite to the weathercock, by using the crockets for a foothold. He came down quite safe and unconcerned.

In 1361, the Cathedral was again in peril, for in that year a violent hurricane blew down the upper part of the steeple, and greatly injured the choir. The present lofty steeple was then erected, and reaches an altitude of 313ft. In 1460, great damage was done by lightning; in 1509, fire was again at work in the aisles of the transepts; and, for the second time, in 1601 the steeple was struck and greatly damaged by lightning. Having encountered the fury of fire, wind, and lightning, it now met with a new assailant —man. Those fanatical zealots, the Puritans, completely wrecked the interior, defaced the ornaments and sculptured effigies, smashed the beautiful stained-glass windows and organ, filed the bells, and stole no less than one hundred brasses. At the Restoration, the Cathedral was again restored and refitted, and since that time has not been interfered with. Its principal dimensions are as follows :—Length from east to west, 407ft. ; breadth across transepts, 178ft. ; length of nave, from west door to screen, 204ft. ; breadth of nave and side aisles, 78ft. The cloisters form a square of 174ft. within the walls. Strangely enough, nearly all the windows are divided, by upright mullions, into three divisions. Notice the beautiful roof, the altar-tombs of Bishop Goldwell (1472) and Bishop Bathurst (1805), and the very fine stained-glass windows.

In various parts of the interior may be seen good specimens of carved work. The accompanying engraving represents a panel bearing an heraldic device, noticeable for its distinctness and simplicity of design.

The roof of the nave is studded with carved bosses, upwards of three hundred in number, representing Bible history, from the time of Solomon to Christ. A pair of opera glasses will be necessary to see these properly.

PANEL—NORWICH CATHEDRAL

The Bishop's Palace is an ancient building, adjoining the north side of the Cathedral, one of the rooms of which is lined with fine carved oak wainscot, brought from St. Benet's Abbey, by Bishop Rugg. The Bishop's Chapel is at the east end of the Palace, and was built in 1662.

I would particularly call attention to the gateways leading to the Cathedral. That leading to the west front of the Cathedral is called Erpingham Gate, from Sir Thomas Erpingham having built it, in the year 1383, as a penance for having espoused the cause of Wickliffe. This gateway is considered a fine piece of work; no less than thirty-eight small stone figures are

FLINTWORK MASONRY IN ST. ETHELBERT'S GATEWAY, NORWICH
CATHEDRAL.

dispersed over it, standing in niches beneath canopies. In a niche in the pediment is a kneeling figure, supposed to be Sir Thomas as a penitent; the word *pœna* (punishment) is carved on many of the scrolls. The two figures which crown the buttresses, or piers, on either side, are representative of a secular and an ordained priest of the Middle Ages, but are now so worn with wind and weather, that their distinctive features are almost obliterated. St. Ethelbert's Gate was built by the citizens as a penalty for having destroyed the old gate and church of St. Ethelbert, when they made their fatal raid on the monks in 1272. Some of the elaborate stone and flint-work for which the gateway is remarkable is shown on the opposite page. The niches in this gate are mostly empty; but one or two figures still remain, notably one which represents a man (possibly St. George), with sword and round shield, attacking a dragon. There is a large room over this gateway, which forms a council-chamber for the clergy of the city, and for other clerical purposes.

There are upwards of forty churches in Norwich, most of them very ancient, and containing many things nearly as old as the fabrics themselves—stained-glass windows, fonts, screens, wall paintings, brasses, monumental tombs and tablets, and no end of archæo-logical treasures in stone and wood carvings. And the bells of these churches! Edgar Allen Poe might have added another verse to his poem "The Bells," had his lot been cast in this city, for it is the home, *par excellence*, of English bellringers. I sup-pose no other place in England can boast of so many bellringers, or of such good ones, as Norwich. On certain occasions the clamour of the bells is nearly deafening. Fancy a score of peals ringing at the same time!—why, it out-Wagners Wagner for volume of sound.

Rapidly we will glance at the chief architectural points and most notable objects in the principal of the ancient churches. First mention is claimed by

St. Peter Mancroft, which is the largest and most prominent, standing, as it does, overlooking the market-place. It was restored only a few years since, at a cost of £14,000, the commission being placed in the hands of the late Mr. Street, of Law Courts fame. The tower was completely restored, at a cost of several thousand pounds, and surmounted by a leaden Fléche, 40ft. in height, making the total height from the ground 150ft. From the tower a grand view of the city, spread map-like around, is obtained, and well repays the toil of whirling upwards in the narrow, circular stairway, a height of 110ft. from the ground line. Take the view from the top first, then on the downward course you may examine the finest peal of twelve bells in the kingdom at your leisure. The weight of the full set is within a few pounds of 184cwt. No doubt there are peals of eight bells of equal tone, but this peal, as a set of *twelve*, is unequalled. In the ringing chamber, emblazoned upon large boards attached to the walls, are the records of the ringers, of which the Norwich ringers are justly proud. One sets forth how, in February, 1827, the herculean Sam. Thurston rang the tenor bell, weighing 41cwt., unaided, and without a rest, through a set of triple Bob Royals, containing 5040 changes. This was the first feat of the kind on record. The immense east window is filled with genuine fourteenth-century stained glass; and there are also several other modern painted windows, of mediocre calibre.

The organ is a very fine one, with the ugliest set of false front pipes in the world. They are typical of a tidy builder's yard, being merely square wooden troughs, set on their pointless ends, in a *nearly* perpendicular arrangement of crescendo and rallentando as to size.

The very ancient font is covered with a wonderful piece of carved and painted (Vandals!) tabernacle work, of such dimensions as to form a kind of raised baptistry. The tiara, or diminishing upper storey, has fallen into such decay that it is taken down; but funds are being raised for its restoration. On the wall behind the font is a large panel of tapestry, representing the Ascension, and bearing the date 1573; and over the south entrance hangs a large oil painting, by Catton, a local artist, of Peter being released from prison.

There is, in the vestry, a collection of rare old manuscript books; one of them, an illuminated Bible, beautifully engrossed on vellum, bears the date A.D. 1340. Many other relics of past ages, as painted panels, the disused fourteenth-century clock, a carved slab of alabaster, &c., will be shown by the obliging verger. The reredos is a very fine modern one, but its beauty cannot be appreciated until a close inspection is made, as the minutiæ of its carved detail is lost in the vastness of the cathedral-like church, when seen from the middle of the nave. The present church was dedicated in 1455, and its register, dating from 1650, may be seen in the vestry. The only thing that could improve the noble interior is the insertion of more stained glass, or, at least, obscured glass, as the grandness is spoilt by the admission of too much white light, which leaves every nook and corner exposed, and thus detracts from the solemnity and vastness of the building, by allowing the eye to penetrate too easily to the greatest height and length of the church, whose size, to an ordinary mind, is thus grasped at a glance. The deep shadows are entirely missing—those dim depths of unknown extent are absent; and this shadowless nave is robbed of its solemn awe and mysterious proportions by the admission of a much too brilliant and unsubdued light. The clerestory windows, in fact, are in such close contact, and of such unusual size, that they appear, when seen from the outside, like one huge window, running the whole length of the church.

St. Michael's Church should be seen by those interested in the actual fabric of the building, as the flintwork, formed into various Perpendicular patterns, is second to none in the realm. The chancel is especially well planned, the walls being occupied by patterns in flint, which embrace their whole area. Many other fine points will repay a visit to this venerable edifice.

St. Peter-per-Mountergate, in King Street, is a fine Perpendicular building, finished in 1486. In the chancel are twenty-four ancient oak stalls, formerly occupied by the monks, who had a kind of college, which stood in the corner of the churchyard, but has long since disappeared. The tomb of R. Berney may be seen near the altar. During the rebellion of Kett, the tanner, Thomas Codd was mayor of Norwich, and led a large force against him. Codd is buried in the nave, and his will is annually read in the church on the Sunday before St. Thomas's Day.

St. Andrew's, in Broad Street, is second only to the parish church (St. Peter Mancroft) in size, and greatly resembles it in appearance. A plentiful use has been made of the St. Andrew's Cross, as a pattern, in the flintwork. The tower was built in 1487, and the body of the church in 1506, as recorded in a verse over the north porch :—

> This church was builded of Timber, Stone, and Bricks,
> In the year of our Lord XV. hundred & Six,
> And translated from extreme idolatry
> A Thousand five hundred and seven and forty;
> And in the first year of our noble King Edward,
> The Gospel in Parliament was mightily set forward—
> Thanks be to God. Anno Dom. 1547, December.

The Communion plate, weighing 160 oz., was presented to the church in 1704; the flagons each weigh 60 oz. The tower contains a fine peal of ten bells. A large tomb, erected to the memory of Sir John Suckling and his wife, is surmounted by their effigies, of life size. Several stained-glass windows give dignity and warm colouring to the otherwise white and cold interior. A few old mural tablets complete the sights of this very fine church.

St. Clement's Church, in Colegate Street, is a very old building, but has nothing very remarkable about

it, except that many persons go to it to see the
"Leper's Tomb," in the churchyard. Who the leper
was nobody knows; but the legend is, that on condition that he was buried here, in consecrated ground,
he would bequeath his fortune to the Church. As he
is buried here, we may presume that he kept his
word, or doubtless the monks of those days would
have had little compunction in disinterring him.

St. Edmund's Church, in Fishergate Street, is a
little, ancient building, boasting a life of 800 years, as
it was built in the time of William the Conqueror, and
for a great number of years contained a relic even
more venerable than itself. This was a portion of the
shirt of Edward the Martyr, which has since been
shifted—at least, it is not there now. The register
in the vestry dates from 1550.

St. Etheldred's, in King Street, is also very ancient,
being partly of Norman and partly of Perpendicular
design. The flint tower is round at the bottom, and
surmounted with an octagonal bell-chamber, containing
a solitary bell. A curious carved monument in the
chancel contains large figures of Alderman Johnston,
kneeling, and behind him his son, also kneeling, and
reading a book. Opposite him are the kneeling
figures of his wife and three daughters; date 1611.

St. George's Tombland stands close to St. Ethelbert's Gate of the Cathedral. It is perched on a
piece of rising ground, and seems to stand uncom-
fortably in a corner, as if trying to hide itself. It
is flanked by some nodding Elizabethan houses, and

forms a very picturesque "bit" for an artist. It was erected in 1445, and is a very fine building, of the Perpendicular style, though with some portions of an earlier type.

St. Giles, in St. Giles Street, is a grand building, and stands in such a position that it can be seen without the usual impediments of encroaching houses. It was originally built in the reign of William the Conqueror, but rebuilt in the reign of Richard II. (about 1380). It is now in a complete state of repair, having been thoroughly restored about 1870. The massive square tower rises to a height of 125ft., and forms quite a landmark to the surrounding country. Round the eaves are some curiously carved gargoyles, of a very grotesque character. On entering, notice

STONE GARGOYLE, ST. GILES'S CHURCH.

the groining of the porch roof; it is of the fan tracery style, for which King's College, Cambridge, is so celebrated, and is the only specimen in Norwich! There are a number of old brasses in this church, and several mural tablets. The chancel was demolished in 1581, by order of the dean and chapter, and the old material given to certain poor traders to start them in business. These dignitaries thus killed two birds with one stone: they obtained the name of

G

philanthropists, and at the same time got rid of their obligation to keep the said chancel in repair, which at the time it much needed.

St. Gregory, in Pottergate Street, is an ancient church in the Perpendicular style, but with the clerestory and some of the other windows in the Decorated style. As it has several attractions, it should certainly not be missed. On the end wall of the nave is a very large fresco painting, perhaps 16ft. by 8ft., in a very good state of preservation, which was discovered at the restoration of the church in 1861. It represents St. George, on horseback, slaying the dragon; the figures are all much larger than life. The brass eagle lectern, with four lion's-head feet, is dated 1496, and is probably one of the oldest brass reading-desks in the kingdom. There are a few brass inscription plates and mural memorials to Sir Francis Bacon and Sir Peter Seaman. The tower contains the original stone gallery, formerly used by the choir, and is an object of interest to many. The pall is a notable example of needlework, and may be seen by "speaking kindly" to the sexton. It is curiously strewn with angels, bearing small figures, and beneath each angel is represented a large fish swallowing a small one. Various theories as to the symbolic meaning of these great and little fish are given. The fish was the ancient symbol of the Church, so, perhaps, it represents the Church of England swallowing the Dissenters; or, more probably, it represents the Church taking tithes, as represented by St. Peter's fish, which is the little one.

St. John's, Maddermarket, is a good specimen of fifteenth-century architecture. It contains two small chapels, dedicated to St. Mary the Virgin and to All Saints. The roofs of these chapels are of old painted designs. In various parts of the building are nine or ten brasses; so that (with permission) a morning might be spent here in taking rubbings.* A tablet in the north wall of the choir denotes the resting-place of Margaret, second wife of the Duke of Norfolk whom Queen Elizabeth caused to be beheaded. She was buried here in 1563, but the monument was not erected for more than two centuries after. The tower is a massive, square, flint building, with a public way through its base, which was also the case with St. Peter's till recently. There is no chancel, which gives the church a curious, curtailed appearance.

St. John Timberhill, in Ber Street, has the distinction of being the only towerless church in the city. The tower was blown down during a gale, in 1784, and has never been restored. A small excrescence, called a bell-cot, does duty for a tower, and contains a small, solitary bell.

---

* Mentioning brasses brings before me the fact that the two largest and finest in England are to be seen in the county of Norfolk, although not in this part. They are at St. Margaret's Church, Lynn, and may be seen in the tower. One, dated 1349, to Adam de Walsoken, is of large extent, and represents a vineyard. The other is to the memory of Robert Braunche, and is dated 1374, and is called the "Peacock Brass." It represents a feast, the principal dish of which is a lordly peacock being served in full plumage. The dimensions of this brass are 8ft. by 5ft. 6in.

G 2

St. Lawrance, in Upper Westwick Street, is a large building, of great architectural elegance, especially the windows, the tracing of which is extremely graceful. It contains several fine brasses of the fifteenth century. The interior has a somewhat cold appearance, which has been accentuated by employing very cool tints in the cathedral glass of the windows, which is a mistake. The oak roof is supported by lofty, massive columns, which give a fine open appearance to the interior. In the spandrels of the western door are some curious old stone carvings; one represents St. Lawrance, patron saint of the church, being grilled to death; while the emperor, who gave orders for his cruel death, is also receiving his death-blow by the hand of God, who is represented as wielding a sword. The other carving represents a party of soldiers transfixing the body of King Edward with arrows. His head may be seen in a bush, which is guarded by a wolf, as related in the legend (see Butler's "Lives of the Saints"). The tower is 112ft. to the top of the battlements. One of the windows —that at the end of the north aisle—has been unceremoniously blocked by a building, an outhouse of some kind, in the corner formed by the junction of the nave and chancel, which spoils the look of the church from the north. The windows were at one time filled with stained glass, which those narrow-minded Vandals, the Puritans, took great pains to destroy in the year 1643.

St. Lawrance's Well was a public spring as early

as the reign of Edward I., but in 1576 was granted
to Robert Gibson, on condition that he should conduct
its waters, through a leaden pipe, to the main thorough-
fare. This he did, and a pump was erected over it.
A few years since, Mr. Harry Bullard, a brewer, and
well-known patron of his city, transformed it into a
public drinking fountain; but as Norwich is a notori-
ously—well, to put it in a mild form—anti-teetotal
city, it is doubtful whether many of the inhabitants
could give evidence as to the purity of the spring.

St. Martin's-at-Oak, in Oak Street, was so named
from an oak which formerly stood in the churchyard,
in the branches of which hung a painted figure of
St. Mary. This figure the pious came to worship
beneath, and many fat donations fell to the Church
in consequence. The present oak was planted about
1798, so is quite a modern institution. Finer specimens of Perpendicular windows, with the straight
line tracery, cannot be found anywhere, and architects will do well to study them. The interior of
the church, which is somewhat bare, contains an
alabaster tomb to the memory of Jeremiah Ravens
and his wife.

St. Martin-at-Palace takes its name from having
been built exactly opposite the Bishop's Palace. It
is not in any way uncommon as regards architecture.
It contains, however, several stained-glass windows,
of various degrees of merit. The east window is
filled with subjects from the life of our Lord. They
are as follows:—The Annunciation, the Adoration,

Via Dolorosa, Crucifixion, Resurrection, and Burial. The register dates from 1538.

The plain in front of the church is historic ground —in fact, tragically historic, for here was fought the battle against Kett, which was the death-blow to the rebellion, as also to Lord Sheffield, who was here killed. An adjoining public-house, with the amorous appellation of the Cupid and Bow, has an inscription upon it setting forth that Lord Sheffield was there slain.

St. Michael's, Coslaney Street, is a large and elegant building, and should on no account be missed. It is not so ancient as many of the Norwich churches; but what it loses in antiquity is more than compensated for by the greater elegance of its later style of building. The south aisle and chantry chapel were built, in 1498, by William Ramsey, who was afterwards twice mayor of Norwich. They are in the Early English style, though the remaining portion of the church is in pure Perpendicular work. The nave and north aisles were not built, or, rather, rebuilt, till 1511-1514, by two brothers — Stephen and John Hallow. It is a remarkable thing among Norwich churches, that this one (St. Michael's, or, as it is usually called, St. Miles's) has no clerestory windows; but plenty of light is admitted by the nave windows, each of which is of four lights, and unusually large. The altar-piece, which takes the place of the east window, which was ages ago filled in, is the work of Heins, and represents the scene of the Resurrection, and the four Evangelists, life-size. Several very old brasses, and a number of mural tablets, help to give the church a furnished and most interesting appearance. There are parts of two stained-glass windows of ancient work, which fortunately escaped the hands of the gentle Puritans, who appear to have left the subjects unmolested, with the trifling exception of taking off the heads of the figures. The chancel floor is paved with parti-coloured marble, brought from the seat of the Earl of Yarmouth, at Oxnead.

The glory of the building is the chantry chapel, which is dedicated to the Virgin Mary. This was built and endowed by Robert Thorpe, about the year 1500. The exterior is a most remarkable piece of flint and stone work; so much so, that architects have come from all parts of England to see and profit by it. The various patterns are set out in stone, and the intervening spaces neatly and exactly filled in with flints; but an adequate idea of the finish of this work can only be gleaned by actual inspection.

St. Michael's-at-Plea, in Queen Street, is so named from the fact of the Ecclesiastic Court of Pleas being held there. It is of cruciform construction, and has a square, embattled tower, with two bells. Near the pulpit are eight old painted panels of saints, which are worthy of inspection, as are also the brasses and tablets.

St. Michael's-at-Thorn, an old church in Ber Street, was anciently called St. Michael-cum-Montem. It has still a large thorn-tree growing in the burial-ground; but whether it is the original one I cannot say—probably not. The entrance-porch is a fine specimen of Norman work, dating from about 1250; but the tower was not erected till 1436.

St. Saviour's, in Magdalen Street, is a small fabric, and is really, according to its full dedication, the Church of the Transfiguration of our Saviour. It contains a number of mural tablets, none of them of great beauty or importance. The font is an old specimen of stone carving, 400 years having passed since it left the mason's hands. The stem is formed of a cluster of four columns, resting upon lions' heads.

St. Simon and St. Jude, in Wensum Street, is considered the oldest of the Norwich Churches, as it was in existence before the building of the Cathedral by Bishop Losigna, in the eleventh century. It contains several good brasses, and a number of mural tablets. The tomb of Sir J. Pettus has the effigy of that military knight, encased in *cap-à-pie* armour. Four knights, who fell at Mousehold Heath during Kett's Rebellion, in the reign of Henry VI., are buried in one grave beneath the chancel; the record of this fact is preserved in the register, still extant.

St. Stephen's, in Rampant Horse Street, is a large Gothic building, built of flint, in the Perpendicular style. The aisles are parted from the nave by lofty, fluted columns, with pointed Gothic arches. The church contains several good old brasses and neat wall tablets, and several stained-glass windows, including that at the east end. In the vestry is a curious carving, in alabaster, of figures of saints, and

also a description of the church by the antiquarian
Mackerell, who helped Blomfield to compile his huge
tome "The History of Norfolk," at the end of the
last century. The oak roof deserves attention, as it
is a beautiful specimen of open timber-work.

St. Swithin's, in Westwick Street, is of several kinds
of architecture, and affords a kind of architectural
puzzle to discover the various periods and styles of
its construction. During the year 1834, a portrait of
Edward the Confessor was discovered nailed under
one of the seats, where it had probably been placed
during Cromwell's administration ; it forms part of the
old rood-screen. The altar-piece, a large oil painting, has for its subject the brothers Moses and Aaron.
The Communion plate is ancient and valuable, as it
is very massive. Fragments of old stained glass are
still discernible in some of the windows, and three old
oak stalls are still preserved. Some of the brasses
are quite perfect. The font, on its four panels, bears
carved emblems of the Trinity, Eucharist, and Passion,
with the arms of East Anglia.

These are the most noteworthy of the city churches ;
but short walks from the city will bring one to the
small hamlets of Earlham, Eaton, Heigham, Lakenham,
and Hellsden, with their parish churches.

The walk of a couple of miles to Earlham is very
pretty, and the old, ivy-covered church, overlooking
the bridge over the river Yare, is very picturesque,
and will give pleasure to those persons who may be
disposed to go and view it.

At Earlham, and elsewhere, may be seen circular-sailed water-mills, which are so contrived, that they serve the double purpose of drain-ing the marsh - land, and also supplying the farms on the adjacent hills with water, by means of a hydraulic ram, which is attached to the pumping appa-ratus. I am not sure, but I think the idea is more American than English.

Another pretty rustic walk is to Cringleford, *viâ* Eaton. The old water-mill stands on a spot which has been thus occupied ever since Saxon times. The scenery round about is very fine, and has afforded the subject for many pictures, both in oil and water-colour.

A good picture may be obtained when standing near the bridge over the Yare, taking in the glistening stream, with its green meadows and richly-wooded slopes, with Eaton Church, of picturesque aspect, standing—as it does in the afternoon—in the golden sunlight.

Harking back to the city once more, we will notice the Museum. It is not of very great extent, but its contents are such as no one who cares for the study of Norfolk can afford to miss. It has a very complete ornithological collection, of which that of the Raptorial birds is considered one of the finest in Europe. It has also a fine collection of various relics which have been discovered at various times in the villages all over the county. Treasures from the sea and from the cliffs also go to swell the list. Many bones of antediluvian animals are shown ; among them is a tusk of a mammoth, over 11ft. in length, and of proportionate thickness. There is also the humerus of a mammoth, which makes the corresponding bone of one of the largest elephants of modern times look quite small. Here is the comparison between the mammoth bone and that of Chuny, who was kept at Exeter Change, London, about the beginning of the present century, until he went mad, and had to be destroyed by a party of soldiers firing volley after volley into him till he expired :—

	HUMERUS OF MAMMOTH.	HUMERUS OF CHUNY.
Length	53in.	35in.
Circumference at middle	26in.	13in.
Circumference at large end	41in.	32in.

By comparing the bones of these two monsters, it has been ascertained that the mammoth must have been within an inch or two of 17ft. in height.

Besides local curiosities, may be seen articles of general interest from all parts of the world, from the well-cured mummy to the cast of the head of the modern murderer. There are a few very ordinary pictures, hung, perhaps for the best, in a rather dull light.

The Cattle Market, on the hill, is one of the principal sights of the city, and is, without exception, the largest in the kingdom. Saturday is the market day, when hundreds of horses and cattle are shown, and literally thousands of sheep and pigs; so that, from the Castle walk, the *coup-d'œil* is a living sea of animals.

The Corn Exchange, open also on Saturdays, will be an amusing sight to those unused to such places.

The Public Library, close to the Guildhall, has just completed its centenary. It contains about 55,000 volumes, available for the use of the public on payment of a small annual subscription.

The library of the people is the Free Library, of several thousand volumes. It contains two large rooms, one for males and one for females, both of which are daily thronged. It is a pleasure to go in and see the scores of working men and others, quietly reading the papers, magazines, and books of various kinds, in the well-warmed and ventilated rooms.

The Market Place is 200yds. long, by a little over 100yds. wide; the market is held on Wednesdays and Saturdays, when beautiful country stores of all kinds are exposed for sale. It is a surprise to London people to see the skill with which the poultry is dressed. The fowls appear as if they had been born without feathers, for not the faintest trace of one is to be discerned on any part of them; and this cleanness is heightened by the manner in which they are trussed and set-off with the lace-like fat, which is artistically arranged over the breast. There are also skin, seed, and fish markets.

In the centre of the Market Place stands a statue

of the Duke of Wellington, and at one end is the old Guildhall, of fifteenth-century flint-work, the building of which was commenced in 1408. The latter building contains various portraits of early mayors and other notables, among the latter being John Crome, the artist, who is better known as "Old Crome." One of the chief objects of interest is the white-sheathed sword of Admiral Don Zavier Winthuysen, who commanded at, and was killed in, the Battle of St. Vincent, 1797. It was presented by Lord Nelson to the Mayor of Norwich during the same year. The Regalia and Corporation Plate is stored here, and is, some of it, over 200 years old. A civic mace, which was presented by Queen Elizabeth, is still in good preservation, although nearly three centuries have elapsed since it assumed its sway.

There is a fairly good theatre, in which plays are rendered by starring companies from London and other large cities.

St. Andrew's Hall, where the Triennial Musical Festival is held, has a long history, of both ecclesiastical and civic importance. The building was commenced in 1413, by Sir Thomas Erpingham, and was finished by his son, Sir Robert (who was a Dominican), about 1430. It was dedicated and used as a church till the reign of Henry VIII., who, at the dissolution of the monasteries, caused it to be closed; but the citizens, partly by prayers and partly by payment, caused it to be granted to the Corporation of Norwich as a Council Hall, and thus pre- • served it from destruction. It has been the scene of many feasts, civic, political, and Royal. It is now used for meetings and concerts of all kinds, the chief being the Triennial Musical Festival in which the principal vocalists of the day take part.

The hall proper is 124ft. long, and 64ft. wide. Most of the windows are in the Perpendicular style, but three are of Decorated construction. The roof is of chestnut, and of ancient workmanship. The tower fell in 1712, and has not been again reared. The chancel, 100ft. by 32ft., is now the Dutch Church, and has a sermon preached in it once yearly by the Chaplain to the Dutch Embassy.

St. Andrew's Hall contains a large number of oil paintings and portraits. Two of the former are large historic subjects: " Queen Eleanor Sucking the Poison from the Arm of her Consort, Edward I." and " The Death of Lady Jane Grey." The principal portraits are those of Lord Nelson, by Sir William Beechey ; Queen Anne and Prince George of Denmark ; Sir Harboard Harboard, by Gainsborough ; Hon. Henry Hobart, and others, by Opie ; and Mr. Harry Bullard, by the late Frank Holl ; besides those of many mayors, aldermen, and other civic functionaries. The windows contain the coats of arms of the various mayors from 1855 to the present date.

Norwich is peculiarly rich in old architecture, and, among other old buildings, the following may be noted as some of the grandest specimens of bygone styles yet to be seen :

The Old Music House, in King Street, is very

ancient, and makes a fine study for the artist. Very close to it is a house dating from the twelfth century, and one of the oldest private dwellings in England. As early as the reign of William II. this was known as Isaac's House, because it had been bequeathed by a Jew of the period to his son Isaac. The vaults are pure Norman in style. These two houses are now severally a public-house and a corn merchant's. Another remarkable room is to be seen at Elm Hill ; it is now used as a carpenter's shop. In Queen Elizabeth's time it was a dining-hall, and, during her State visit, she was here entertained by the Mayor and Corporation. It is panelled and ceiled with oak. The Rosemary Inn also contains some ancient rooms with carved ceilings, of a graceful and delicate nature. The Strangers' Hall, in the Maddermarket, also claims attention.

One of the finest specimens of mediæval architecture is the Dolphin Inn, at Heigham, formerly the Palace of Bishop Hall. It is rarely that a wood-carver comes in contact with such a study as this old building affords. Staircases, ceilings, chimney-pieces, overmantels, panels, and everything else, are carved— except, as the host informed me, the joints and fowls, and they are frequently hacked.

The cloisters of the Dominicans, and the Priory of St. Helen's, will amply repay a visit, and, upon inquiry, many other rare old fabrics will be pointed out to the antiquarian student.

Almost every street contains examples of old houses

of Elizabethan and other picturesque styles. At the corner of Surrey Street and St. Stephen's Street is a group of five old, thatched houses, with oak timber-work and the usual plaster filling. Others, suitable for sketching, may be seen in Oak Street and Pottergate Street, and in a number of other places.

As you stroll along, notice the queer names of the still more queer lanes, alleys, and yards, which branch off from all the principal thoroughfares. These places are the residence of the poorer classes, and each "yard," which is reached by a narrow passage-way under the house in the main street, contains a little colony or town of mechanics and their families, who are, at times, very jealous of their courtyard being scrutinised by strangers. The names of some of these yards are very funny, but doubtless have their origin in some local fact. Such are Little Arabian Horse Yard, Ten Bell Lane, Three Kings Lane, Gaffer's Yard, Pipe Burner's Yard, Keel and Wherry Yard, and others by the score.

Having briefly examined the principal sights of Norwich, we must now again hie back to Pull's Ferry and the "Lily." As we are very late, the only thing we can do is to have our supper, a hand of cards, a "nightcap," and retire; for we must be up betimes in the morning, so as to enjoy our thirty miles trip to "Bloaterville." Don't forget to take a last look at the Cathedral from this point (Pull's Ferry) before leaving in the morning, for it is considered a very fine view.

CHAPTER VI.

NORWICH TO YARMOUTH.

Wha'll buy my caller herrin'?
They're no brought here without brave darin';
  Buy my caller herrin'! ye little ken their worth.
Wha'll buy my caller herrin'? O ye may ca' them vulgar
  farin';
Wives and mithers, maist despairin', ca' them lives o' men.
  Caller herrin'! Caller herrin'!
                                        LADY NAIRNE.

AS most of the Yare between Norwich and
Yarmouth was traversed by us on our upward course, but little remains to describe
until we again arrive at the mouth of the New Cut,
from which we have about four or five miles to
journey before reaching Breydon.

Could we but see this now comparatively narrow
river as it existed a thousand years ago, we should
notice a wonderful difference. At the time of King
Canute—according to ancient manuscripts—a large
arm of the sea extended quite to Norwich; the Yare
being at that period divided into two broad channels,
which freely admitted the tides, over what are now

H

meadows, quite up to the city. About the time of the Norman Conquest, one of these channels was gradually filled up by sand, and became solid ground, upon the most eastern portion of which the town of Yarmouth was built. The other opening has, in the course of time, become the mouth of the present river Yare. The flow of the sea having been thus checked, Norwich was obliged to forfeit its claim to being considered a fishing town, a distinction it had hitherto enjoyed. The country, from the New Cut to the entrance to Breydon Water, is so flat that one may see for miles in every direction. This is the best river for canoeing, as the tide serves as far as Norwich; so that a couple of days may be spent very comfortably by starting from Yarmouth on the first of the flood tide, visiting the various places of interest on the route, landing at Norwich at dusk (28 miles), and sleeping there, so as to come away an hour or two before the ebb tide next day. A sailing canoe is a capital craft, as in most of the reaches one can scud along, enjoying the *dolce far niente*. I am surprised that canoeing is not more generally indulged in by the thousands of visitors who throng to Yarmouth in the season. True, the canoes on these waters are not what they might be; but if the public took more interest in canoeing, the owners would soon find it pay them to construct canoes on the lines of those used on the Mersey and other northern rivers by the various clubs. Anyone with sufficient capital and confidence to build a dozen good canoes would, by letting them out during the season, secure a good return of profit on his capital: £150 would be required to build and equip a dozen canoes, and during the season they would bring in from £15 to £20 per week, or even more.

Canoes of the "Rob Roy" type are best adapted for travelling, as they are strong and light, with good beam for sailing. A canoe 15ft. long, by about 28in. broad, is large enough to carry a heavy man anywhere, as, with a burden of, say, fourteen stone (twelve for occupant and two for stores), it would not draw more than about 4in. of water. This lightness and shallowness of draught enables them to go anywhere—that is, if there be only a few inches of water; and as the paddle only requires a space of about 5ft. in width, instead of the 12ft. required by sculls, the canoeist may explore even the narrowest dykes and the most sinuous channels of the Broads. The Mersey canoes have a centre-board, which can be raised and lowered at pleasure, so that the amount of canvas they can carry, in comparison to their size, is very great. For the general public, however, these canoes would be only a source of danger, as great experience is required to manage them. Speed on a trip of this kind must necessarily be subservient to other matters. By the way, has anyone yet realised the idea of pro-pelling a canoe by means of a very small marine engine and screw, the boilers of which could be heated by some kind of oil?—or electricity might be

H 2

brought into the service. If this were carried out, one would be independent of wind, tide, or manual labour.

Crossing Breydon in the evening, which is alive with gulls and their larger relatives, the yachts, we anchor at Sir Edmund Lacon's Ale Stores, near the Bure mouth, until the morning; up this river we will, with the early tide, venture.

The town of Yarmouth, as previously stated, is built on a small peninsula formed by the sea and the river Yare. It lies in longitude 1° 43″ E., so that the time here is about 6 minutes 55 seconds earlier than Greenwich mean time. The old town is built in a very peculiar manner; indeed, its like cannot be found in England. The main streets run from north to south, and are connected by a great number of very narrow lanes, or alleys, locally termed "rows"— a very appropriate name for a town so much connected with herrings. Instead of these rows being given distinct appellations, they are simply distinguished by numbers running from 1 to 160. These streetlets are so narrow as not to admit the passage of an ordinary cart, so recourse is had to a curious-looking skeleton affair, called a "lorrie," which is a vehicle 12ft. long, and not more than 3ft. to 3ft. 6in. over all in width; and even then, when one of these narrow vehicles is passing through a narrow row, pedestrians have to seek refuge in the nearest door-way or court. The drivers stand upright, holding the reins as their sole support; but constant use makes them quite at home on these curious conveyances.

A Yarmouth "Row"

The market is, I believe, the largest of its kind in the kingdom, and covers nearly three acres of well-paved ground. On Saturday, the principal market day it is quite a sight to walk up the long paths, flanked by curious old booths containing huge quantities of provisions—fish, flesh, fowl, and fruit; the two latter especially may be had here in rare perfection. The market women of Yarmouth are second to none as poultry dressers, as all who have seen their wares must acknowledge.

Three bridges span the river, at a short distance from each other; one of them—the Suspension Bride —marks the spot where a dreadful calamity occurred in May, 1845. A clown (Barry) from one of the London theatres had undertaken a journey down the river in a washing-tub drawn by geese; the banks, and also the bridge, were lined with spectators, and as he shot the bridge, the people rushing in a body from one side to the other caused the chain to snap, when 400 persons were precipitated into the Yare, 79 of whom were either crushed or drowned.

NORTH GATE, YARMOUTH.

Among other curiosities in Yarmouth may be noted

the remains of the old city walls and towers or gates ; that of the North Gate, which is still in good preservation, bears the date 1396 as the period of its construction. From this gate the ancient wall may be traced till it reaches the remains of the King's Tower, in the churchyard.

No. 4, South Quay, is a remarkable house. It was built in 1596, and contains some fine rooms in the Elizabethan style, which, by courtesy of the occupier, may sometimes be seen by those interested in old architecture. In one of these rooms, according to tradition, the death of Charles I. was determined upon. The house was then in the occupation of the Carter family. A granddaughter of Oliver Cromwell also resided here early in the eighteenth century.

The Star Hotel should not be missed, as it contains some fine carved work in its ceilings and fireplaces ; and other things of interest will be pointed out by the obliging landlord. The Quay—or, rather, quays, for it is divided at the Vauxhall Bridge into North and South Quays—is thought to be, with, perhaps, one exception (that at Seville), the finest in Europe. At the extreme end of the North Quay stands one of the ancient city towers above mentioned, of which there were formerly sixteen, also ten gates ; this was when the City was environed by a strong wall.

The Town Hall, built in 1882, is by·far the finest building in Yarmouth, and stands at the commencement of the South Quay, opposite the berth of the General

Steam Navigation Company's steamers. It is built of red brick and Portland stone, and is surmounted by a tower rising to a height of 125ft. It contains some very fine rooms; one—the Assembly Room—is 100ft. by 40ft., and is elegantly decorated. There are other large rooms for municipal uses—viz., the Court Room, 50ft. by 30ft.; Dining Room, 33ft. by 25ft.; Police Court, 37ft. by 32ft.; Committee Room, 32ft. by 27ft.; Entrance Hall, 80ft. by 25ft., &c., &c.

It seems a pity that, after an existence of only five years, this noble structure should have to undergo extensive repairs, on account of the subsidence of the foundations contiguous to the river; but such is the case.

From the Town Hall the Quay is planted with a double row of trees, and presents a very fine vista. Walking down this avenue, noticing the various craft as we go (and they are legion), we come to the Fish Wharf, where, during the "herring harvest," scenes of great excitement and clamour may be witnessed, as the laden vessels come in and disgorge their finny cargoes, which are at once sold by auction. Upwards of 2000 lasts of herrings have been landed here in one day; and when we consider that a last contains 13,200 fish, thus giving a total of 26,000,000 herrings caught in a single day, we may well be amazed, and wonder wherever they all go to. Perhaps it is not generally known that, according to local legend, a herring, like Baalam's ass, once spoke, and then not in common prose, but, as my informant said, "it spook in powertra" (spoke in

poetry). This is the complete and unabridged version
of the poem :—

> There was a herring spoke,
> And only one,
> And that said : " Roast my back
> Before you roast my bone."

Good advice! and, let me add, eat them as the
natives do, with mustard as a condiment. The best
way to serve a bloater is to cut off the head and tail,
open it down the back, take out the bones, and grill.

Trinity Wharf, the store and repairing yard of the
Trinity Company, is an interesting sight. Very few
persons have seen a light-ship, except at a distance;
but here they may make a closer acquaintance with one,
as there is always a spare vessel moored here. Notice
the immense buoys, of all shapes, sizes, and colours,
and the curious "mushroom" anchors, with which the
light-vessels are moored. At the extremity of the
South Quay is the racecourse and Nelson's Column ;
the latter was erected in 1817. It consists of a handsome Doric, fluted column, springing from a square
base, and is surmounted by a colossal figure of
Britannia. The total height is 144ft. The ascent
may be made for a trifle, and a splendid view
obtained. Leaving the racecourse, and returning
along the beach, the visitor soon reaches the Wellington Pier, named after the Iron Duke. It is
about 700ft. in length, and, the head of it having been
greatly enlarged in 1883, now affords ample room
for the large number of persons who assemble, during

the summer season, to hear the band and the concerts which take place there every evening.

The Jetty, or Old Pier is much shorter—only about 560ft. — and comes in for a much smaller share of patronage from visitors, who like to go as far out to sea as possible, so long as they can get a firm footing. The Britannia Pier was originally 750ft. long. It was twice cut in two during gales, one vessel actually sailing quite through, and smashing the massive piles for 80ft. or 90ft. The pier was then shortened some 50ft., and is now of the same length as the Wellington. Many young, and would-be hardy, fishermen (if the sea did not toss about so, and make one feel ill) may be seen at the pier-head when the tide is rising, and occasionally make rare havoc among the flats and whiting. At any rate, if, after two or three hours' toil, their hauls are not great, their appetites are.

In the centre of the Parade, facing the sea, stands the Sailors' Home, a large building in the Italian style of architecture. Great as are the resources of this institution, during stormy weather, on several occasions, they have been tried to their utmost, nearly every bed being occupied by wrecked sailors and fishermen. The Museum, on the first floor, is free, and contains many curious things, brought from all lands under the sun. In passing out, an offertory-box will be observed at the door, and any little odd coin you may drop in will go towards helping some poor fellow who has been snatched from a watery grave, perhaps with the loss of everything he possessed in the world, even to his clothes. Adjoining the Home is the Lifeboat Station.

OLD TOLL HOUSE.

The Toll House, which was formerly the Gaol, is now a Free Library. It has been entirely restored, except the Dungeon, which has been kept in *statu quo*, and may be inspected on payment of a small fee.

Before retracing our steps to our yacht, we will take a peep at the venerable Church of St. Nicholas, standing at the foot of the Market Place. It was founded by Herbert de Losigna, first Bishop of Norwich, in 1101, but was not finished until some years after; indeed, it was not completed when Losigna died, in 1119. It is of a cruciform shape, and has been several times enlarged, especially during the years 1123, 1250, 1338, and 1370. It is, as a parish church, unrivalled for size by any in the kingdom. It also boasts a very large porch, which is 21ft. long by 15ft. wide. In the Isle of Wight is a church which would comfortably fit into this, it being only 20ft. by 12ft.; I refer to St. Lawrence.* During the fifteenth

---

* Since writing the above, I have come across a still smaller church, and that is Lullingworth Church, Sussex, which is 16ft. square. The parish contains sixteen inhabitants, so the church is large enough.

and sixteenth centuries, no less than sixteen chapels
were attached to, and embraced within, the walls of
St. Nicholas, each with its altar and attendant priest.
These chapels, being richly endowed, and containing
valuable jewels, plate, and ornaments, were suppressed
by Henry VIII., who converted their appurtenances
into money and diverted it to other uses. In 1683,
the tower was so crooked that it had to be taken
down, and was then replaced by the present one,
which is between 160ft. and 170ft. high. It is the
vicar's aim to raise, by public subscription, a
fund sufficient to build a tower (separate from the
church) which shall reach an altitude of nearly 500ft.
Until within the last few years the church was divided
lengthways into three parts, so that three services
might be carried on simultaneously. These divisions
have now been swept away, and new pews replace
the old ones ; the vast size of the building can, therefore, be seen at a glance. The organ is considered
a very fine one, and was originally built in 1733,
but has since then been several times enlarged and
thoroughly repaired. I do not know of a finer pulpit
than the carved one in this church, and which was
placed there a few years since. A library of rare old
books is attached to the church; one of these books,
a black-letter Bible, is dated 1541 ; and another, a
work printed in Italy, is dated 1547. A remarkable
revolving reading-desk is also shown. There are some
very fine stained-glass windows, those at the west
end of the south aisle (Mills Memorial) and in the

north transept (an Ascension window) being especially worthy of notice; but those in the south aisle, with the exceptions mentioned, are unworthy of the church. The skull of a whale, which has been in the church for two or three centuries, brings ill-luck to anyone who sits in it. Some carved oak panelling at the end of the north aisle is worthy of note; it contains the arms and names of the churchwardens in the seventeenth century, the earliest being dated 1597. The centre panel contains the precept: "𝔉eare 𝔊od; 𝔥onor the 𝔎png "—1 PET. ii. The graveyards, of which there are three, all contiguous to one another, cover several acres, and attract many visitors, on account of their size.

St. Peter's Church contains a fine copy, by T. Myers, of Rubens' "Descent from the Cross;" it is the gift of Col. Mason.

The accompanying illustration represents one of the curious little Dutch whipping-tops used by the Yarmouth urchins. I believe this kind is quite unknown to London children.

DUTCH WHIPPING-TOP.

Many other interesting objects may be seen in Yarmouth; but as I think we have been long enough away from the "Lily," we will cut through Charlotte Street to Lacon's Wharf, and board her.

While we discuss our evening meal in the little cabin, I will, to keep up the discursive character of this chapter, say a few words upon shooting, skating, &c. Without a doubt, wildfowl is not so plentiful as it was some twenty years since; but still, in the late autumn and winter, a good bag may be made. It is almost necessary, however, to procure the services of a man who can take you to the most likely places. On some of the marshes and riverside lands good snipe-shooting may be had; but of course the permission of the owners must be first obtained. A friend of mine, who still lives at Stalham, some twenty years ago bagged fifty-three brace of snipe in one day, and only quite recently brought in seventeen-and-a-half brace as the result of five hours' sport. For the visitor, however, this kind of thing is not obtainable, except by the favour of a landlord. The river, in all navigable parts, is free for shooting to all, and at dusk or early morning good sport may be had among the coots and kindred aquatic wildfowl; while a stray heron, curlew, or pewit, will help to swell the bag. Oulton Broad, Lake Lothing, Breydon Water, and one or two other lakes, are free; but of course little shooting takes place on them in the summer, except for gulls, the close time for which ceases on the first day of August. A dog will be found very useful to retrieve the birds which fall among the reeds, and which would otherwise be lost; and he will often go among the reeds and rushes, to put the fowl out, so that a shot may be obtained. Duck-shooting is pursued in severe weather with both sport and profit, large flights at times making their way here. Teal, widgeon, &c., are to be found occasionally, and in severe weather many foreign birds from the Baltic make their appearance.

Skating can be enjoyed in the depth of winter on the Broads and rivers, as much as in any place in England, the natural features of the country, with its rivers and water-courses, making it almost equal to Holland in this respect. I have sometimes been on the beautiful crystal surface of Hickling Broad, about a square mile in area, with perhaps only a dozen other persons on it besides myself; no fear of being knocked down by the crowded state of the ice here! In very cold weather, one may skate for miles and miles along the rivers; or, if the skater be nervous, he may try his fortune on the glassy covering of ice which surmounts the flooded marshes, with a depth of only about a foot of water; so that, if he should happen to go through, he can step quietly out again. Many of the farmers take off the wheels of their traps, and, fixing on a pair of runners, go sleighing for miles along the rivers. Care has to be taken that the horses' shoes are well-roughed, or removed altogether, and their hoofs "bumbled" with sackcloth.

Some of the fen-men are noted for their speed-skating; they having such splendid opportunities of practising in the winter, almost at their own doors. Even little fellows of six years of age may be seen on skates; so that, when they grow up, they are as much at home on runners as if it were their natural mode of travelling. In the accompanying woodcuts, the upper figure shows the usual form of running skate used in the Fens: the lower one—an elongated steel runner—is frequently seen, and is nearly identical with the skate used in England before the Conquest. The waterfowl are at times found frozen in the ice, which in this bleak eastern county forms very rapidly. I am informed that excellent sport is to be had by cutting a hole in the ice, and well ground-baiting the place a couple of hours before fishing. I cannot vouch for this, as I have not had practical experience of this Esquimaux mode of angling; nor should I much care to try it, for fear of catching more catarrh and rheumatism than perch and rudd. I should think that, when the ice bears well, a roughly improvised ice-boat would furnish infinite amusement, even if no very great speed were attained. A flat-bottomed punt, with two pieces of wood screwed across the bottom, and upon which a pair of iron runners could be fastened, would form the hull; while I should fancy a working lug would do for the sail. No doubt, with a good breeze, a fair rate of speed might be obtained, even with an improvised craft of this description—say, ten to fifteen miles per hour. Even a 2-in. plank, with arms to hold iron runners, would make an ice-boat after the Canadian type. A short mast, stepped forward, would serve for the purpose of an experiment, and *some* fun, on a bright, cold day, could surely be extracted, even from these rough and ready materials.

CHAPTER VII.

UP THE BURE TO ACLE BRIDGE.

Glide gently, thus for ever glide,
  O Bure! that anglers all may see
As lovely visions by thy side
  As now, fair river, come to me.
Oh, glide, fair stream, for ever so,
  Thy quiet soul on all bestowing,
Till all our minds for ever flow
  As thy deep waters now are flowing.

T is a glorious August morning, so we take the top of the flood, and at 8 A.M., having breakfasted, are on our way up the river Bure. For the first few miles the landscape is singularly uninteresting, being composed of water, marshes, and sky, with very little to break the monotony. It seems as if we should never lose sight of Yarmouth; indeed, after going three-and-a-half miles, we are only a mile and a half in a straight line from it, the Bure here describing two-thirds of a circle. A glance at the chart will show this, and we shall also perceive certain points, marked "2-mile house," "3-mile house," &c. These distances are only approximately correct; the houses

or landmarks are so few (the former sometimes half-
a-mile or more apart), that the nearest house to a
given distance is dubbed a "mile-house," and shown
as such on the chart. . The actual distances of the 1-,
2-, 3-, 4-, 5-, 6-, and 7-mile houses from Bure mouth
are, respectively, 7 furlongs, 1¾, 2¾, 4, 5, 6¼, and 7¾
miles.   Nothing but this flat Dutch scenery presents
itself till reaching Acle Bridge—eleven miles and a
half.

At Runham Swim Ferry we lay to, and, packing our
rods and provisions, take a two-and-a-half miles walk
to Filby Broad, there being no means of getting by
water to the leash of Broads known as Filby, Ormsby,
and Rollesby, which are all connected, and form a
straggling, irregular lake, of about 700 acres in extent,
their united length being upwards of three miles.
Filby, the smallest of the three, is nearest the Bure;
next comes Rollesby; and farther north is Ormsby.
Some splendid fish are caught here, but for some reason
pike do not appear to be so plentiful as they were
a few years since.

From the south end of Filby Broad a wide dyke,
called by the appropriate, but not very euphonious,
name of the Muck Fleet, leads to the Bure, but, being
choked with weeds, it is not navigable.   It is about
three-and-a-half miles long, and 16ft. wide, and, by the
outlay of a few pounds for dredging, might be made
navigable for small and flat-bottomed boats; this
expense might be met by the exaction of a small toll.
Communication between the Broads is effected by a low,

I

single-arched bridge, with 4ft. of head room, which space is only just sufficient to allow of a boat and its passengers passing under.

Filby Church (All Saints') contains several stained-glass windows, and has a lofty, embattled Gothic tower. There are also several sculptured memorials to the Lucas family; one especially deserving of

VIEW ACROSS ROLLESBY BROAD—SUNSET.

mention is the work of M. Herrman, of Dresden. Filby is celebrated for the cultivation of raspberries, which, to the value of several hundred pounds, find their way to the Yarmouth and Norwich markets. To those who have never seen a field of raspberry canes, and the mode of culture, a visit to one of those at Filby will be of interest.

Rollesby Broad is a much larger area of water, but is partly preserved ; visitors to the Eel's Foot Inn, kept by host Monsey, can, however, readily obtain boats and permission to fish.   Scores of anglers come here, in the summer, from Yarmouth, either by waggonette (some seven miles), or by rail to Ormsby Station, and thence on foot (two miles.)   It would be as well if those who drive to Ormsby from Yarmouth came *viâ* Caister, so as to view the remains of the Castle, built for Sir John Fastolfe, a valorous knight in the reign of Henry V.   This hero must not be confounded with Shakespeare's pusillanimous Falstaff.   The Sir John referred to, at the battle of Agincourt, took prisoner the Duke d'Alençon, who, as a ransom, built Caister Castle ; at least, so local tradition has it.   History has a different version, for we find that the Duke d'Alençon was slain outright at Agincourt.   At the battle of Verneuil, the son of this Duke was brought prisoner to England, and it was probably he who built Caister Castle.   It was twice besieged—first by the Duke of Norfolk, in the fourth Edward's reign, and, later, by Lord Scales.   It was really more of a castellated mansion than a castle in the strict acceptance of the word, but was complete, with its moat, drawbridge, and strong outer defences.   A lofty, circular tower, and two sides of the body of the building, still stand in picturesque decay.   The edifice was of brick, strengthened by stone.   The population of the villages hereabout is very small, probably not more than 100 souls inhabiting any one of them.   As the villages each occupy an area of about three square miles (or, rather, the parishes containing the villages), some idea may be formed of the scarcity of the inhabitants. Over the door of one of the cottages in Rollesby is the ghastly sign, " A pall to let." Such a thing as a hearse is unknown at a village funeral, as the body is either borne on the shoulders of the relatives or conveyed in a cart. The pall is therefore let out, and does duty for all the villages in the immediate neighbourhood.

Ormsby Broad is the northern limit of these waters, and contains some splendid perch and pike, and a fish which London anglers seldom get among—the rudd. He is a very game fellow, and grows to a large size. It appears to be a moot point as to whether the rudd is a distinct species or a hybrid produced from the roach and the bream. These fish travel in shoals, so that, when on the feed, a good basket may soon be secured: but more on this subject anon. Great Yarmouth draws the supply of water for its 40,000 inhabitants from these Broads, and, upon a visitor applying at the office of the Water Company, in Yarmouth, a ticket will be given him admitting him to view the large waterworks at Ormsby—a sight worth seeing. The parish church of Ormsby (St. Margaret's) is an ancient edifice, having a lofty, square tower, with four monks at the corners instead of pinnacles. It contains several brasses in memory of Lord Home, Lady Alice Clere, &c. The ruins of two or three other churches may be seen near by, viz., All Saints', at Scratby, and Holy Trinity and St. Peter's, between the two Ormsbys. At Billockby, the church is in such a ruinous state that the service is held in the chancel, which for that purpose has been specially

THE LANDING STAGE AT ORMSBY BROAD.

renovated. The whole adult population of the hamlet does not exceed thirty-five, so that even the chancel is never inconveniently crowded : a score is a large congregation. At Scratby is a cliff from which a splendid view of the sea and the surrounding country may be obtained. In the church at Clippesby is an altar-tomb, upon which is a brass portraying the full-length effigies of John Clippesby, his wife Johan, and their four children. It is dated 1594, and contains also a number of shields, emblazoned with coats of arms, &c. The north doorway is well-preserved Norman work, and has frequently been engraved and painted. An ancient font, and the quaintly-carved pews, should be noticed.

Having spent a long, delightful day, we return, late in the evening, to our yacht, thankful to once more enjoy the comfort of our snug cabin and the meal our man has prepared for us. The largest of our catch of fish we reserve for breakfast; at this dish our man will probably turn up his nose, as the natives care little for fish when they have the run of the larder—as our honest Sam has. He actually wonders how we can eat "them things; they're rare things for gret men like yow to keep yar strength up on, they are." No doubt the steak hanging in the locker in the stern-sheets is in his mind's eye. He evidently does not know what ardent anglers we are, nor the sweetness to the palate of a fish caught on one's own hook and by one's own skill.

While our meal is being discussed, the vessel slowly and silently makes her way to Acle Bridge, where we anchor for the night. On the right we pass the village of Stokesby, which, beyond being a pretty little waterside village, possesses nothing especially worthy of note. It contains a population of about 400, and, consequently, the inhabitants are rather proud of it. The church register dates from A.D. 1558.

A note to anglers! During the year 1886, several trout were caught in the vicinity of Acle Bridge, and no doubt others are only awaiting the advent of the angler to hook themselves. In the bar-parlour of the solitary inn at the foot of the bridge, two little "spotted beauties" may be seen, each weighing a trifle under 4lb.; large eels are also caught here, running up to 4lb. and 5lb. in weight.

CHAPTER VIII.

ACLE TO AYLSHAM.

Islets so freshly fair
That ne'er hath bird come nigh them,
But from his course through air
Hath been won downward by them.—TOM MOORE.

T being a rainy morning, we feel lazy, and do
not rise till 8 A.M. Our man has cleaned nine
or ten of the largest perch we caught yesterday at Ormsby, and is cooking them for breakfast.
As it is not everyone who knows how to cook fish
in a proper manner when they have caught them, I
will, at the end of this little work, give a few hints
on the art, not as a professed cook, but as one who
has found out, from experience, the quickest, simplest
and most toothsome manner of preparing for table
the result of his day's sport.

At Acle Bridge (stone, with three arches) all vessels
must lower their masts. This is not a very formid-
able task, as, after striking sail, the mast lowers in a
kind of fulcrum, called a "tabernacle"; the heel of
the mast, being weighted with lead or iron, rises or

falls with very little exertion. The masts of some of the wherries have as much as a ton and a half of lead to balance them. Care should be taken in shooting this bridge, and others of similar construction, as with a strong tide and wind accidents may soon occur. Keep to the middle arch whenever practicable, as the water is there deeper and the arch itself wider.

ACLE BRIDGE.

Acle is a town of nearly 1000 inhabitants, and, consequently, an important place. The church, dedicated to St. Edmund the King, was built about 1350, and has a round tower with an octagonal top. It contains an oak screen, of florid Gothic carving, and an ancient font (1410 A.D.), which at some period has been elaborately painted, the colours being clearly discernible. Over the porch is an effigy, and in the spandrels are, respectively, a kneeling figure and a Tudor rose. In the churchyard may be seen this curious verse :—

> Farewell, dear children, to you I bid adieu;
> *When living, what was in my house always did for you ;*
> But now my time is past, that I did toil in vain,
> But hope in Heaven with you to meet, in Glory to remain.

The town stands a mile to the west of the bridge, and is in direct railway communication with Norwich (thirteen miles) and Yarmouth (eight miles). The remains of Weybridge Priory, founded by Roger Bigod, in the time of Edward 1., are here; but as visitors are fond of taking "samples" of it away with them, the greater portion will doubtless be found somewhere else, as only a waggon-load or two of it is now left.

Nowhere, formerly extra-parochial, is now annexed to Acle; it contains fifteen inhabitants.

A mile from Acle is Fishley (476 acres), noted for little save the paucity of its inhabitants, who number not more than a score, all told.

It is as well to warn yachtsmen of the danger of being run down by a wherry on the narrow rivers. They come swooping down like a huge bird of prey, appearing suddenly round a bend of the river, like a huge "brown" ghost. There seems no particular "rule of the road," but the craft with a free wind usually gives way.

As a wherry is a vessel seen in no other part of England, it may be as well to describe one. It is

neither more nor less than a cargo barge, of local
build, and for local requirements and waters. They
are from 50ft. to 60ft. in length, with a beam of from
10ft. to 12ft., and only draw from 2ft. to 3ft. of water,
which enables them to navigate shallow rivers. They
are from twenty to thirty-five tons burthen, on an

A NORFOLK WHERRY.

average; but one monster, called the "Wanderer,"
has a carrying capacity of eighty-one tons. The body
of the wherry is one long hold, covered by movable
hatchways, which are taken off in 2ft. sections. Aft
is the cabin, forming sleeping accommodation for two
men, and containing a stove for cooking and warming

purposes. Forward, within a few feet of the bows, the huge mast is stepped, in what is called a "tabernacle," which acts as a fulcrum for lowering and raising the mast, sail, and tackling. To raise this huge mass more easily, a number of leaden weights, weighing from 25cwt. to 30cwt., are attached to the heel. The mast is raised by the aid of a windlass standing at the foot. It may be noted that there is no standing rigging whatever. The sail is an enormous one, of tanned canvas of the thickest kind; and in light winds a "bonnet," or supplementary piece, about a yard deep, is attached to the foot of this mainsail. Jibs or topsails are never carried—simply the one mammoth sail, with its boom and gaff.

At the top of the mast, a flag of peculiar construction is invariably placed, as by its aid the wherry is sailed Every little flaw of the wind is denoted by it, and upon this the wherryman relies. The flag-pole is an iron rod, 2ft. high, upon one side of which a painted tin figure is fixed, which always points in the direction from which the wind is blowing. The flag is composed partly of tin and partly of silk. The end nearest the pole is of tin, covered with

MASTHEAD AND GAFF, SHOWING ATTACH-
MENT OF SAIL.

silk, the free end of which flutters in the breeze, as shown in the accompanying woodcut.

In a dead calm, or when it is required to go against a head wind, recourse is had to quanting; that is, pushing with a pole, 18ft. or 20ft. long, called a "quant," in the use of which the wherry-men are very expert. They obtain a sett into the river bottom, or bank, with the pointed end, apply

FLAG ON MASTHEAD OF A WHERRY.

the knobby end to the shoulder, and thus propel their craft forward, many a grunt and deep breath accompanying the arduous task.

The wherry is noted as a fast sailer, and it is claimed for it that it can sail nearer the wind than any other vessel afloat.

Going easily along under a small foresail, having unfortunately run out of coal sooner than we expected (as we did not take any on board at Yarmouth, knowing that we had a

BUTT AND HEAD OF A QUANT.

store at Wroxham), we come to a part of the river called Thurne Mouth, as it is here the Bure and Thurne meet. We turn sharp to the left, almost at right angles, and, a mile and a half from the mouth arrive at Cowholm, a marshy place, on which feed vast herds of cattle. On the right bank we land to obtain a close view and sketch of

the celebrated Abbey of St. Benet's-at-Holm. A hermitage occupied this site long before the time of Canute, but, by that king's order, the Abbey, of which these ruins remain, was built in 1020. The occupants were of the religious order known as Black Monks, or Benedictines. The custom of the times being "might rather than right," and each community having to look after itself, the Abbey was built like a castle for strength. In 1066, the monks, with the help of the surrounding peasantry, offered a most stubborn resistance to William the Conqueror. So well did they fight, that it was only by treachery that the place was captured. One of the monks was promised the abbacy if he allowed the Normans to enter. The bait was too much for the poor follower of St. Benedict, for he gave up the Abbey to its besiegers, who kept their word so far as to invest him with the insignia of office, but then hanged him in his sacred vestments. The Abbey was at one time a very rich one, as many of its royal benefactors liberally endowed it—Edward I. and the Empress Maud in particular. In the reign of Henry VIII. its annual income was put down at £677 9s. 8d., which in those days represented a very large sum. In 1535, the Abbey was annexed to the bishopric of Norwich, and has remained so ever since. All the abbots had a seat in the House of Lords; so that the present Bishop of Norwich has a double claim to his seat. He is the only abbot in England, being styled in legal documents "Bishop of Norwich, and Abbot of St. Benet's-at-Holme."

The walls which once surrounded the Abbey inclosed thirty-eight acres of ground, and were defended on the south by the river Bure, and on the other sides by a deep moat. Part of their foundations may still be traced. Of the Abbey, which was a cruciform building with a round tower in the centre, little now remains; the fine gateway, however, still stands, though it is blocked by the ruins of a huge windmill built during the early part of last century. One of the side walls of the chapel stands close by, and many other fragments are scattered about, especially of the wall bounding the river.

For a picnic or lawn-tennis party, no better place than this can be got; the grass is short and velvety, and plenty of level spots may be found.

Nearly opposite the Abbey is the Fleet Dyke (a mile and a half long), leading to South Walsham Broad (between fifty and sixty acres in extent), which is very rarely, in comparison to other Broads, visited by anglers, being a long way from any railway station. I would advise those who have plenty of time to visit this and other smaller Broads. I dare say that for every party of pleasure-seekers who visit this particular Broad, at least fifty pass it without, perhaps, being aware of its existence. The church of St. Mary is a fine old building, with chancel, nave, side aisle, and tower containing five bells. The register dates from 1550. The church of St. Lawrence was destroyed by fire in 1827, but the chancel having been restored, Divine service was carried on in it, and furnished sufficient accommodation for all the villagers who were likely to attend, the entire population not exceeding 160. The fire was caused by a shovelful of hot cinders being thrown on some dry manure which was lying by. It spread with such rapidity, that in a few hours several stacks, a dwelling-house, and barn, and the church, were consumed. It is a

SOUTH WALSHAM.

TWO CHURCHES IN ONE CHURCHYARD.

remarkable sight to see two parish churches in one churchyard, as is the case here.*

Coming back again to the Bure, and proceeding a mile or so, we reach another dyke, also on the left,

---

* This remarkable feature occurs in several instances in Norfolk. Legend says the two churches in question were built by two sisters; but legend does not always keep to the truth.

which takes us to wild, picturesque Ranworth Broad.
Bring out your sketching materials and colours, for
here is a picture ready for you. Masses of reed-beds,
and glittering water, upon whose surface water lilies,
with their spotless white flowers and broad, circular,
green leaves, float and quiver; a floating coot's nest,
and many sub-aquatic plants, make a splendid fore-
ground. The middle distance is filled in with more
glittering water; some swans; Piscator in his punt,
just playing a fine fish; a rustic, with fodder-hidden
boat, quanting noiselessly along, like a modern
Charon. For your distance: in the soft, blue haze
of a summer's day is seen an old farmhouse, half
hidden by trees, and above this the grand old church
tower, also springing apparently from a nest of
trees. This place seems to present an epitome
of the salient features and characteristics of the
Norfolk Broad district. The Broad is a mile long,
and a quarter of a mile broad, and contains about
100 acres. In parts, it is greatly grown up, but, being
very quiet, some large fish are to be found in it.
It is very amusing, on a calm day, when the yacht
lies at anchor, to lie flat down over the counter,
or in a boat, with one's face close to the water, and
watch the fish, who may be seen a long way down in
clear water, disporting themselves. A "water telescope" (an instrument which you can get made by
any tinman for a trifle) is a capital aid in watching
the gambols of the "water babies." It may be made
thus: Procure a tin cylinder, about 3ft. in length,

K

with one end about 4in. in diameter, and the other
1½in. Blacken the inside of this tube, and have a
slight rim soldered round the inside of each end, upon
which to rest a disk of ordinary window glass, which
should be carefully puttied or cemented in, so that
no water may enter the tube; the telescope is now
complete. To use it, thrust the large end below
the little waves, apply the eye to the upper extremity,
and, the water being perfectly still a short distance
below the surface, a clear view may be obtained of
the denizens of the deep.

A boy from the village, who has been fishing for
a couple of hours with very coarse tackle, has taken
about thirty fish as we pass, and has threaded them
through their gills on to rushes; two or three of
them weigh a couple of pounds each. His outfit
is a hazel pole (cut from the adjoining wood), about
10ft. long, on the end of which he has a line, or
"tow," as he calls it, of thin whipcord, to which is
fastened a large hook on gut, weighted with pieces
of lead stolen from the glazing of his mother's
window. His float is a common bottle-cork with a
quill (stopped at one end with pith) thrust through
it, and, with this gear, by sundown he will capture
as many fish as he can stagger home with. "They
du fare kindly to bite bett'rn they du sum days," he
tells us, in answer to our question of, "Do you
always capture them as fast as this?"

The church of St. Helen is a fine building, standing
in a commanding spot overlooking the Broad, and con-

tains several objects of interest. Here is to be seen a splendid chancel screen, of carved and painted work, said to be one of the finest in Norfolk; also an ancient oaken,

CHANT ON READING-DESK (300 years old).

READING-DESK—RANWORTH
CHURCH.

double reading-desk (see illustration), on one side of which is the Latin chant here represented.

The chancel contains some curiously-carved oaken stalls. Some of the figures of saints are in excellent preservation, and form a capital series of subjects for sketches, especially that of St. George. The register dates from 1556.

The belfry contains a peal of five bells, none of which are less than 200 years old. They all bear inscriptions, which read as follows:

1. EliƷa Souldich filia ac hæres Sen: Sol: Armigri et Dña Sui maneri 1610.

2. MB. Anno Domini 1615.

3. IB. W omnes sonus crudet dominum anno dñi 1616.

4. John Darbie made me 1670.

5. Magdalena Maria Dona rependi dia Rogo.

K 2

Near the screen is a sculptured tablet to the memory of the donor of one or more of the bells :—

Here under lyeth Buried the bodie of
Thomas Holdiche one of the sonnes of
Robert Holdiche of Ranworthe Esquier
who died the 9th day of August 1579.

The font (see illustration) dates from the fifteenth century, and is still in excellent preservation.

FONT—RANWORTH CHURCH.

Again we resume our journey along the Bure, and soon arrive at Horning, with its prettily embowered church peeping down on us from an adjoining hill. Please get your coppers ready, for, as the village is being passed, a crowd of noisy little lads and lasses will run along the bank singing "John Barleycorn," and create great fun in scrambling for any coppers you may throw to them. From the river this village presents a pretty appearance; but in this, as in many other cases, "distance lends enchantment to the view." This particular village lies very low, and is surrounded by fens, so that many windmills are necessary to keep the water from flooding it. This accounts for the church standing a mile away, on the top of the hill. At Horning Ferry is a prettily-situated inn, where we will take a glass of ale, and, being smokers, indulge in a cloud while our man digs for worms in a garden close by. If time permit, this is reckoned a capital place for fishing, either from a boat or from the banks, which on both sides are firm; the river is at this spot wide and deep.

The scenery here is very beautiful, and, if your vessel be large enough, a somewhat uncomfortable seat on the gaff for half-an-hour will be amply compensated for by the loveliness of the surrounding

LAYING TO—BESIDE HORNING FERRY.

country, which may be scanned in all directions from that eminence as you proceed. On the right is Hoveton Little Broad, ninety acres in extent, and studded with islets, upon which the gulls love to congregate and, in the spring, breed. The Broad, being nearly, if not quite, land-locked, is very quiet, and is the home of numerous wildfowl. Away a mile or so inland beyond this Broad, are one or two other isolated

Broads, of small extent. Burnteen is one of them, and, lying quite away from the river, is seldom or never visited by strangers.

Just past Hoveton, on the left, is the entrance to Woodbastick Broad, a fine sheet of water, of about thirty acres in extent. It is very secluded, and well

ENTRANCE TO WOODBASTICK BROAD.

stocked with fish. As the water is fairly deep, it makes a delightful spot for a cruise round. The village stands a long way from the Broad—quite a mile—and contains nothing of special note. The church is an old one, dedicated to two saints (Fabian and Sebastian).

The next Broad is that of Salhouse, also on the left,

delightfully surrounded by trees, and quite a romantic spot for a picnic. Just beyond is a small lagoon, of very inviting appearance (Salhouse Pool), which forms quite a little harbour; one end of it runs up to a picturesquely situated farmhouse, snugly embowered among trees. All about this part is, in summer, very lovely, and frequent halts should be made, so that the individual beauties of the surroundings may be

SALHOUSE POOL—AT END OF SALHOUSE BROAD.

admired and appreciated. All along, quite to Aylsham, the scenery is worthy of more than a passing glance. Time, alas! will not always allow us to halt at will, so we must be content with a flying visit. On the right hand is Hoveton Great Broad, with its romantic little islands. This is the largest Broad of those just mentioned, being upwards of 130 acres in area. During the breeding season it is a favourite resort for sea-gulls. They arrive in large numbers about the middle of March, and at once commence to lay

their eggs, which are of various tints, and considered, by some persons, a great luxury. The man
appointed to collect these eggs only takes from
each nest the first two or three laid, and sends
them to market, where they sell for about a shilling
per dozen. The gulls are so numerous that thousands
of eggs are thus obtained during a single season.
Hatching commences about the beginning of April,
and lasts till the end of July, when the birds leave,
usually during the night. The young ones are very
funny little fellows, and are covered with a yellow
down, which gives them the appearance of being so
light and fragile that a breath of wind might almost
waft them away, as it would a puff-ball.

The church of Hoveton St. John contains several
handsome memorials to the Aufrere family. It is a
brick structure, and was erected in 1624.

I may here mention what is to be seen in the
neighbourhood of this group of Broads. The church
at Salhouse (All Saints') is greatly indebted to the
late R. Ward, Esq., of the Hall, for a great deal of
its embellishment, and contains, among other relics, a
sanctus bell, an hour-glass (with which the sermons
were formerly measured out), and a curious Knight
Templar's coffin. There are also several monuments
and tablets to the memory of local families. Some
portion of the chancel is Early English. The register
dates from 1568. Salhouse Hall was built in the
reign of Queen Elizabeth. If time allows, many pretty
walks may be taken in this neighbourhood, which lies

in the very heart of the beautiful Broad district. Hereabouts the banks of the river are, in the summer, for miles covered with wild flowers.

I would caution amateur yachtsmen against an unseen danger, which appears to be peculiar to Norfolk, and that is "Roger"—"beware of Roger!" Who or

A QUIET NOOK NEAR HOVETON.

what is "Roger?" Well, "Roger" is the name given to a whirlwind which occasionally strikes yachts before the crew are aware of its approach. By keeping a good look-out, however, you may, when you see the reeds and trees at the river-side violently agitated, know what to expect, and will, of course, take steps to trim your sail accordingly. I was once nearly overturned, near Stokesby, in a ten-ton yacht,* simply through our man making the mainsheet fast while he prepared dinner. A fast sheet has caused many fatal spills. At Wroxham Regatta, in 1881, no less than three competing yachts were overturned and sunk by a "Roger," whilst a tent on shore was taken up in the air and carried a distance of 80yds. These whirlwinds do not last more than a minute at most, generally less, but are during that time perfect little tornadoes. While staying at Happisburgh, in 1885, I was one night awakened by a noise like thunder, but, on rising and looking out of the window, could see nothing to cause alarm, so concluded that I must have been dreaming. In the morning I discovered the cause of my alarm; it was a "Roger," which had stripped a bullock-shed, 30yds. long, of its tiled roof, made a hole in a barn roof 14ft. by 11ft., torn off the limbs of some oak trees which stood in its path, and scattered the corn, then in full ear, in all directions. Such is the force of a "Roger."

We will now proceed to the last Broad of any importance in this district—Wroxham. This fine, open, deep sheet of water is in many parts 12ft. or 14ft. deep, and for regatta purposes is not to be excelled; it is also a splendid place for fishing, for which a small fee is usually demanded. Its length is about a mile, and its acreage about 120.

---

* "The Warrior." Last autumn, a gentleman standing on her deck, gun in hand, waiting for a shot, was struck by her unusually long boom, as she took a jib, and knocked overboard. He was a good swimmer, but the blow had stunned him, and he never rose again.

Regatta day here presents a sight worth witnessing. The water is then literally alive with craft of all sizes, from the lilliputian canoe, with its single occupant, to the stately twenty-tonner, with its merry party of twenty or thirty persons. The snowy sails of the vessels rival in whiteness the fleecy summer clouds, as their keels do the clouds in swiftness. The show of bunting is, of course, very large (who cannot sport a flag on such an occasion ?), so that, from a distance, the Broad looks like a huge flower-garden in full blossom. Visitors staying in Yarmouth should not miss this sight, as it is one of the best of the season. From Vauxhall Station, Yarmouth, Wroxham may be reached in about an hour and a half, and from Norwich in fifteen minutes.

Many persons, who have only a day or two at their disposal, prefer to come straight on to Wroxham, and confine their movements to the river and Broads between Coltishall and Thurne mouth—a very wise proceeding, as this is, without exception, the finest stretch in Norfolk, and for fishing and scenery cannot be surpassed. There are two very fair inns at Wroxham, but, being only country inns, and not "Grand" Hotels, their sleeping accommodation is somewhat limited. The names of these inns—which will be found very comfortable—are the Horse Shoes and the King's Head. Many of the cottagers in this and other villages keep a spare bedroom for visitors, which they let at a very moderate fee; if required, they will also provide breakfast or tea for a small party. A bouquet of old-fashioned flowers, which, though considered common in London, are quite as fragrant as their more delicate hothouse relations, may be gathered in the garden. Boats may be had here, though the supply of these is also limited. Passing under the old stone bridge, and also under the railway bridge, we come to a small lagoon, of no importance, called the Bridge Broad. Wroxham Church (St. Mary's) stands on a knoll, and is built in the Early English style; its register dates from 1558. In the churchyard is a large mausoleum to the memory of Sigismund T. Southwell, Sheriff of Norfolk, who died in 1827.

NORMAN DOORWAY—WROXHAM CHURCH.

The view from the elevated churchyard is a sight not on any account to be missed. It is lovely; and so is the appearance of the church from the river. It stands on a hill covered with giant oak trees — which spring from the beautiful grassy slope—and makes a very sylvan scene. Notice the Norman doorway of the south porch, which is in excellent preservation, as may be seen from the illustration.

Belaugh Broad, about a mile past the stone bridge, is the last of the Broads, in this river, of any size, though several others of small extent may be explored. The church of St. Peter, on the summit of a hill, is in the Gothic style, and contains a handsome screen and ancient font. The well-preserved register takes us back to the year 1500. This, again, is a prettily situated village. The grounds of the vicarage slope down to the water's edge, and are in summer a blaze of colour.

The river is navigable as far as Aylsham, and persons on sailing bent cannot do better than make the trip, as the surroundings are very picturesque; but nothing drawing more than 2½ft. of water can reach it. There are eight locks to stop the way, but they may each be passed in ten minutes. Toll is taken at the first one, for the series. Aylsham is about eighteen miles by river from Wroxham, and forty-four from Yarmouth. As we pass several villages on our way up, I will just mention what is of interest in connection with them, and, should my readers wish to see for themselves, they may land and do so, as all of them are within a few minutes' walk of the Bure. The first is Horstead-cum-Stanninghall, which contains a new church, and the remains of an old one which ceased to be a place of worship 300 years since; the ancient font is preserved in the present church.

On the right is Coltishall, a very old town (population about 1000), which received a charter, granting them various privileges, from Henry III., in 1231. In this document, of which the following is a portion, these privileges are quaintly expressed: "To all men, women, or children, born, or to be born, in this my town of Coltishall, freedom from all villainage of body and blood, and from toll, stallage, picage, and pannage, in all fairs and markets throughout England; and that all frays, transgressions, bargains, quarrels, and suits concerning the said town of Coltishall shall be determined twice every year, before the King's officers, at the leets there." The church (St. John the Baptist) has some curious, rudely-worked stone figures round the western doorway and inside the battlements.

The first lock is at Coltishall, and I would advise visitors who have viewed the beauties of this truly delightful village, with its red-roofed houses, thrown into relief by the sombre green of the pinewood background, to take train to Aylsham rather than pass through the never-ending locks and bridges.

Great Hautbois is also an ancient village, "for, at the head of the Causeway in this parish, in the reign of King John, Sir Peter de Alto Bosco founded an hospital, or *Maison Dieu*, for a master and several poor people. It was dedicated to the Blessed Virgin, and made subordinate to the hospital at Horning, which was under the government of the Almoner of St. Benet's Abbey." The church of St. Theobald is in ruins; the chancel has been converted into a mortuary chapel.

The river, from Wroxham to Aylsham, is usually quiet, as large yachts do not go above Wroxham Bridge. As we proceed, if watch be kept, many beautiful little birds may be seen. Our launch, of course, makes too much noise for these little warblers; but if the naturalist, in his little boat, will drop silently down the river, he will gain a deal of information concerning our feathered friends. Among others, he may espy the gay, peacock-coloured kingfisher, of whom Shakespeare has something to say; indeed, what has he *not* something to say about? Alluding to the old custom of turning a dead kingfisher into a weather-cock, by mummifying it, and suspending it so that its beak shall point out the direction of the wind, he says, speaking of rogues, in " King Lear " (Act ii., scene 2):

> · · · And turn their halcyon beaks
> With every gale and vary of their masters.

The kingfisher rarely takes long flights, but its motion is exceedingly quick, and, as it flits about in the sunshine, its gleaming feathers look as if made of burnished metal. Although a species of this bird is known in the tropics, it is not nearly so brilliantly coloured as the English one (*Alcedo hispida*), which is an anomaly, seeing that most tropical birds quite eclipse ours in point of brilliancy of plumage. Like the heron, it is fond of fish as a food; but, unlike that bird, it prefers to kill or stun its prey before devour-ing it : hence, it may be seen, after capturing a fish, to knock it on a stone, limb of a tree, or rail, till it is either killed or stunned ; then, tossing it in the air, it catches it adroitly in its beak, head downward, and swallows it.

The kingfisher, like several other predaceous birds, has a curious way of lining its nest with fish and other bones, which is brought about in this way. The bird swallows the fish whole, and, when it has satisfied its appetite, retires to its nest, which is in a hole bored in the bank of a river. Then it quietly digests the food, or, at least, that portion which can be readily assimilated ; the remainder, consisting of the larger bones, skin, &c., it throws up from its stomach. These pellets, or " casts," are always found on the floor of the nest, and upon them the eggs are hatched and the young reared. The owl is another instance of the pellet-casting bird, and, being very fond of mice and birds, its nest may be readily recognised by the fact of its being covered with skins, bones, and other indigestible portions, formed into balls or pellets.

Little Hautbois and Lammas are both on the right, but contain little of interest. Buxton is a pleasant village on the left, and has an ancient church, of Early English architecture, containing several fine stained-glass windows. Oxnead, on the right bank, is also prettily situated, and its church is quite surrounded by woods. The chancel is paved with black and white marble, and contains a handsome marble tomb, upon which lies the effigy of Clement Paston, who died in 1597. By his side is the effigy of his wife, and at their feet a pelican. Clement Paston was the person whom Henry VIII. called his " champion," Protector Somerset his " soldier," Queen Mary her " seaman," and Queen Elizabeth her " father." He built the Hall, of which a part still remains, about the year 1590. His grandson, the first Earl of Yarmouth, added to it, for the entertainment of Charles I., the Banqueting Hall, which contained the first sash-windows ever made in England. At Brampton, many

Roman coins, urns, and other antiquities have been found at various times, showing that, probably, the Romans encamped here for some time after the disastrous defeat of Boadicea, Queen of the Iceni, who inhabited these parts more than 1800 years since.

Aylsham, our farthest point, is an interesting town, of some importance, and contains upwards of 2500 inhabitants. It was a town at the time of the Norman Conquest, and later, in the reigns of Edwards II. and III., was noted for its linen cloth, called "Aylsham webbs," or "cloth of Aylsham." The Bure, which at one time was not navigable beyond Coltishall, was deepened in 1779, and has since then been dredged, so that now vessels drawing not more than about 2½ft. of water can pass up it. A free school was founded here as far back as 1517.

The church of St. Michael was built by John of Gaunt, Duke of Lancaster, and the court of his duchy was once held in this town. The tower contains a clock and a peal of ten bells. The font is enriched with bas-reliefs of the Four Evangelists, the emblems of the Passion, and the arms of Gaunt, &c. The screen, which was painted in 1507, contains some quaint figures of saints and martyrs; the cost of this work was defrayed by Thomas Wymer, who is represented on his monument wrapped in a winding-sheet. There is also a monument to Richard Howard, who, in 1488, built the church porch. There are several stained-glass windows, some of them containing genuine old painted work. The east, west, and south windows, however, added

L

in 1842, are the work of a Norwich artist, and were doubtless thought a great deal of at the time. Notice the fine Lych-gate, as you enter the churchyard precincts.

Aylsham has a Spa, which was once a noted resort of persons afflicted with asthma and other chronic complaints; it is now but little used. It stands about half-a-mile to the south of the town. There is also a very level bowling-green, and those who are fond of this ancient pastime may spend a happy hour here. I may add that the Aylsham bowlers are such adepts at this game, that they are willing to meet all comers. Aylsham is altogether well worth a visit, and may be reached by rail from Norwich in about an hour. On Stow Heath, two miles to the east, are several large tumuli, or barrows.

There are several other places of interest within walking distance of Aylsham, notably Blickling Hall, to be reached in about half-an-hour, or less. The mansion is a large, quadrangular structure, built in the Elizabethan style. It has two open courts in the centre, turrets at the angles, and a large clock-tower over the principal entrance; the tops of the walls are embattled, and the mansion itself is surrounded by a moat having bridges, &c. The whole is environed by noble old trees. The park is a very large one, containing 1000 acres (much larger than Regent's Park and Hyde Park, London, put together), and is well stocked with deer. Blickling Hall contains many large rooms; the library is 127ft. long, and 21ft.

wide, and has a panelled ceiling, enriched with figures
in relief, representing the Seasons, the Elements, the
Passions, &c. The hall is 42ft. long, 33ft. wide, and
33ft. high, and opens on to the carved oak staircase,
which is surmounted by carved oak figures of Queen
Elizabeth and Anne Boleyn. Here are some fine oil
paintings, by various artists, including George III.
and his Queen, and George II. on horseback, by
Sir Joshua Reynolds. The park contains a lake, in
the form of a crescent, about a mile long, and nearly
a quarter mile across at the widest part. Blickling
Hall has passed through the hands of various families
since its erection. During the reign of Henry VI.
it was in the possession of Sir Thomas Erpingham,
who built the Erpingham Gate of Norwich Cathedral,
and who sold it to Sir John Fastolfe, the builder of
Caister Castle; Sir John sold it to Sir Geoffrey Buleyne,
or Boleyn, who was Lord Mayor of London in 1457.
Sir Thomas Boleyn, father of the unfortunate Anne
Boleyn, next possessed it. On the anniversary of her
death—according to local traditional belief—Queen
Anne Boleyn is seen, with her severed head in her lap,
sitting in her coach, which is drawn by four headless
black horses, driven by a headless coachman, accompanied by a decapitated footman. The Hall then passed
into the hands of the Cleves, one of whom sold it to
Henry Hobart, a Chief Justice, whose son, Sir John
Hobart, rebuilt it in 1620; one of the latter gentleman's
descendants was created Earl of Buckinghamshire in
1746, and his son, the second Earl, rebuilt the west

L 2

front, and greatly improved other portions. On his death, without issue, the Hall came into the possession of the Suffield family, and is now the seat of Constance, Marchioness of Lothian. In an ancient poem, mention of Blickling is thus made :—

> Blickling two Monarchs and two Queens has seen :
> One King fetched thence, another brought, a Queen.

A mile from the Hall is a mausoleum, in the form of a pyramid, 45ft. high, erected to the memory of the second Earl of Buckinghamshire and his two wives, who lie beneath it. The church (St. Andrew's), which stands near the Hall, on a hill, contains some fine brasses and stained glass, and also a handsome memorial to the Marquis of Lothian, who died here in 1841.

Blickling Hall is thrown open to the public on one day in each week throughout the summer, during which time excursion trains are run from Norwich, so as to give visitors an opportunity of viewing this fine old English residence, with its valuable collection of articles of virtu of all kinds. The tapestry, which covers the walls of some of the rooms, is considered very fine, especially the piece given by the Emperor of Russia to a former owner of the Hall, who acted as ambassador at the Russian Court; it represents Peter the Great on horseback.

The parish of Blickling contains 2085 acres, with a population of about 350. The Marchioness of Lothian is owner of the whole parish.

Artists, botanists, and others, would be repaid by

making Aylsham their headquarters for a few days, and thence taking walking excursions in various directions. The country round about is very pretty, and also very quiet, as the adjacent villages are very small.

Sleeping at Aylsham, we in the morning steam back to the mouth of the river Ant, which flows into the Bure on the left as we return, just before we reach St. Benet's Abbey. It is navigable for vessels of moderate size.

CHAPTER IX.

UP THE ANT, TO BARTON AND STALHAM BROADS.

There is a pleasure in the pathless woods,
There is a pleasure on the lonely shore;
There is society where none intrudes,
By the deep sea—and music in its roar.
—BYRON.

THE run from Aylsham to the mouth of the Ant (twenty-eight miles) has occupied the whole morning, so we lay-to and take lunch; our man, meanwhile, digs us some worms from the monks' garden or orchard at St. Benet's Abbey, so that we may have some angling in Barton Broad in the evening.

While we are discussing our meal, I will tell you a little about the eel-catchers and their house-boats. The latter may be seen on most of the rivers hereabouts. The hull is simply an old ship's boat, standing high out of the water, with the sides raised, and a roof put over them, so as to form a house, or cabin, in which the eel-catchers live and sleep. The boats are usually painted white (or, rather, whitewashed), so as to be easily distinguishable at night, in order to avoid collisions, and also to be the same colour as the snow-covered ground in winter, for wildfowl shooting. Eel-catching is carried on in the autumn, when the eels are returning along the rivers to again enter the sea; for, strange to say, the young ones are born in salt water, and then make for the rivers in the spring. The eel-nets, as seen hanging on the stakes, by the side of the huts, seem exceedingly complicated affairs, but are not so in reality. The whole net is somewhat like a trawl net, has a mouth as wide as the river it is to be placed in, and tapers away to a small tail, to which is attached a movable piece, or "cod." The mouth of the net is fastened, at the two sides, by stakes driven into the river bank, which keep it distended; while a heavy chain is lashed to the bottom, to keep it in position on the mud. The top rope of the mouth hangs loosely between the two posts, so as to enable wherries or boats to pass over it. The top and bottom of the mouth of the net are kept from too wide distension by a couple of cords, which, by being shortened, will draw the mouth down as close as may be desired; so much in fact, as to close it, if necessary. Hoops are placed at intervals along the inside of the net, and to

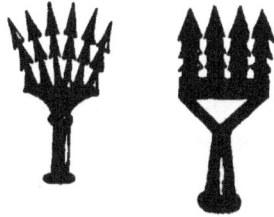

EEL PICKS, DARTS, SPEARS OR GLAVES.

these are fastened transverse nets, having a small,

pursed-up aperture in the centre, to allow the eels to pass through, but placed at such an angle as prevents their returning. The net finishes off with the above-mentioned "cod," a detachable bag, which, at intervals of an hour, is hauled up, taken off, and the eels contained in it emptied into a wicker basket

EEL-SPEARING.

or trunk. The mesh diminishes from mouth to tail, so that at the end a darning-needle would stand a poor chance of getting through. Dark, wet nights in September are the times when the largest takes are obtained, and tons of eels are sent to the large markets in different parts of England during this month. Eels are also taken by spears or darts, mounted on long handles. They are easily managed; but care must be taken that the boat does not drift away, and leave you hanging on the handle of the eel-pick, with no alternative but a ducking. Choose a dark night for this sport.

Now, having finished our meal, we will ascend the Ant, a river connecting Barton Broad with the Bure. After proceeding about a mile, we come to Ludham Bridge—a small, stone structure of one narrow, low arch; all masts must here be lowered, for the crown of the arch is not more than 6ft. or 7ft. from the water; its small aperture has brought many amateur yachtsmen to grief. Several years ago, a young gentleman, desirous of showing his skill as an oarsman to a party of ladies who happened to be crossing the bridge, put on a spurt, feathered beautifully, and pulled a long, clean stroke till he got to the bridge, when suddenly, as if struck by lightning, the sculls flew from his hand, and he was thrown to the bottom of the boat, amid a frantic peal of laughter from those on the bridge. He had been sailing, and had forgotten to unship the mast. The crestfallen oarsman was —myself! This, though somewhat unpleasant, was not nearly so bad as what happened to a yachting party, the recital of which may act as a warning to others who may visit this spot under similar circumstances.

A party of gentlemen, who had hired a very large yacht, came to Ludham Bridge, and being desirous of seeing all that was to be seen on the Ant, requested

their man to take them under the bridge. The man
said the yacht was too large, and in different ways
tried to dissuade them from the attempt. But to no
purpose. The mast was therefore lowered, everything
made snug, and the quant got out and used. There
was so little head-room beneath the bridge, that it took
a long, long time to coax her through; but at length

LUDHAM BRIDGE.

she was squeezed through, to the detriment of her
paint. But there she was, afloat, on the opposite side
of the bridge, and her merry party quite happy. Away
they sailed, and were gone several days, as they, unfortunately, were detained by very rainy weather, after
a long period of dryness. In due course they returned
to Ludham Bridge. But what was their chagrin to
find that the river had become so swollen that they

could not possibly pass through the arch by several inches! There was no help for it, and so they had the misfortune of having to pay something like £25 for the hire of the yacht for the next three weeks, the time which elapsed before the rivers had subsided enough to allow of the yacht again passing under the bridge.

There are a number of very large water-mills along the river banks, having red brick towers 40ft. high. Land, and see the means by which the sails are made to work the powerful machinery which drains the marshes.

For a test of skill in boat-sailing, I do not think it possible to beat this river, as it is as full of turns and twists as the limb of an oak tree. No matter which way the wind blows, you are sure to get a head wind in some of the reaches, a fair one in others, and a following one in others. Perhaps the head is pointing due east; five minutes after we head north; in another five minutes, west; and so on, quite to Barton Broad.

The whole district is very marshy, and from the Bure to the Broad there is only one village—Irstead, on the left bank. In the church (St. Michael's)—a small, flint building, possessing a register dating from 1538—is a stained-glass window to the memory of William of Wykeham, who was rector of this parish in 1347, and afterwards became Bishop of Winchester. Some portions of ancient stained glass have been carefully preserved, and worked into the windows. The pattern of the quarries proclaims it to be late fifteenth-century work. The oak benches were repaired and restored about fifty years since. The church stands within fifty or sixty yards of the river, and the keys may be had of the sexton, who lives in a cottage close by. The ancient name of the village, as given in Doomsday Book, was Orsteada. In the next village (Neatishead) is a church, with a lofty tower and spire, dating from the time of Edward IV.; over the entrance-door is some very curious carved work.

STAINED-GLASS QUARRIES—IRSTEAD CHURCH.

Some good catches of fish are to be obtained in the Ant, which may be fished from the banks, as the river is not very wide. A good pair of water-proof boots are needed, as the river-bank is boggy. These boots will be found handy in many parts of Norfolk. By-the-way, the best and simplest recipe for waterproofing boots that I have come across is that by " Wildfowler." Here it is: Put ½lb. of tallow and ¼lb. of resin in a pot, which place on

the fire. When melted and stirred together, it is fit
for use; but, before applying, warm the boots. While
the mixture is hot, lay it on with a painter's brush,
until neither the sole nor the upper will absorb
any more. Then, in order that the boots may take
a polish, mix one ounce of wax with a little lampblack.
This preparation must not be applied until twenty-
four hours after the tallow and resin mixture has been
used.

Barton Broad is a large lake, quite a mile and a
quarter long, and averaging a third of a mile wide,
and contains nearly 300 acres of water area. There
is a fair depth of water for fishing and sailing, which
may be indulged in with even more freedom than on
the other Broads, as it is more open. A large artificial
island, near the centre, affords a capital *locale* for
picnic parties, as yachts may be brought close to the
side in 5ft. of water. Beware of certain shoals, having
little tufts of weed showing above the surface, in
various parts of the Broad. Do not be lured, on a
breezy day, by their placid appearance, while everywhere around the water is in little, lumpy waves. If
you once get on one of these weed-shoals, it is a
difficult matter to get off again, as you cannot find
a firm bottom, or anything else, to push off from.
If you put an oar or boathook down, the treacherous
weeds, after standing a fair amount of pushing, will
suddenly give way, and if you are at all off your
balance, a ducking will follow. If you do run on to
one of these places, the best way to clear your boat

is to push the stern from side to side until you get it clear, and then a vigorous push off from the bows (everyone else being in the stern) will usually back it into deep water.

WHERRY ON BARTON BROAD.

The large western arm of the Broad leads to Beeston Hall, the seat of Sir Jacob Preston, who owns the whole of the parish of Beeston St. Lawrence. The Hall stands in a beautiful park of 300 acres, some of the trees in which are truly patriarchal and gigantic specimens of the British oak. The house, which has been the seat of the Preston family for generations, is built of flint, with stone quoins. One member of this family was a great supporter of Charles I., who, on the scaffold, gave him (Jacob Preston) an emerald ring, which is still treasured here. There is a large lake in the park, well stocked with fish, but it is, of course, strictly private. This park and hall are the *beau ideal* of an English gentleman's home. The church (St. Lawrence) is a small structure, with a round tower, and was restored by Sir Thos. Preston at the beginning of this century. The east window is filled with stained glass, and beneath is an oil painting of the Last Supper. Many elaborate memorials of the Prestons may be seen in the church.

STAINED-GLASS PANEL—
BARTON CHURCH.

The Broad is fringed round with reed-banks, and surrounded by undulating country, but is not quite so picturesque as some of the Broads we have visited.

Barton is a very straggling village, and contains

a very noble church, which, standing on a hill, causes
it to be a notable object in the surrounding landscape.
It is delightfully embowered amid trees, and should be
visited, if only for the remarkable view of the Broad
and district which may be obtained from its lofty
tower. There are a few odd panels of ancient stained
glass, of which the engraving on page 159 is a
tracery piece.

By all means devote a day to angling on Barton
Broad, as you are almost certain to get a good basket.
For obvious reasons, it would be useless for me to
mention the best spots for angling; but any of the
old reed-men may be induced to show you a warm
corner.

At the North end of the Broad is the dyke leading
to Stalham Broad, which is of considerable size, but
greatly grown up. In passing up the river from
Barton to Stalham Broad, bear to the right. The
channel on your left, which you will pass, is a con-
tinuation of the Ant. Thousands of water-lilies, both
white and yellow, grow in this Broad, and a very
pretty water-bouquet may be made by those who are
returning to town; if gathered when the flowers are
just opening, they will keep for a long time if the
stems be placed in water.

Stalham Church contains a very old font, round
which are stone carvings of the Apostles and the
Baptism of our Saviour; this font, until restored by
the Vicar in 1860, was an unsightly mass of cement
and whitewash. The roof has just been renewed,

and placed at its proper angle, in place of the dreadfully depressed structure which had for years covered the nave

Stalham town is five minutes' walk north of the Staithe, or landing-place. Mr. Teasdel, who has quite a fleet of small sailing and rowing boats to let, will

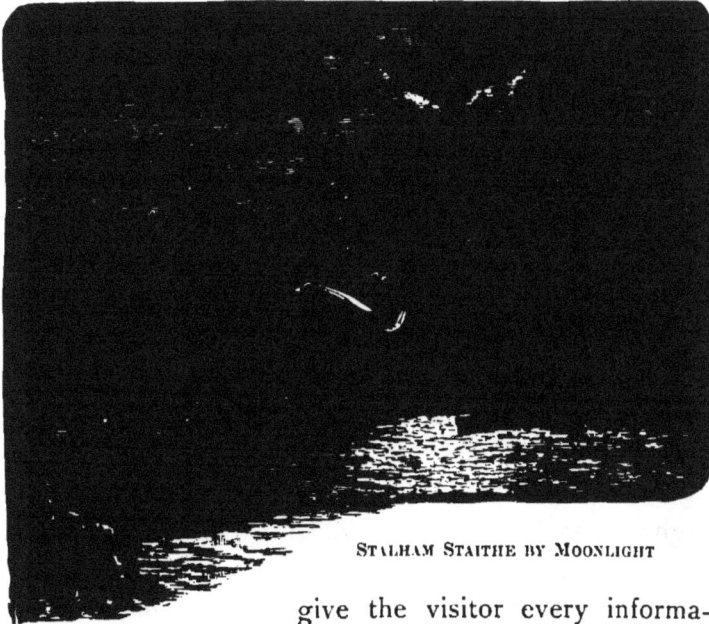

STALHAM STAITHE BY MOONLIGHT

give the visitor every informa- tion that he can, and is quite an authority on angling and shooting. He will tell the stranger the most likely spots, and will supply him with anything he may require, from a boat to a loaf of bread. It is expedient, when out for a day's angling, to take a couple of stout ash-poles, about 8ft. or 9ft. long (never mind how rough they are),

M

to which to moor the boat. Having chosen your spot, stick the poles firmly into the ground, and moor the boat stem and stern to them.

The railway station lies to the west of the town, about three-quarters of a mile from the Staithe, and seventeen miles from Yarmouth.

The main street contains several good shops, so it would be as well to take our man with us, and replenish our larder here. There is a butcher's, a baker's, an ironmonger's (who keeps a supply of fishing tackle), a capital grocer's, a chemist's, and several other handy shops. Having made sundry and very miscellaneous purchases, we send the man back to the Staithe, accompanied by a boy, both heavily laden, while we take a walk to Ingham, one mile to the east. Here the church is the sole object of interest, and is a remarkably fine building, standing on rising ground, and reckoned, for proportion and workmanship, equal to any in the county. The lordship of Ingham can be traced back to the time of Richard I., when John de Ingham was lord of the manor. Oliver de Ingham (a successor) was a great favourite of Edward II., who made him governor of several castles, Seneschal of Gascoine, and Warden of Guyenne, in France, as a mark of approval for the valiant manner in which Oliver fought for him.

The church (Holy Trinity) was rebuilt in the year 1360, and appropriated by Thomas Percy, Bishop of Norwich. Sir Oliver founded a College, or Priory, for the use of a prior, a sacrist, and six monks of the order of Trinity and St. Victor; the ruins of it may still be seen in the churchyard. Under an arch in the north side of the chancel lies the sculptured effigy of Sir Oliver de Ingham (Edward III.'s reign), who was Marshal of Guyenne; on the side of his tomb was inscribed: " 𝔐ounsier 𝔒liuer be 𝔍ngham gist icy, et 𝔇ame 𝔈lizabeth sa compagne, que luy 𝔇ieu be les almes, bit mercy."

At the east end of the church, by the rood-loft, is an altar-tomb, with sculptured figures of Sir Roger de Bois and Margaret his wife; the knight is in complete armour; his head rests on the body of a Saracen, and at his feet lies a hound, with its paws resting upon a gauntlet. His arms (*argent*, two bars with a canton *gules*; over all a fillet *sable*) may still be discerned on his surtout. The lady's robe also shows her arms quartered with those of Sir Roger. In the year 1800, the brasses, which were among the finest in the country, were stolen from the church.

From Ingham to Happisburgh, or Hasbro', as it is locally known, is a pleasant walk of four miles. This place, formerly a busy little fishing village, is now a purely agricultural spot, with its shore washed by the German Ocean, which is only kept from making incursions by the narrow banks, which commence here, and extend quite to Winterton. The original village of Hasbro' was swallowed by the encroaching sea ages since, and the fishermen affirm that, when the sea is clear and calm, they can, at low tide, by peering down into the depths, distinguish the ruins of the village, especially those of the church. As a

M 2

matter of fact, portions of the walls, and other relics of this lost village, have from time to time been dredged up and brought ashore.

The modern village is gradually being swept away; scarcely a winter passes but what a few yards of the land along the coast are swallowed by the north-west gales which prevail. Fields which, during recollection, contained several acres, have either entirely vanished, or have dwindled into mere patches. Several other villages on the Norfolk coast have been gradually swept away, until not a wreck of them remains—Keswick, Whimpwell, and Shipden, among others.

There is a lifeboat and a Coastguard Station here. The latter is an almost new building, the sea having encroached so much that the old buildings now stand nodding upon the brink of the cliffs.

Happisburgh is noted for its ancient church and two lofty lighthouses. The church, dedicated to St. Mary, is a particularly handsome edifice, erected in an imposing position, on an eminence overlooking the sea. This hill is 130ft. above high-water mark, and the noble tower, rising to a farther altitude of 112ft., commands a grand view, both of sea and land. The keys of the church may be obtained of the sexton, who lives in a cottage adjoining the churchyard.

At the chancel end of the church is an old tombstone, with a very rude attempt at versification. It is erected to the memory of two brothers—Thomas and Johnson Canning, lost off Hasbro', February 18th, 1807, and runs as follows:

A storm arose, with Snow and Rain ;
The " Abeona " to presarve we strove ;
In Vain we stood for land, our lives to
Save—our efforts sunk beneath the wave ;
Short was our stay on earth below ;
To our souls may Heaven its mercy show.

This would read much better if put into correct lines ; but either the tombstone was too narrow, or the letters too large, for what they had left over from one line they used to give them a start on the next.

Standing by this grave, a very fine sea view is obtained ; and if you have a short time to spare, you may while it away with the old sea-dog, Galbraith, who lives in the little tarred, wooden cottage, adjoining the churchyard. He will yarn you till you are both dry ; but be not alarmed at that, for the inn is next door.

Nine miles from the shore, opposite the village, are the dreaded Haisbro' Sands, the most dangerous of any on the English coast. Despite the fact of their being indicated by the two land lighthouses previously mentioned, and one floating light, these sands are, in hazy and stormy weather, much dreaded by those mariners whose vocation takes them near the spot. Hundreds of vessels have been wrecked here, and I have known as many as seven vessels to be on them at the same time, not one of which was ever floated again. Volumes might be written concerning the fell disasters which have occurred here, and which have made the sea for some distance around one vast grave. One narrative will serve to show the danger of this coast, which has only one harbour in its coast line of 100 miles. In October, 1876, the barque " Young England," with a crew of twenty-five all told, was wrecked here. Amid the fury of a north-west gale, thirteen of the hands (twelve men and a boy) successfully launched the long-boat, and pulled for the shore. Such was the strength of the gale, however, that, instead of being able to land at Hasbro', they were carried, in a diagonal line, to within 200yds. of the shore of the village of Winterton, twelve miles to the south, arriving there in an exhausted condition. It was dark; no friendly forms were visible on the shore; nothing was to be seen but the cruel, white-crested billows, roaring on the flat, sandy beach. They paused a moment, to consider the best means of reaching shore safely; but the pause was fatal, for, the next moment, a tremendous sea struck the counter of their craft, which broached-to, and was instantly overwhelmed. For a brief space of time, a few screams were heard, amid the chaos of broken water, from the doomed crew, and then all was still, save for the voice of the storm, which raged with unabated fury. But, as day broke, the coastguards-men saw that an object had been cast upon the tide-deserted beach; this proved to be a boy, upon each of whose wrists was fastened a bag of linen. The bags had floated him ashore, and he still lived (though with a broken thigh-bone), the sole survivor of the long-boat's crew. The captain and his wife, and ten of the crew, who had remained on the vessel, were saved by a tug from Yarmouth. A day or two after, the bodies of six of the men from the long-boat were washed ashore (irony of fate!) at the very place they had endeavoured to land at—Hasbro'. Six finer men never were laid forth for the last rites of mortals; the mate, a young Norwegian, 6ft. 4in. in height, was a very handsome man, and of giant frame. On searching him, a letter to his sweetheart was found in the breast of his jersey, and was duly forwarded to her, with particulars of his untimely fate. They were all buried in one grave, at the chancel end of the churchyard, and their resting-place is marked by a handsome stone, upon which is carved the appropriate emblem of a "foul anchor."

As, after the walk from Stalham, and the climb to the top of the church-tower, the pedestrian will need refreshments and a rest, he cannot do better than stay for an hour or two at the only inn near—the Hill House. After refreshing the inner man, and viewing all that is to be seen through the telescope kept in the Green Room, if time permits, a game of bowls may be indulged in on the capital bowling-green belonging to the Inn. Bowls seems to be *par excellence* "the" game in Norfolk, and comes much more under notice than cricket, as it can be played by persons of any age and size, and without the slightest fatigue. For a portly gentleman of some sixty summers, and 20st., or a trifle more, in weight, cricket is out of the question; but a quart of "Old Tom," as the best ale is here called, a yard of clay, and a four-handed game of bowls, will suit him admirably.

Nearly every village throughout Norfolk has its bowling-green, and, on the weekly meeting afternoon, the show of "churchwardens" and burly bucolics is amazing. Here the latter meet all through the summer, except during harvest, and, like Drake and Frobisher, of Good Queen Bess's reign, are such enthusiasts, that they play very late, so that the "jack" has to be marked with a piece of white paper or a lanthorn, to finish "just this one game."

The High Light is half-a-mile from the church, and stands on an eminence some distance from the sea. It is an unusually lofty tower, upwards of 100ft. in height, and shows a very powerful revolving light for a distance of about twenty miles. Visitors are allowed to go over this building, not only to see the lens, and the mechanism for making the light revolve, but also to see the process of making gas for the supply of the sixty-four burners which constitute the "light." The word "revolve" is a misnomer, as the light does not revolve in any way; a cap simply comes over the light, as an extinguisher does over a candle, and remains there for a period of five seconds, during which time no light is seen at sea. It then shows a bright light for twenty-five seconds, again disappears for five, and so on *ad infinitum*. The Low Light, which was erected about 1790, stood upon the brink of the cliffs, a well-known landmark by day, and beacon by night, to the thousands of colliers and

fishing vessels annually passing along the coast. It
was lighted in many different ways. At first,
the lantern was a huge iron frame, upon which a
fire was kept burning all night, the fuel used being
principally tarry wreck-wood, which would burn well
in all weathers. Next, a glass screen, or lantern, was
erected above the watch-room, and in this a large
number of tallow candles were constantly kept burning,
the keeper being in attendance all night for the
purpose of snuffing and replenishing them. Oil lamps
were then successfully introduced, which gave a more
brilliant light, and required less attention. The keepers,
however, had a great deal to do in the way of
cleaning and burnishing the numerous silver-plated
reflectors by which the lights from the lamps were
both enhanced and multiplied. An oil lamp, on an im-
proved principle, came into use some twenty-five years
since, which gave a still greater illuminating power,
and this was a kind of Argand, and the wicks were
in concentric circles, one inside the other, to the
number of four or more, according to the power
required. Ten years since, gas took the place of
oil, and is still the best illuminating power available,
as other lights, though more brilliant and powerful,
have the drawback of suddenly going out, especially
the electric light.

In consequence of the High Light having been transformed into a revolving light, and an extra light-vessel
being placed at the extremity of the dreaded Haisbro'
Sands, Haisbro' Low Light was, in the summer of 1886,

condemned by the Trinity Board, and sold by tender to the highest bidder. The mode of razing the tower was very simple and very effective. First, a line of bricks was taken out all round, about 14ft. to 16ft. from the ground. Into this gap the heads of a number of strong props, or rough battens, were placed, the other ends being firmly planted in the ground. Men then dug away the foundation of the tower, as much as they considered prudent, so as to leave it in a very weak state. A load of faggots was then placed beneath the supporting logs, and lighted. Soon the logs began to burn through and fall away one by one; and then, without a moment's warning, the whole fabric, 80ft. in height, came to the ground with a dull roar, amid a chaos of smoke, dust, and flames. When the clouds of smoke had blown away, it was discovered that the watch-room had come down intact, without even breaking the floor or glass windows, and this from a height, from ground-line to floor of watch-room, of 60ft.! Thus was removed one of the best-known landmarks of the East Coast, the loss of which is deplored by the thousands of mariners who pass by annually, almost as much as if an old friend or relation had been removed by death.

During the autumn of 1886, Jenkinson, the chief coastguardsman, who, wherever he may have been stationed, has always been an ardent seeker after treasure-trove, came across some huge fragments of bones in a fossil state. This was at the foot of the high cliffs near Hasbro' Church. This find consisted of a jawbone, with several teeth (each weighing upwards of 10lb.), and some thigh and other bones of enormous dimensions. Professor Taylor, of the Ipswich Museum, immediately identified them as parts of the skeleton of an antediluvian animal about double the size of an elephant, and called the mammoth. Finds of a like nature are constantly being made along the East Norfolk coast, and these generally go to enrich the County Museum at Norwich.

If we wish to lengthen our walk somewhat, we can visit the small village of Walcott, and interview the old blacksmith; John Gibbons, one of the strongest men of his day, and the very *beau ideal* of Long-fellow's Village Blacksmith; his stalwart frame and kindly, ruddy face, with its ragged white beard, form a fit model for an artist. John, like Longfellow's hero, sings in the village choir; "roars out the bass like the drum of a threshing machine," a neighbour informed me. The church is medium in size, but capable of containing the whole population of the village twice over. It contains nothing very striking in the way of architecture, being of the usual type of Perpendicular work.

The churchyard is sometimes visited by epitaph-hunters, who find several unique specimens to enter in their note-books. Upon entering it recently, to see if there was anything worth recording in that line, I was at once struck by one which nearly caused me to retrace my steps without looking further, it was so touching, and so startlingly *original*. It commenced thus :

Affliction sore, long time I bore.

I should not at all wonder if the reader has met this very verse before.

The next to attract my attention was better—a very curious one, upon a, presumably, curious man :—

> Here lies the body of W. W.;
> He comes no more to trouble U, trouble U;
> Where he's gone, & how he fares,
> Nobody knows & nobody cares.

Another admonished brotherly love :—

> On Paul Blake.—1835.
> Go home, dear children, shed no tears,
> We must lay here till Christ appears;
> Now we are gone, no sorrow take,
> But love each other for our sake.

A very uncommon and cynical epitaph rewarded further search. It was this :—

In Memory of William Wiseman, who died 5th of August, 1834, aged 72 years—

> Under this marble, or under this sill,
> Or under this turf, or e'en what you will,
> Whatever an heir, or a friend in his stead,
> Or any good creature, shall lay o'er my head,
> Lies one who ne'er cared, & still cares not a pin
> What they said, or may say, of the mortal within,
> But who, living and dying, serene, still, & free
> Trusts in God, that as well as he was he shall be.

Two very beautiful verses rewarded my final search. The first was upon a child named "Blanche, aged 6 :"—

> This lovely bud, so young & fair,
> Cut off by early doom,
> Just came to shew how sweet a flower
> In Paradise will bloom.

The other was also on a child's grave, "C.C.B., aged 5 yrs.:"—

> When the archangel's trump shall blow,
> And souls to bodies join,
> Many will wish their lives below
> Had been as short as mine.

We may now either retrace our steps along the road to Happisburgh, which is a mile and a half, or take the road, past Walcott Church, to the beach, and return along the sands, beneath the high cliffs —a walk of two miles. It is a curious thing about the name of this village, that it is spelt by the postal authorities, Happisburgh; by the villagers, Hasbro'; and by the Trinity Board, Haisbro'. It is pronounced locally, Haisbra'.

Leaving Hasbro', we walk along the beach, southward, and, as the tide is out, find it capital walking on the hard, outer bank of fine sand.

The country hereabout is exceedingly flat—a dead level, in fact—and, in many parts, appears to lay actually lower than the sea at high tide. By the side of the beach runs a kind of sea-wall of sand hills, or dunes, as they are called, ranging from 20ft. to 50ft. in height, and from 50yds. to 100yds. wide at the base. These hills of sea sand are locally called " Marram Banks," from the rush-like vegetation with which they are covered. The plant forming this vegetation (the *Arundo arenaria* of Linnæus) is very little known upon other parts of the British coast. It grows to a height of about 3ft., and greatly resembles the bulrush in stem and leaves.

The leaves finish off with a hard point as fine and sharp as a needle; while the stem, instead of ending with a large, brown spindle, like the bulrush, has a head resembling that of rye-grass, but larger and rounder. The root of the marram, however, is its "saving clause," as it is several feet in length, and, with its many lateral shoots, binds the sand, and keeps it from blowing or drifting away. These banks are, now and then, during heavy Nor'-west gales, pierced, and great damage done to the fields and property adjoining. They are kept in repair by a tax, which is partly levied on the good people of Norwich, twenty miles inland.

The beach all along this coast is very safe for bathing, the currents rarely being very strong, even at half ebb or flood, as the tide does not rise or fall above 6ft.—a marked difference to some parts of the Bristol Channel and the Channel Isles, where the rise is between 30ft. and 40ft.

Two miles from Hasbro' Town Gap we arrive at Eccles, and view the churchless steeple, standing alone on the beach, just above high water mark, and wonder how it came there. It is a circular, flint tower, with an octagonal turret, and is 64ft. high. Once a year a sermon is preached here, for which the Bishop of Norwich receives the sum of about £50. Eccles was once a thriving fishing town; but, in consequence of the encroachments of the sea (the land having been washed away during stormy weather), it has dwindled from 2000 to 250 acres, and only boasts a population

of twenty-four persons.   In 1605, the inhabitants
prayed for a diminution of their taxes, on the ground
that only fourteen houses and 500 acres remained of
their once considerable parish.   One stormy night during
Elizabeth's reign the roof was blown down and one
of the walls became dangerously infirm.   This state
of things continued for a short time, when, as the
inhabitants were unable to defray the cost of repairs,
the walls were taken down, and the steeple left
standing.   At this time the steeple stood some distance
inland, but now stands on the beach, and forms a
well-known landmark to coasting vessels.   During,
or rather after, a Nor'-west gale, in the winter of
1880-1, the sand was scoured completely away from
around the foundations of the walls. Being in the vicinity
at the time, I visited the spot, and was surprised to
see the overthrown walls of the church exposed to
view, and also the foundations of the cottages which
once formed the village.   There were to be seen the
decayed wooden thresholds of cottage doors, circular
wells, and other signs of a buried village.   Close to
the church walls several graves were washed open,
and the bones floated about the beach by the tide.
It was a curious sight for anyone of a contemplative
turn of mind.

From Eccles we retrace our steps to Stalham,
which we reach in the twilight, having enjoyed our
long walk and long day's pleasure.   The cabin of
the "Lily" never looks so snug as when we have
been away all day, and return at dusk to find the

little oil lamp alight over the table, and a smell from the fore peak pervading the air, which, to a hungry man, is a smell of comfort. There is, at times, another smell in cabins, which is not so pleasant, and that is that which is caused by a smoky oil lamp. To prevent this, soak the wick in vinegar and thoroughly dry it; when you again light it, you will find the smell has been banished.

CHAPTER X.

THE ANT, TO NORTH WALSHAM AND CROMER.

I murmur under moon and stars
In brambly wildernesses ;
I linger by my shingly bars ;
I loiter round my cresses ;
And out again I curve and flow,
To join the brimming river :
For men may come, and men may go,
But I go on for ever.
—TENNYSON.

LAZY morning with us after yesterday's long ramble ; actually, breakfast not finished till past 9 o'clock. " Is the steam up, Fred ? " " Yes, sir —this half-hour." " Very well—go ahead then ! " We go down the river from Stalham Staithe about a mile, and then, turning suddenly to the right, resume our journey up the river Ant. This small river, like most of the larger ones, is very tortuous, bends and reaches following each other in such quick succession that it is rarely a straight course of a furlong presents itself. Two miles up we come to Wayford Bridge, pronounced locally " Wafer; " here the mast of our boat must be lowered.

N

The high road to Norwich passes over this bridge, and a splendid road it is, as any cyclist can attest. Norfolk is a splendid county for getting about on wheels, as it is very level, and all its main roads are kept in excellent repair. In the Broad District, however, this method of locomotion is at times awkward, as some of the roads lead " nowhere," and others end abruptly at the edge of a Broad or river; in these cases, nothing remains but to grind one's teeth or whistle something soothing, and retrace one's steps to the cross-roads again.

On the right hand, not far from the bridge, is an old tumulus, or encampment, which rejoices in the name of the " Devil's Ditch." It may have been a Roman earth-fort, as the raised mounds certainly seem to indicate something of the kind; but how it came there, or why, deponent knoweth not.

Our next halt is at the Tonnage Bridge, a very picturesque spot, flanked with a countrified dwelling, having a large garden and orchard attached, reaching quite down to the water's edge. No other houses are in sight—simply a vast common, tenanted in autumn by innumerable geese, destined later on for the London market. One goose-breeder near Norwich has sent up as many as seven tons in weight of dead geese during the Christmas season. The geese are marked either on the feet or beaks, but never appear to get mixed, for at night each flock returns of its own accord to its appointed sleeping-place in the village.

Just past the Tonnage Bridge we get our first view

of Ruston Common, an immense tract, reaching to the east as far as can be seen. The village of East Ruston lies about a mile from the river, and the clay cottages—"daub and wattle" they are called —may be an uncommon sight to some, the cottages being made by simply erecting walls of stakes, or brushwood, upon which the kneaded clay is plastered and smoothed. These cottages, despite wind, rain, and frost, will stand for several generations, but are, in these civilised times, fast disappearing.

Before coming to Dilham our course is arrested by a lock, but by the payment of a small fee this difficulty is easily overcome. It is quite exhilarating to feel one's self "rising in the world," as the great flood of white water comes rushing in between the massive gates from the upper river, and we once more find ourselves on a level with the surrounding country. And a very pretty country it is, right away to North Walsham, being in many parts beautifully wooded; some of the plantations come quite down to the water's edge. These, however, are kept as preserves for game, especially pheasants, and, being private property, may be looked upon as sour grapes; so we have to content ourselves with the voices of the smaller birds, who make the woods ring with their noisily joyous songs.

Presently we come to Dilham Bridge—built of stone, and with only one arch—where we must again lower the mast. A pleasant walk over Dilham Bridge, to the right, leads to Honing, a snugly-placed village, surrounded with timber. The approach to the church is along a road beautifully over-arched with trees, called the Long Lane. It is a beautiful spot in the summer time, when the hedgerows are crowned with all kinds of wild flowers. The church, dedicated to St. Peter and St. Paul, was rebuilt in 1796, except the tower, which dates from the fifteenth century.

HONING LONG LANE.

I copied this epitaph in the churchyard, as a specimen of the Norfolk peasantry's disregard for the tense of the verbs :—

A tender mother she have been,
And many changes she have seen ;
And when on earth she did her best :
We hope her soul is now at rest.

And we fervently hope that the *poet* who wrote the lines is at rest too.

We have, as you will no doubt have noticed, passed a great deal of fen and common land, and are scarcely out of it yet, for just beyond that cottage on the right is Ruston Common, of I don't know how many acres, but large enough, at any rate, to supply turf to the "natives" for miles around, and to maintain multitudes of geese, and those very musical "Norfolk Dickeys" (donkeys). Richard Porson, M.A., the eminent Greek scholar, was born here in 1759, and received his early instruction from his father, who was the parish clerk. A Mr. Norris discovered his ability and sent him to Eton; from there he went to Trinity College, Cambridge, and in 1803 was unanimously chosen Greek Professor to the University. He died in 1808. The opening to Dilham Broad is on our left before coming to the bridge, but is nearly grown up with flags, reeds, and rushes. The Broad itself is very small, not covering more than fifteen acres. We keep our course, with woods on either side of us, till stopped by Briggate or Bridge-gate Lock. This is one of the old gates of Worstead, Bengate, Lyngate, and Withergate being the others. Worstead is a bare mile from here, on the left, so we will stroll to it, and, on the way, I will mention one or two facts concerning the town.

Worstead, or, as it was formerly called, Worstede, was at one time a large town, and celebrated as the seat of manufacture of worsted stuffs; it is now an ordinary agricultural village, with a population of about 850 souls. Worstead Hall, the seat of the Rous family, stands in a beautiful situation, surrounded by a park of 300 acres, in which are some fine old trees, and a lake 8¼ acres in extent. This lake is literally alive with fish—some of them are veritable monsters, as very little or no angling takes place here; it is, however, private, so that strangers have no opportunity of enjoying an hour's sport. But there, if one *could* fish, the great fellows would break one's tackle; so perhaps it is better to eat our sour grapes contentedly. The Hall contains several fine paintings by Vandyke, Rubens, and other great artists. In the middle of the eleventh century, Worstede belonged to the Abbot of St. Benet's-at-Holme, who leased it to a captain of crossbowmen, one Robert of Worstede. Worsted stuffs were first made in the reign of Henry I., but their manufacture died out with the last century. The Church (St. Mary) is a splendid Gothic building of flint, with stone dressings, and has a lofty, embattled tower, rising to the height of 120ft. The period of the foundation is not known, but it is of early date, as Sir Robert de Worstede granted the appropriation of the church to the Priory of Norwich, in the reign of Edward III. The tower may be distinguished from any other in the neighbourhood by its four pinnacles, each weighing 1¼ tons, which were added some years since. There is a peal of six bells, and a clock, in the tower. I give an illustration of one of the windows in the church, which is considered to be very pure in style.

The interior of the church presents a remarkably neat appearance, and has a gallery at the west end. The chancel is divided from the nave by a fine, carved oak screen, adorned with paintings of saints ; it was erected in 1412. Facing the west end is another screen, upon which are painted several figures, repre- senting the Virtues. This screen, the work of the wife of the Rev. Mr. Gunn, of Irstead, was erected about sixty years since. The ancient font is hexagonal in shape, and divided into sculptured compart-

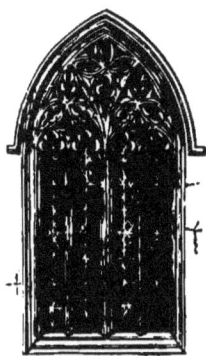

DECORATED WINDOW, 1350—WORSTEAD CHURCH.

ments ; the cover of it is a fine piece of wood carving, rising tier above tier, and ending in a floral finial. The Rev. Henry Wharton, author of " Anglia Sacra," was born here in 1664, and possessed (a great boon for a public speaker) two tongues. One of these tongues however, " grew smaller as he grew older, until it was not at all inconvenient." When he died, in 1694, he bequeathed twenty-two acres of land to the parish, the proceeds of which (now £30 per annum) were to be devoted to repairing and beautifying the church.

Notice the north doorway, which is considered a very fine example of mediæval work. In the churchyard is a tombstone to one Peter Clarke, which teaches a lesson to all village gossips :—

> These lines are not to praise the dead,
> But to admonish those by whom they're read ;
> Whatever his failings were, leave them alone,
> And use thine utmost care to mend thine own.

John Starling, who for upwards of fifty years has been sexton of the church, will explain the points of interest to the visitor.   .

We now retrace our steps to Briggate, and again embark.

A journey of another three miles upon the river brings us to Cubit's flour-mills, and another lock ; and as this is the nearest point to North Walsham, it shall be our terminus. By passing through the lock, we might continue our trip some distance farther, but as there is nothing of interest to be seen, we will not do so. The source of the Ant is at Bradfield, so that, altogether, it is about twenty miles long. On our right, coming nearly to the water's edge, are Witton Woods, of immense extent, and the property of the Earl of Kimberley. The road on our left, up the hill, leads direct to North Walsham, which we will now visit. This town, consisting of three principal streets and several smaller ones, is irregularly built, and contains about 3000 inhabitants, so that it is the largest town for many miles round. The Market-place, in the centre of the town, has a neat cross (with a clock), built by Bishop Thirlby, in the reign of Edward VI., and repaired by Bishop Redman, whose arms may still be seen upon it, in 1600. The market, since the advent of the railway from Norwich, has not been so well attended. The church (St. Nicholas'), a large, ancient structure, was greatly damaged by the rebels in 1381, but was afterwards restored. Its massive flint tower, now in a ruined condition, was

originally very lofty (146ft.); it was partly destroyed
by lightning in 1724, and in 1835 another large
portion fell. Two bells have, however, been hung
in the ruined tower, as high as possible. The aisles
are separated from the nave by very lofty, clustered
columns, so that no clerestory windows have been
inserted. The large east window was formerly filled
with stained glass, but this was unfortunately destroyed,
during a storm, in 1809. A remarkably fine sculptured
monumental memorial to Sir William Paston, who
died in 1608, graces the left side of the chancel; Sir
William is portrayed in full armour. The font is
surrounded by iron railings, in an octagonal form,
and is covered by a lofty piece of carved tabernacle
work, rising, in four tiers, to a height of several feet,
and terminating with a finial in the form of a pelican.
The church has a very ancient painted screen, which,
having been for many years hidden away behind
some lofty pews, was discovered in 1844, when the
whole of the interior was being cleaned and restored.
A stone reredos, of beautiful design, greatly enriches
the interior of this noble church. In the spandrels
of the entrance-porch may be seen the arms of John
of Gaunt, and the Abbot of St. Benet's Abbey. The
Grammar School, standing on the outskirts of the
town, was built and endowed by Sir W. Paston, in
1606.

On the road to Norwich, and about a mile to the
south of the town, stands a lofty, stone cross, erected
to commemorate the rebellion of 1381, on which

occasion an assembly of 50,000 men, under the leadership of John Litester, pillaged the surrounding districts,
and carried all before them till Bishop Spencer, at
the head of a large body of troops, forced Litester
to take shelter in North Walsham. This town the
Bishop then besieged, and, after nearly destroying the
church and other buildings, forced the rebels to give
battle on the Heath, where between twenty and thirty
thousand of them were slain, and their leader taken
prisoner. Litester was afterwards, according to the
gentle custom of the good old days, hung, drawn,
and quartered, and his remains placed above the
gates at Yarmouth, Lynn, Norwich, and his own
house. The remainder of the rebels then cried *peccavi*,
and dispersed.

We walk back to the yacht, and after supper,
and the usual game of cribbage, retire for the night,
well satisfied with our day's pleasure.

As we wish to get back to Thurne Mouth as soon
as possible to-morrow, our song on retiring is :—

> We'll be up in the morning early,
> Just before the peep o' day;

and, true to our warbling, we are up with the lark. A
mist still hangs over water, meadow, and woods, and
the sun's golden rim is only just appearing over a
low, purple cloud, portending a fine day, as we push
aside the hatch, throw open the cabin-door, and emerge
for our dip. The glorious plunge over, we dress, and,
while munching a biscuit, prepare our tackle, and

start off for a spot close to the mill, which our man
has ground-baited overnight, and there have a couple
of hours' capital sport, landing several mighty bream.
At the end of this time we have as many fish as we
can conveniently carry, so we trudge back, in capital
spirits, to breakfast. What zest the morning air and
morning dip do give one for this first meal, to be
sure! How we enjoy everything that is set before
us, and revel in the enjoyment of good health! At
7.30 we start on our backward journey—or, rather,
commence to start, for we are brought up short by a
curious accident. We have cast off, and the propeller
has only made a few revolutions, when there is a jerk,
a snort from the engine, and a sharp snap, all in an
instant; then, although the piston is working rapidly,
we make no headway. We see at a glance that
the propeller shaft has broken, and that, for to-day
at least, there is no prospect of moving. A council
of war is held, the result of which is that our man
expresses his willingness and competency to repair
the damage, if we let him have the help of an
engineer from North Walsham, and leave him to
himself during the day. We accordingly call upon
Messrs. ———, who send an experienced man back
to the "Lily," while we walk on to the station, and
book to Cromer, only about nine miles distant. It
may be noted that the Ant rises at the Antingham
Ponds, near Bradfield.

Cromer was formerly part of the parish of Shipden,
which was overwhelmed by the sea about the reign

of Henry IV. Its ruins lie about half-a-mile from the coast, and, on a very clear day, at neap tide, huge masses of stonework may be seen deep down in the sea; the fishermen call these ruins the Church Rocks. Cromer, which is fast becoming a favourite watering-place, stands on the cliffs, in a hollow between hills which environ it on three sides. It has a population of about 2000, and is still rapidly increasing. Previous to the reign of James I. there was a small harbour here, but in 1611 this was destroyed by the sea, and no attempt has since been made to construct another. Several landslips have been caused by the encroach-ments of the sea during this century, notably in 1800, 1825, and 1832. After the last of these falls of rock, the present lighthouse was erected 250yds. farther inland than the old one. It is only a trifle over 50ft. high, but the altitude at which it is built (250ft. above high-water mark) makes up for its insignificant height. The lantern is about 300ft. above the sea level, and on a clear night shows a light to a distance of twenty-five miles.

The Jetty, which is a stumpy little affair, about 200ft. long, is the great promenade during the summer months. But the glory of Cromer is its beautiful sands, which are so firm that as many as a dozen tennis-courts may be seen marked out on them at one time. This is a good idea, as each successive tide makes the ground beautifully level, and then all that is needed is to mark out the courts, when all is ready for several hours' enjoyment.

A steamer plies daily, during the summer months,

between Yarmouth and Cromer, and is always well patronised; it stops here about a couple of hours, so as to allow of its passengers taking a stroll, and gets back to Yarmouth about 7 P.M. The fare is only half-a-crown for the return journey—in all, nearly seventy miles.

Cromer Church (St. Peter and St. Paul) is said to have been built in the reign of Henry IV., after the destruction of Shipden. It is a very fine building, of flint and freestone, and is a good specimen of Gothic architecture at its best period (the early fifteenth century). The tower is a handsome one, rising to the unusual height of 159ft. The church was nearly destroyed in 1681, and for many years service was held in the tower. It has, however, been thoroughly restored, and now presents a fine appearance from the outside, but has no internal decorations worth mentioning, with the exception of some stained-glass windows; it is even now minus a chancel. The ruins of the old chancel, which was destroyed by gunpowder in 1681, still remain; and buried beneath the walls is the painted east window, which, in the forthcoming restoration, will be brought to light, but doubtless too much fractured for restoring. The reason that the chancel was blown up was because of its getting into a bad state of repair; and, as the proprietor of the great tithes would not go to the expense of restoring it, he took the more forcible method of ridding himself of the chancel and his responsibilities at a single blow. The porch is one of the fine features of this noble building.

In Cromer churchyard are several quaint epitaphs:
here is one, dated 1755:—

> Farewell! vain world!
> I've seen enough of thee;
> And careless I am what you
> Can say or do to me;
> I fear no threats from
> An infernal crew,—
> My day is past, and I bid
> The world adieu.

Cromer is surrounded by beautiful walks and drives,
and appears to afford a good field for scientific research
to geologists.   Both Professsors Lyell and Buckland
have visited it and its vicinity with profit.   Visits to
the following places may be made: Felbrigg, with its
woods, and a Hall containing Flemish windows painted
by Rembrandt, Vandervelde, Brill, &c., and other things
of interest.   The church here contains a fine brass of
Sir Simon de Felbrigg, in full armour, who died 1443.
Gunton, with a Hall and Park, open to visitors on
certain days, should not be missed.   There are, altogether, about 1000 acres attached to this fine Hall,
which is the seat of Lord Suffield.   The roof of
Knapton Church is widely noted for its beauty.   It
is of a very elaborate description, and is said to have
been taken from a Spanish ship wrecked on the coast;
but this is extremely doubtful.   Knapton is three miles
north-east of North Walsham.

Mundsley, seven miles to the south-east, is a nice
drive along the coast.   A new church was built
here, in 1881, of material taken from the old church,

the tower of which still stands, in solitary state, on the cliff. Sherringham should be seen, journeying by way of Beeston Regis, where stop to view the ruins of the old Priory, which are situated in a pretty vale; this Priory dates from the reign of King John. Sherringham, a fishing village, lies in a picturesque cleft in the high cliffs, and has formed the subject for many paintings. Beckham, whose church is in ruins, is about five miles distant; lovers of the romantic should not miss seeing these ruins, which are the finest in the neighbourhood.

At Bacton, two miles from Happisburgh, are the ruins of Bromholm Priory, built by William de Glanville, in 1113, as a cell for Clugniac monks—who were subject to Castle Acre Priory—and which was dedicated to St. Andrew. It was once famous as possessing a portion of the true Cross, which drew pilgrims from all parts of the kingdom, who came to worship before it, and to be healed by it. Such were its virtues, that nineteen blind persons received their sight, and thirty-nine others were raised from the dead by its power. The ruins of the Abbey may be seen by obtaining permission of Mr. Cubitt, proprietor of the farm, of which it forms part. The gateway, dormitory, and chapter house, together with other masses of masonry, may be seen.

And now our watch tells us that the time for returning has arrived, so we bid adieu to Cromer, and in half-an-hour are back again at North Walsham. The broken shaft has been mended during our absence, and

over the happy accomplishment of his task our man
returns from "somewhere," in such a hilarious state,
that we carefully put him to bed and tuck him up
for the night. We then play our usual hand at cards,
just to last out a cigar, and then retire for the night.
Not to sleep, however, for we have no sooner dozed
off than we hear a footstep on deck, and then a
heavy plunge in the water. We rush on deck, and
in the dark see a man's head bobbing about. "Good
gracious! Is that you, Sam?"

"Yes, master; don't yow pay no regard tu me.
I'm haven a kuler, jest ter set me ter rights agin."
So we left him bobbing about in 4ft. of water, and
once more wooed Morpheus.

CHAPTER XI.

THURNE MOUTH TO HICKLING, MARTHAM, &c.

Oh! summer is a pleasant time, with all its sounds and sights—
Its dewy mornings, balmy eves, and tranquil, calm delights;
I sigh when first I see the leaves fall yellow on the plain,
And all the winter long I sing: "Sweet summer, come again."

AT 8 A.M. we are once again under weigh, returning along the river Ant, across Barton Broad, and thence, still along the Ant, to where it joins the Bure; then we turn sharp to the left, and at noon pass St. Benet's Abbey, and arrive at Thurne Mouth. Leaving Thurne Mouth, we pass the little village of Thurne on the right hand. The church here stands out boldly against the sky, as it is perched conspicuously on a hill, apart from the village. Thurne, Ashby, and Oby form one parish, having been consolidated in 1604. The three villages contain about 250 inhabitants between them. Oby Manor House is an ancient building; the barn attached is of great size, and bears the date 1622. Proceeding up the river Thurne, or Hundred

O

Stream, for about a mile, we come to Womack Broad, on our left—a long inlet, of delightfully picturesque aspect. Being an out-of-the-way place, it affords a snug and appropriate sketching-ground, and to the art student will give as much pleasure as many of the larger Broads. The village of Ludham stands at the north end, and the nearest railway station is Potter Heigham, two miles distant. Ludham, after the dissolution of St. Benet-at-Holme's Abbey, was given by Henry VIII. to the Bishop of Norwich, who converted the Grange into an episcopal dwelling; the greater part was burned down in 1611, but the Palace was restored and enlarged by Bishop Harsnet, who built a chapel of brick; this chapel, after the Bishops ceased to dwell here, was converted into a granary, and the remainder of the edifice into a farmhouse, which is now called Ludham Hall. The church is a large building, and is dedicated to St. Catherine. The font, a very ancient one, is enriched with bas-reliefs. The screen is greatly admired: on it remains of paintings of the Twelve Apostles may still be discerned, as also vestiges of gilding.

Continuing eastward along the Hundred Stream, we pass under Heigham Bridge, a favourite angling spot, where many a finny monster has been lured to his doom. The bridge is of stone, and has three arches; the two side ones, however, are too small to admit of boats passing through. A few score yards farther on we pass under the railway bridge; the station lies half-a-mile to the left. The Falgate Inn

has, for a sign, a model five-barred gate, hung in the
usual manner; and on the four lower crossbars is this
verse :—

> This gate hang high,
> And hinder none;
> Refresh, then pay,
> And travel on.

This verse was evidently the effort of a Norfolk man,

POTTER HEIGHAM BRIDGE.

as evidenced by the final *s* of the verbs "hang" and
"hinder" being absent.

On our right we pass the hamlet of Bastwick, with
its solitary tower, mourning the loss of its ruined
church, and continue straight along until we arrive
at the dyke, on the left, leading into Heigham Sound,
a celebrated haunt of the pike. From the Sound we
pass into Whiteslea, and thence, through another

O 2

dyke, into the largest sheet of fresh water in Norfolk —Hickling Broad.

Calling Hickling Broad, Whiteslea, and Heigham Sound one, we have a magnificent lake three miles in length, by nearly a mile in width at the widest part, or at least 700 acres of water (twice the area of Hyde Park, London), free for angling and sailing. Except in the channel, which is marked out by stakes, the Broad is very shallow, not averaging more than 4ft. or 5ft.; so that, in case of an upset, nothing more serious than a good ducking would result. In the channel are spots 7ft. or 8ft. deep; and in the dyke between the Broad and Whiteslea it is deeper still. The bottom is hard gravel, greatly overgrown with weeds, and therefore a remarkably good place for perch. A good plan is to go at night, with a pole, and clear out the weeds for a space of several feet each way, so as to leave a clear space for fishing; by the morning the fish will have entered this space for feeding purposes, when, by quietness and care, a good capture will result. Roach and rudd are quite as plentiful as perch in these waters. A good place for angling is at the Pleasure Hill, a semicircular "rond" of reeds growing near the centre of the Broad; another is the Wor Bush, nearly opposite. There are many other favourite spots, but by mentioning them I should expose my own "quiet nooks," which I regularly haunt two or three times a year. At these places I have had many days' excellent sport. The Staithe is at the north end, where refreshments and

boats may be obtained at the Pleasure Boat Inn.
The country round the Broad is rather flat, and the
sky line only broken by a few trees, some tremendously
tall mills, and the grey towers of a neighbouring
village church or two. I can myself speak with great
certainty of the enormous catches of fish which have been
taken here, having lively recollections of some of
them. Fancy a day's catch amounting to more than
a strong man could carry when placed in a sack;
and this is no fancy, but a solid fact. Many long
days have I spent on this Broad, without even once
returning with a really poor bag. The watermen
who hang about the inn will, in consideration of a
glass of ale, give you valuable information as to the
best places for fishing, and for half-a-crown you may
secure the experienced aid of one of them for the day.
Some of these men are very droll fellows—full of quaint
humour and water-lore, and are well worth the money
paid for their services, if only to "pump" them, and
hear their yarns.

Catfield Station, about two miles from the Staithe,
is the nearest hereabout.

Fishing here, in a match against a friend, in 1881,
I landed 115 fish in two hours, which weighed in the
aggregate 34lb. 10oz.; but this take would appear
ridiculous by the side of some others of recent years.

A ground-bait composed of small barley, boiled
with treacle, and when cold mixed with a little earth,
is a favourite lure.

Hickling village is about three-quarters of a mile

from the Staithe, and is rather a large one, but much scattered; it contains about 1000 inhabitants. The church of St. Mary is a very fine one, only recently restored. The vicarage was founded in the reign of Edward I. Hickling Priory, half-a-mile north of the church, in which were located a prior and nine canons, was founded by Theobald de Valoins, in 1185, and dedicated to St. Mary, St. Austin, and All Saints, for the use of canons of the order of St. Austin. Robert Botyld was the last prior (1503), and, with three of the canons, signed to the King's supremacy, in 1534. The ruins of the Priory are rapidly diminishing; the last window was taken down in 1825, and may now be seen in the porch of the farmhouse connected with the Priory.

A mile to the north of the Priory is Calthorpe Broad, which is only about twelve or fourteen acres in extent, and nearly grown up with reeds. I have caught some large fish here; but it is scarcely worth a visit—that is, to the angler, although the artist will find it a very secluded and pretty spot, and should not miss it.

We leave Hickling Staithe, cross the Broad, and come back through Whiteslea, and notice a dyke on the left, up which we go for a mile and a half, and emerge suddenly upon Horsey Mere, a noble expanse of water, 130 acres in extent. The fishing here is preserved, but leave to angle may readily be obtained; a favourite spot is Benwell's Reach, on the left upon entering the Broad. This is a very pretty Broad, and also one of the quietest. The east end being only a mile from the sea, we will not neglect to have a dip, especially as we are to sleep here to-night.   Until purchased by Robert Rising, Esq., who has only been deceased a few years, the whole parish was at times flooded by incursions of the sea, which, entering the Mere, killed the fish.   That gentleman, by having the marram banks repaired, and the land drained, brought this fenny district to a high state of productiveness.   He also had a road made, so that vehicular communication with the next village (Somerton) was established.   The Hall, the seat of Captain Rising, contains a good library, and also a fine collection of Norfolk birds, all of which were shot in the immediate vicinity.

Frequently, in the shallow pools around this and other Broads, may be seen the stately heron, plying his calling of fishing.   Although this bird will eat many other things besides fish, he is a most ardent fisherman.   His method is to stand quietly in a shallow pool until the minnows, small roach, or other fish play round his legs; then, like a flash of light, his long, spear-like beak is darted among them, with unerring aim, and a poor little victim is secured. The fish are caught sideways; but as the bird cannot swallow them in that way, they are jerked into the air, deftly caught, head downward, in the open mandibles, and then disappear for ever.

Many naturalists affirm that herons neither swim nor dive; but this idea is certainly erroneous, as, upon more than one occasion, I have seen them swimming on Hickling Broad, in the open channel, where the water is 6ft. or 7ft. deep, and free from weeds. Although never an eye-witness of their diving powers, I am assured that, in warm weather, they will occasionally dive, and travel some distance before again appearing. Herons sometimes visit the beach, peering into the little pools left by the retreating tide, and regaling themselves with shrimps, crabs, little fish, or anything by which the pools (or, as they are here called, "lows") are inhabited. Although their staple food is fish, they will also eat worms, snails, mice, young birds, or anything else toothsome.

For nesting purposes, they invariably select the highest elm trees in the district, and build their huge, flat, round-table-top-looking nests quite at the summit. The nests are composed of successive layers of large twigs, small twigs, coarse fibre and leaves, and an inner lining of grass; each layer is more concave than the previous one, so that the inner one is fairly comfortable and hollow. The hen lays about four or five eggs, of a beautiful blue-green colour. It used to be popularly supposed that a heron, when incubating its eggs, sat straddle-legged upon the nest, like a man riding on horseback; but this, like the tales anent the Barnicle goose, is an exploded myth.

Horsey being a treeless place, the heron does not breed there, but simply makes it, with the surrounding district, its summer residence.

Horsey Mere is a fine open, expansive lake, and

is, therefore, a very suitable place for fishing or sailing.

Horsey Church (All Saints') is a very old, thatched building, with a register dating from 1559. The nearest railway station is Martham, at least four miles distant by road.

Again returning, through Heigham Sound, to the Hundred Stream, or river Thurne, we turn sharp to the left, and keep to the east until we arrive at Martham Broad, which is nearly square, and of about the same area as Horsey Mere; it is, however, not nearly so clear, being in many places quite grown up. This Broad is about two miles from Martham Station by road, but is not often visited by anglers, although some good fish are to be obtained there, and also in the Thurne. It is situated at the foot of a hill, on the highest part of which, a mile distant, is the church. This structure is one of the finest we have seen on our trip, and should not be missed. It is built of flints and other stone, in the early Perpendicular style, and has a lofty, square, embattled tower, of fine proportions. Great care has been displayed in forming the flint stones into various patterns on the outer wall. The chancel is a veritable work of art, and quite a surprise on entering the church for the first time; it was rebuilt and beautified, at a cost of £8000, by Catherine Alice Dawson, as a memorial to her husband, the Rev. Jonathan Dawson. The ancient octagonal font, sculptured with representations of the Seven Sacraments of the Catholic Church and the Last Judgment, dates from the fifteenth century. The church itself was, no doubt, built in the reign of Richard II., as we read that Roger Gunton, in 1160, gave it to the prior and convent of Norwich, "for the redemption of his soul." It contains several windows of ancient stained glass, which have been recently restored One of them, at the east end of the north aisle, is evidently of foreign design, and probably Flemish fifteenth-century work.

There is a rabbit warren on the coast, upon which, on a fine day, innumerable "bunnies" disport themselves, until summoned to help feed the mighty metropolis.

Close to the south-east corner of Martham Broad is West Somerton, or the "Land of Giants," for it was the home of the Hales family—the Norfolk giants. The daughters were all over 6ft., and the sons ranged from 6ft. 6in. to 7ft. 3in. A relative still lives in the village, whose shoulder I just overtopped when standing beside him, and I am quite 6ft. high. It was quite a treat to feel so small.

When the church of St. Mary was being repaired, in 1867, a mural painting, 12ft. long, was discovered, between the windows in the nave, which had been covered with several layers of plaster and whitewash. The subject was, "The Son of Man coming in the clouds of Heaven with great power and majesty." Several other wall paintings were subsequently found, all of which have been carefully preserved. In 1868 a very interesting Early English painting of the "Virgin and Child" was found under the floor of the pulpit.

An hospital for lepers was founded here, in the reign of Henry II., by Ralphe de Granville, Lord Chief Justice of England.

Now, having seen all that is noteworthy on the Thurne, we return to Yarmouth, where I will take leave of my reader, as I have, I think, fulfilled the promise given when I took him aboard the "Lily," by escorting him to all the Broads of interest, and over 250 miles of delightful river-way.

If the *voyageur* wishes to see more of the rivers, this number of miles may be greatly exceeded, as there are no end of dykes, channels, and nooks, which are worth exploring, to which I have made no reference. I have confined myself simply to the rivers which connect the various Broads; but the Yare, the Waveney, and the Bure, are navigable for canoes and row-boats for many miles beyond the places at which we have stopped in our present cruise, and these districts will form delightful excursions for the hunter of things rustic and picturesque.

I would point out, for the benefit of those fond of walking, that some delightful strolls may be indulged in without any great amount of fatigue, as the Broad district is everywhere flat, and some parts of it well wooded. I think a stroll through the villages and a chat with some of the peasants always disclose something of interest. The *patois* of the people is very curious to those who are not accustomed to it.

Trusting that this brief Guide may be of service to the many who visit this "happy hunting ground" of the East, I will now say farewell, hoping that my reader may have fine weather and a pleasant time whenever he may feel disposed to take a trip on the Broads and Rivers of Norfolk.

I may add, as a kind of postscript, that I do not mind answering queries (by post), so long as the questions are concise, and not too numerous. This I undertake as a sort of penance for any little short-comings or omissions in this book.

CHAPTER XII.

COMMISSARIAT DÉPÔTS.

FOR the comfort of a trip, it is of the greatest importance that the Commissariat be properly managed, as a great deal of the enjoyment of a yachting trip depends upon the creature comforts, as well as the necessaries of existence, being adequately provided for.

With a view of helping the benighted visitor, new to these parts, the following list of places where stores may be laid in, has been prepared :—

Acle.—The town is a mile from the bridge. Necessaries may be obtained, but not luxuries. There are several shops in the town.

Aylsham.—This town is a large one, though visited by few, because of numerous locks, which impede progress. Supplies may be secured here.

Beccles.—Anything required may be obtained here, Beccles being a large market town, with a number of good shops, well supplied. In stopping at Beccles give the tannery a wide berth, as it has two distinct smells: one of the tan—which is pass-able—and the other of the foul hides. Cave!

Bungay.—Although somewhat inaccessible, this town is frequently visited by small boats, the occupants of which may rely on finding enough, and to spare, of all they are likely to want.

Coltishall.—Here, ordinary requisites, at a reasonable rate (especially country produce), may be obtained, as the village shopkeepers have not yet learned the art of bleeding a tourist, as taught in the larger towns.

Hickling.—This town is a mile from the Staithe, and contains only two or three of the ordinary village shops, where they sell everything—from an egg-cup to a faggot of wood; but it is as well not to rely on more than bread, butter, and meat here. Pass the bacon, as it is local cured "black meat," and apt to upset anyone who has not a cast-iron stomach. Oil for lamps and stoves may be procured here.

Lowestoft.—Anything may be obtained here. When lying at Oulton, the train may be taken to Lowestoft and back for twopence, and an abundant supply of anything eatable or drinkable obtained.

Norwich.—Stores of all kinds, and at same prices as in the London shops, may be had here. Delicious butter is to be obtained. Fish is usually cheaper here than at Yarmouth, where it is caught.

Oulton.—Although a prominent yachting rendezvous,

Oulton is a poorly-furnished village as far as edible commodities are concerned. Ice may be obtained here.

Reedham.—This town being contiguous to the river, it is easy to go ashore in the jolly-boat, and procure requisite stores of an ordinary nature. The supply is somewhat limited.

Stalham.—The town is a quarter of a mile from the Staithe, and contains quite a street of shops. There are two butchers, a grocer, a baker, and a chemist. Lost fishing gear may be replaced at the ironmonger's. The watchmaker will put right anything in the way of damaged guns or watches.

Wroxham. — There are two public-houses and a butcher's here; but little else to help the hungry or thirsty traveller can be got.

Yarmouth.—Stores of every description, and of the best, may be obtained here. Market days: Wednesdays and Saturdays. Fruit in great abundance, of especial excellence, it being brought in from the neighbouring villages, fresh plucked for the morning market.

At most of the villages, bread, excellent butter, toothsome sausages, doubtful cheese, new-laid eggs, and fair water, may be obtained. In the summer, however, dependence cannot be placed on getting them, as the hungry occupants of a large pleasure wherry, when they run short, will often clear a whole village of everything eatable. Fruit, during the season, is very cheap, and nothing, in hot weather, is more wholesome. A salad may be gathered from some of the gardens; the cottagers look upon a salad, when mixed up, as horses' food, but will eat the various ingredients separately. Any of the rustics will tell you what can be obtained in the different villages to which they belong.

Norfolk is noted both for its beef and pork; the former cannot be excelled in England, and, buying it direct from the butcher, there is no middleman's profit or railway carriage to pay for. Taking advantage of this, numbers of visitors with large families bargain with the butcher for a weekly supply to be sent to wherever they reside. Butter, eggs, and fruit also find customers in this way.

FRITTON DECOY.

CHAPTER XIII.

THE BROAD DISTRICT IN SPRING.

MARCH, APRIL, AND MAY.

The earth in robes of verdure now is clad,
And Nature, smiling, makes the whole world glad.

OME people hold that spring is the best time in which to visit the Broads; but I must, for various reasons, take exception to this —although it certainly has its advantages.

It is a gloriously exhilarating sensation to find oneself, on a fine spring morning, after a long winter in Town, careening along before a gentle breeze, and upon a fair tide, amid the early loveliness of bursting bud and blossom; but, at the same time, the spring months are very treacherous in the way of weather. Rain is more likely to fall now than in the succeeding months, and the days are shorter, and the mornings and evenings often very cold and raw. Many of the fish are out of condition, and, accordingly, very poor in appearance, flavour, and sport. On the other hand, the weeds

P

in the rivers and Broads, which have withered and died down, have not yet had time to grow again, so that there is more freedom for the angler's tackle than later on.

During mid-spring, some of the primrose banks are worth going miles to see, presenting an almost unbroken front of beautiful sulphur-coloured blossoms. Some of the fenmen might do quite a stroke of business in these flowers with the London markets, especially on the anniversary of Lord Beaconsfield's death; but these men know nothing of smart business dealings, and appear quite happy in their life of simplicity—we will not say ignorance—and retirement.

Let us inquire more closely into the manners and customs of these people. Lord Macaulay, when asked to give an account of the manners and customs of the New Zealanders, did it in an extremely concise fashion, thus : " Manners—none; customs—nasty." This cannot be said of the fenmen, for, although at least a century behind the present energetic age in business matters, they will be found very civil and obliging, if illiterate and unsophisticated.

The fenman here shown, with his towzled hair and unkempt beard, is seen at his best, for he is in his gala dress, ready for a water frolic, as they call a regatta on the Broads, and a very different object— with his smart hat and double-breasted, long sleeved waistcoat—to what he appears if you could see him on one of his work days. Then, early in the morning

he is up with the sun, and away through the long,
dank grass, covered with its dewy burden, regardless of rheumatism
or ague. If foggy,
a muffler is wound
round   the   lower
part of his face,
and his hat brim
turned   down   all
round, so that only
the tip of his nose
and   his   eyes are
seen. Very likely, if

A TYPICAL FENMAN.

he has far to go, his legs will be cased in leggings of
haybands or twisted sedge, to keep off the wet.
Are his spirits damp like the weather ?   Not they,
for he knows that in a short time the sun will burst
through and disperse the fog, the dewdrops will
glitter like diamonds in the sun, the lark will rise
and carol far, far above his head, the cattle will rise
from their damp couch and low in the sunshine,
and he himself will whistle at his work, with a
serenely calm mind, with nothing but his present
labour to think about or care for.   The fenman has
little regard for the future—the present is *all* to him.
Has he not a snug cabin, a nearly new eel net, two
or three suits of clothes, good health, and an equally
good appetite?   What more can a man wish for ?
Nothing : he is happy.

When we know their mode of life, we cease to

P 2

wonder at their simplicity and their plodding ways. We will go to yonder " eel set," and have a chat with its owner as to his mode of life. His home is simply a large boat, with a rough cabin in it, which is furnished with a bed, a little table, a wooden seat or box, a piece of broken looking-glass, and a locker containing some dilapidated crockery. The boat has been drawn up on to the bank, and is probably so old that she would not float if she were placed in the water. His nets are hung to dry upon a row of stakes driven into the ground. The picture is completed by a rustic paling of wood, which, together with weed and rushes, incloses the little plot, planted with cabbages and potatoes, surrounding his dwelling. Here he lives the solitary life of an Alexander Selkirk, paying no rent or taxes, and owning no landlord, for the little plot, a few yards square, has become his by right of pos- session—for, did not his father and grandfather and great-grandfather live here before him without hin- drance, and why should not he? The landlord, upon the edge of whose property he is located, does not mind his being there at all, for our fenman always has an eye to the grazing cattle, can always be relied on for a helping hand, and is generally em- ployed by the farmer during " haysel" and harvest.

During late winter and spring, when the weather is suitable, the fenmen are busy cutting and carry- ing sedge and reed. The latter is cut from the boat, tied in convenient-sized sheaves, and then taken to a meadow and put in shocks, just as is done with wheat; it is here allowed to stand and dry for some time, and is afterwards stacked till required for thatching purposes in the summer.

Some of these men are experts in the capture of wildfowl, which are sent to Norwich market, and sold at a fair profit. Wild duck, mallard, teal, widgeon, wild goose, water-hen, coot, plover, heron, grebe, and ruff, all fall to the gun and decoy of these men; while another, at times profitable, branch of their calling, is netting larks. At other times they are busy among the fish, especially during spring.

While speaking of the fenmen, we will for a short space disregard the season of spring, and see how they exist through the whole year.

June ushers in the "haysel," or hay harvest, when our fenmen lay aside their nets and handle the scythe, cutting meadow grass for the winter food of cattle, and marsh grass, or fodder, for littering them down in the winter. For this service, they receive pay either by the day, acre, or load, according to pre-arranged agreement.

Now comes a pause till the corn is ripe, when, if our friend is lucky enough to secure a "harvest," he earns from £6 to £7 in from three to five weeks, according to the weather. This is his best stroke of business during the year; and, indeed, this is the only time at which he indulges in what he terms "butcher's meat." During the other eleven months, beef or mutton rarely tickles his palate, pork and fish being the usual food.

The harvest finished, September is here, and this being the best running month for eels, our fenman is busy with his nets day and night—mending and fishing. His spare time is now taken up with gathering mushrooms, which, however, fetch but little here, where they are so plentiful. Still, as he says, "they are to be had for the gathering, and half-a-crown a bushel is not to be sneezed at." Neither is it; but what back-breaking work it is, to be sure!

Turfs, or "hovers" as they are called, are cut at any time, just to fill up a few hours when there is nothing else on hand. The hovers, after being stacked up to dry in large mounds, are then ready for sale.

In the accompanying illustration we have a set of implements used by the fenman in his many-branched calling. There is his marking-out spade, and his long "cutter," for digging down the whole length of an hover—about 2ft. Then we have his curi-ously - set scythes for sedge and gladdon-cutting; his reed-hook, or sickle; his hooked staff, for dragging in stray reeds, so that he can reach to cut them; and lastly, his thick, finger-less, leathern gloves, called "dannocks." These are a necessary protection against the sword-like boulders,

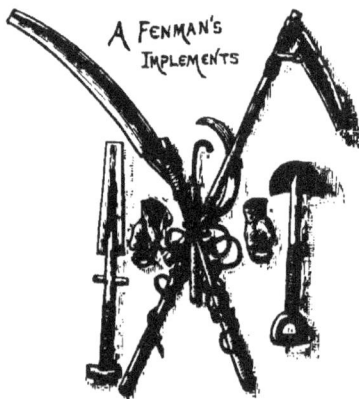

and other broad-leaved grasses, which become very brittle, and will cut like a knife.

Then comes the fall of the year, when sedge and reed-cutting commence again ; and so, year after year, the same round of dull duties goes on, our fen-man being quite indifferent to the things of the world beyond his boundary of life—the river and adjoin-ing fens. It is a strange life, no doubt, and, when talking to one of these " real natives," it is very difficult for a town man to find a theme of conver-sation which will even be understood, much less appreciated. It has been calculated that the English language contains from 40,000 to 50,000 words, and, out of this vast number, only from 800 to 1000 are used by the fenman to express all his wants, and engage in conversation with his brethren. It may be noted, that of this number many are obsolete words—that is, obsolete to the townsman ; and many of them, although used in polite life, have quite a different signification to what they originally had. It is clear, then, that politics, the sciences, and fine art, are beyond him, and altogether incom-prehensible, so that a conversation on anything of the kind would be to him Greek. Still, as a chat with a " native " will be found interesting and instructive, I will tell you how to approach óne, and draw him out. Tobacco is the key ; then talk to him of fish, reeds, and boats, and you will soon get him to tell you all kinds of river and Broad yarns in his own peculiar dialect.

Poor fellows! they often have a hard time of it in the winter, when everything is snowclad and ice-bound, and it is a hard matter to keep the wolf from the door. Sometimes, during hard frosts, they will lie in wait for a whole morning, amid the snow, for the chance of a shot at a wild fowl (for which they will get, perhaps, sixpence or eightpence), returning to their icebound homes with their shaggy beards and unkempt hair tossing in the wind, like old Norse kings awakened after a Rip Van Winkle sleep of a thousand years.

But we have arrived at winter before completing spring, so we will put back our clock of the seasons, and see what more we can say of the latter.

The pike fisher's best time is in the early spring, on open days, with not too much wind, fishing either from a boat or the banks. Sitting in a boat is certainly cramping and cold work at this time of the year, and requires two persons, one to row quietly and slowly, while his companion makes his casts. The bank fisher can keep himself warm with a good thick overcoat, and the exercise of walking along the boggy ground. Knee-boots are an absolute necessity, or wet feet will be the result.

Do not, on any account, miss seeing the gulls and their young during late spring. It is a most curious sight to see the young ones, in their downy coats, looking much like "puff-balls," before they arrive at the estate of featherdom.

The number of cuckoos here is surprising, and, as

everything is so quiet, their notes are to be heard for a great distance. They make their appearance in April, and mark their advent by turning out the eggs from a hedge sparrow's or other bird's nest, and depositing their own in it. Having done this, they contentedly go about their business of crying "Cuckoo," leaving the eggs to be hatched by the unsuspecting foster-mother, who does not find out her mistake till the young ones are larger than herself. I am afraid the school urchins are sad raiders during the spring in the way of egg-stealing, for they appear to take all they come across, from that of the tiny tomtit to that of the lordly heron. The district is thoroughly searched for rare birds' eggs by naturalists from various parts of England, who not only take eggs and nests, but the very branches they are built upon. This exemplifies the title to Shakespeare's play, " Love's Labour Lost."

For the contemplative man, or one who likes to be, like Robinson Crusoe, "monarch of all he surveys," spring will be the most suitable time to visit the Broads, as the sportive tourist is not yet about, and the fish and fowl, after a long winter's rest, are not so shy as they will be later on.

CHAPTER XIV.

THE BROAD DISTRICT IN SUMMER.

JUNE, JULY, AND AUGUST.

Summer comes with cheer and gladness,
Every heart is gay and free ;
Nothing speaks of care or sadness—
Everywhere is mirth and glee.

O says the poet, and so say we. Now is truly the time of enjoyment. Everything is at its best. Flowers, fruit, fishing, and weather, all combine to make this the most delightful quarter of the year in which to visit the Broads. Long and bright days, so suitable for camping out, and short and warm nights, which present only a minimum risk to delicate persons of taking a chill, are now here, and the opportunity of a most enchanting holiday for those fond of the water should not be lost.

The wild flowers in some of the reaches of the Bure between Horning and Wroxham, and even as far as Aylsham, are a sight to be remembered. Some of the banks are a veritable blaze of colour ; and, although all the colours of the rainbow, and many more, are represented, they have a most harmonious effect. A friend of mine, before leaving home, provided herself with two or three old books, and during the trip gathered, with great patience, examples of all the leaves and flowers she came across. These she most industriously placed in albums, and formed in pretty groups on cards during the evenings of the following winter. It was wonderful what pretty results were obtained by a little patience and skill in

WHITE WATER LILY.

arranging these specimens. This is a hint for ladies who wish to know how to fill up their spare time.

Water lilies may be had in any quantity, both yellow and white, and are to be found in greatest luxuriance on some of the smaller Broads and dykes, such as Stalham, Calthorpe, Womack, &c.

Do not allow these beautiful plants to be wantonly destroyed by any members of your own or any other party. These lovely flowers are quite a distinctive feature of the Broads, and, although there is no harm in gathering a few of them, there is no occasion to pull them up by their long, tuberous roots, and then fling them away to decay, as some seem to imagine. Leave them for others to see and enjoy.

Fruit may be obtained in abundance at most of the villages at a very trifling cost, and makes a very nice addition to the regulation *regime*.   Should you be near Rollesby in July, take a stroll through the village, and notice the acres of raspberries growing there under careful cultivation; and do not fail to taste them, for

YELLOW WATER LILY.

they are accounted the finest obtainable in England, both for size and flavour.

Another hint to the ladies. The carriage of a bushel of this luscious fruit is very trifling, and for a small outlay you may send a large hamper up to Town; what are not immediately eaten may be turned into delicious home-made jam for the small fry during the winter.

During this season fishing is at its height, especially during August; and late in the evening you

may see the enthusiast, with his float hardly discernible, straining his eyes, and still angling to get
"just one more, and *then* we'll pack up."

Fish frequently bite quite eagerly as the sun is
sinking and the gloaming coming on, so that the
angler gets quite excited, and naturally wishes for
more daylight; but, as this wish cannot be gratified,
some of the more knowing ones have recourse to
artful little aids to angling, in the shape of phos-
phorus-tipped floats, or floats that have received a
coating of Balmain's luminous paint, or some other
patent tell-tale. Very expert disciples of the craft
are, however, independent of any of these darkness-
defying floats, for they have, by experience, become
so keen to the sense of touch that they can fish
without a float at all.

The morning swim should not be omitted, and
may be indulged in early, before the ladies are
stirring. Take the jolly-boat, or dinghy, and pull to
a secluded spot, where you may indulge in a delightful bathe and swim, to your heart's content · and
body's welfare. At sunrise, there is frequently a thick
white mist hanging over both the water and land,
and, as I do not think this damp atmosphere calculated to do any good to the uninured, it will be
advisable to allow the sun half an hour to dispel
the vapour, when a bath may be enjoyed with
greater safety. Oh, yes, it is an old joke, this *vapour*
bath, and I was *near* repeating it. Those who cannot
swim should be careful where they go in, for they

will find the water very deep in some places. It should also be borne in mind, that the water is always, during summer, much warmer in the Broads than in the rivers, and that, the shallower the Broad, the warmer will the water be. There need be no fear of tides or currents, except within a radius of, say, seven or eight miles of Yarmouth, towards which place, without exception, all the rivers tend.

A better opportunity than this for learning to sail a boat cannot be had, so the amateur yachtsman should embrace it, and, if he commence with a small boat, with a single working lug-sail, he will soon become initiated into the mysteries of luffing, tacking, making a board, going about, &c. If the nautical aspirant happen to be alone, Hickling Broad is about the best place for a first attempt, for, should an upset take place, he can, from almost any part, walk ashore, as this Broad is very shallow; or he may right the boat, climb into her, bale her out, and start again. It is advisable, for many and obvious reasons, to have someone in the boat who understands the business, and can instruct others. I would give one caution, to be observed when sailing. Never, under any circumstances, make the sheet fast, for one of the sudden puffs of wind which occur frequently here, on even a calm day, will overturn the boat before you have time to cast off the turns with which you have fastened it.

The angler will find July about the best month for angling in these waters, as, by this time, the fish have recovered from spawning, and are again in good condition. From 4 to 8 o'clock in the morning, and after 6 P.M. to dark, are the times to make a bag, and the middle of the day may be devoted to sailing, visiting the local sights, and the various amusements which present themselves.

During early spring, after barley and late wheat sowing, you will notice, as your boat glides by the arable land, a boy in charge of several fields, to scare the birds. Your ears will also be assailed by his clapper and song. First, he makes a loud, rattling noise with his wooden clapper, and then commences his war song, which always ends, in true Indian fashion, with a terrific war whoop. Here is the Norfolk bird-boy's song :

> Cadders and crows, take care of your toes,
> For here come the clappers,
> To knock you down backwards:
> So, hallo! Carwho, wo! wo!! whoop!!!

The clappers are constructed of three pieces of ½in. board, of oblong shape, the centre one being elongated to form a handle. The two side pieces are fastened to this by a string, running through two holes in each board, near the bottom. The wood is strung together loosely, so as to produce a loud, rattling sound, when shaken by the bird-scarer.

Another contrivance, used for scaring birds from newly-sown or standing corn, is the "buzzer." This is a flat piece of deal, not more than ¼in. in thickness, about 2in. wide, and 8in. or 9in. long. The edge of this piece of wood is notched deeply all the way round, and sometimes square holes are made through the body of the wood, to produce more noise. A hole is then drilled at one end, through which a string is fastened, when the "buzzer" is finished. To use the instrument, it is only necessary to whirl it round at arm's length as quickly as possible, the result being a buzzing sound, like the highly accentuated drone of a humble bee.

Cricketers should make inquiries at the village inns for news of any cricket matches in the vicinity. The games are stubbornly fought, and great enthusiasm is thrown into the inter-village contests. They are not above receiving aid from visitors, if they are good players.

CHAPTER XV.

THE BROAD DISTRICT IN AUTUMN.

SEPTEMBER, OCTOBER, AND NOVEMBER.

Come, mellow autumn, with thy morning mist,
Thy laden orchards, and thine eve, sun-kissed;
Thy days now shed a ruddy glow around,
And with a leafy carpet strew the ground.

EPTEMBER in East Anglia is frequently one of the most pleasant months of the whole year. The weather is generally warm, without the sultriness of July and August, and the evenings are generally gloriously calm, with brilliant sunsets. The one drawback is, that the days are not long enough, as, by the middle of the month, night draws its dark veil ere seven o'clock has chimed. This is the month *par excellence* for eels, and, as night lines are allowed, providing they are not armed with more than *one* hook, some good hauls may now be made by those who have patience to bait and lay a couple of dozen of these lines. The eels are principally bought up by one Yarmouth firm, who at intervals send boats to the various rivers and Broads,

Q

and collect them from the various eel "sets," or netting stations.

One noticeable feature on the Broads in August is now conspicuous by its absence, and that is, the ever-gliding swallow, which does not return till the spring comes round again. These pretty birds, who nightly muster in immense flocks during the summer months, have now deserted their haunts, and flown far away south, to their winter quarters in Italy, Spain, and the north of Africa. How strange it is that these birds, after an absence of several months, not only return to this country with unerring instinct, but, in some cases at least, actually to the very nests they had occupied during the previous summer. This has been repeatedly proved by birds being caught and marked, and then released, when, upon their nests being visited after dark during the following summer, the same marked birds have been found. The storks of Holland migrate in the same way, as was proved by a Dutch gentleman, in 1885, who fastened a parchment band to a stork's leg, requesting anyone who might catch it in the winter to attach his name and residence. In the spring of 1886, back came the bird to Holland, and, on being captured while asleep, and examined, was found to have another docket upon its leg, bearing the words, in Italian : "I have wintered at Florence, at the house of Signor A——."

During the whole of the autumn, if the weather be open and fine, fishing may be indulged in, especially for pike, as these fish do not go to their deep winter habitations until the waters become cold, and ice makes its appearance.

When the weather is cold, fishing from a boat is very risky work, unless one has an abnormally strong constitution; and I would not advise town dwellers to try it. If they must fish, let it be from the bank, where shelter may be obtained, or a sharp run or walk indulged in occasionally to circulate the blood.

Perch and rudd are caught in large numbers during September and October, and frequently, during these months, the weather is exceedingly calm and mild. As most of the tourists have finished their holidays, the Broads are again very quiet. The visiting season is during the months of June, July, and August; during the other nine months the place is very quiet.

At the commencement of the shooting season, in September, the sportsman sometimes packs away his rod and lines in a dry place, and unpacks his gun, which has for so long lain idle. Now is the season of the dogs' delight, for they will assuredly have plenty of work to do to retrieve the birds falling amid the reed ronds, and which would assuredly be lost but for their valuable assistance.

The navigable rivers, being public highways, are free to all; but many of the Broads are preserved for private shooting, and persons shooting wildfowl on them may be prosecuted as trespassers. The close time for wildfowl is the same here as in other parts of England, but I am sorry to find that the law is frequently infringed, and that with impunity. A shot at a crested

Q 2

grebe or heron seems to be an irresistible temptation to some of the river-men, especially as they find a ready market for any of the rarer specimens of water-fowl they may get, even in the off season. Money, to a poor man, is at all times a great temptation; and especially is this the case here, for these men see money swimming and flying around them all day long, in the shape of fish and fowl. Only this year (1886) a wherry was stopped by the Preservation Officers, who, upon examination, discovered a large net dragging astern as she sailed, and in her hold a ton-and-a-half of freshwater fish, destined for the Midland markets. There are now several persons who carry on quite a trade in illegally netted fish, with Birmingham, Leeds, Sheffield, and other Midland towns, and who, although repeatedly summoned and fined, repeat the offence, as it pays them. Great quantities of freshwater fish are consumed by Jewish families during Lent.

In certain marshes, mushrooms are very plentiful in the autumn—so plentiful at times, that I have known them fetch only half-a-crown a bushel. September is about the best month for them, especially if it be fine, with not *too* much rain. There is no objection to anyone gathering them on the marshes, as they, in many cases, only spring up to rot again, the marsh-men very seldom gathering more than enough for their own use. What a place for an epicure: tender, juicy steaks, and mushrooms for a relish, growing on the same marsh!

October sees the brewing of some splendid ale

(which seems to be very much liked by tourists) at Lacon's brewery, in Yarmouth. It is of quite a different flavour to London beer—rather sweeter, and, strange to say, with a decided taste of malt and hops, which it is so hard to distinguish in the London production.

One of the sights of Yarmouth, from August to Christmas, is the going out and coming in of the fishing fleet, which is, without exception, the largest and finest in the world. Twenty years since, it was difficult to find fishing vessels of more than twenty-five tons burthen ; but now they are built up to seventy-five, and even eighty, tons; they are, moreover, fitted with appliances of quite modern construction and invention. Most of the large vessels carry steam engines for hauling the trawl net, pumping, and other laborious work, thereby saving much time and manual labour. The abolition of the cursed "coopers," or floating public-houses, and the advent of the mission smacks, have greatly contributed to the improvement of the social condition of the hardy and brave North Sea fishermen, who, away in the wild ocean, formerly had very little to look forward to, except incessant toil and hardship.

Yarmouth Autumn Races, one of the closing events of a very busy season, are held on the course between the beach and river, near the Nelson Column.

The autumn fruit and poultry market is exceedingly well supplied ; and the neat way the Michaelmas geese are dressed is a sight seldom to be seen out of Norfolk.

They are picked so clean, that it seems hardly possible to imagine they have ever been guilty of a downy existence. August and September witness the landing of some tons of oysters, which are brought in by the deep-sea trawlers. They are large, but of good flavour, and cheap—seldom more than 1s. per dozen. Of course, nobody thinks of leaving Yarmouth without a few of the celebrated bloaters, as presents for their friends. They are at the best during September. When well cured with oak billets they are delicious.

CHAPTER XVI.

THE BROAD DISTRICT IN WINTER.

DECEMBER, JANUARY, AND FEBRUARY.

> Come, skaters all, your jovial prince adore!
> King Frost his icy court doth rule once more;
> Come, glide; come, gleam,
> In moonlight's cold, pale ray;
> Come, make thy young blood tingle,
> And drive dull care away.—E. R. S.

DWELLERS in towns who are fond of bodily exertion in the form of skating and other ice games, are but too little acquainted with the advantages the Broad district offers in this respect. Here the skater may disport himself over hundreds of acres of ice, varying in thickness from a few inches to 3ft., which has formed on the overflown marshes. No dread of death by drowning need haunt him here, for he may exercise the graceful gyrations of his fancy and feet without risk of running against, or being run into by, other skaters; and, if he choose, he may select a spot all to himself, and there indulge in his favourite sport to his heart's content. For the bolder, and perhaps

more skilful, skater, there are scores of miles of river
to be traversed, though with the drawback of fifteen
feet of water if he should go through. This very
rarely happens, however, as any tyro can tell when
the ice is safe to practise upon. In hard winters, the
Broads are frozen over, when sleighing and shooting
are freely indulged in. Anyone having a friend in
the district, who would let him know when this occurs,
might hastily get together a party of ten or a dozen
(all of whom should be skaters), and proceed by an
early train from Liverpool Street, next day, to Norwich, whence they could select their own locality
for a day or two's good skating. A good plan is
to have a pair of stout leather boots made with the
skate screwed on the soles. The irons are usually
made on the pattern here shown. The boots should
be strong lace-ups, as
they give a great deal
more support to the

SKATE IRON.

ankles than side-springs.
They can be carried in a small bag, and put on or
taken off the feet as occasion demands. On some good
stretches of ice, if the company is numerous, booths
are erected, fires lighted, steaks cooked, and refresh-
ments vended at a reasonable rate. The ends of these
booths are left open, so that skaters may glide in, and
anchor themselves on upturned barrels, which do duty
as seats, and order any refreshment which they may
stand in need of. Sometimes parties are formed to
visit a village on the river some twenty or thirty

miles distant; and, while luncheon is being partaken of, the straps of the skates are unbound from the feet of the skater, or "skateress," as the case may be, so as to give ease and rest. Skating matches are of frequent occurrence, the course usually being half-a-mile out and home, the turning-point being generally marked by a barrel, filled with snow, and with a flag fluttering from a pole thrust into it. It does not by any means follow that the first round the turning-point wins, as it often happens that a competitor, having obtained, as they say, "the length of his opponent's foot"—that is, found out his capabilities—will make a waiting race of it, and only put forth his energy in the last hundred yards or so, when he will dart past his opponent like a flash of lightning, and win by a yard or two.

What are the fenmen doing during this Arctic weather? Well, these are really hard times with them, as all labour has to be stopped, and they can only snare and shoot wildfowl. This they accomplish by fitting a flat-bottomed punt with runners of iron, or hard wood, and filling it with fodder, or marsh hay, to lie upon, and keep themselves warm; then, in the fore part, they erect a screen of rushes, furze, or twigs, with an aperture to see through, and an arrangement of crossed sticks, upon which to rest their fowling-pieces. Their guns are old-fashioned muzzle-loaders, with enormously long barrels, and look as dangerous to the sportsmen as to the birds. Let us watch a "gunner," and see how he sets about his work. See, here he comes out of his boat-hut, from the chimney of which curls the thin, blue, peat smoke, indicating a cosy warmth in his little home. He is warmly wrapped up—an old white cap is pulled down over his ears; a white comforter is folded round his throat; and drawn over his clothes is a long, white smock, reaching below his knees. This is his uniform. In his mouth is the inevitable stumpy, clay pipe (a "nose-warmer"), about 2in. long, and as black outside as in. Over his shoulder is a rope, attached to the bow of his punt, which he now commences to drag after him over the ice, after first carefully depositing his trusty firelock on the crossed stand before mentioned. Presently he comes to a likely place, and, leaving his boat, creeps quietly along to a reed bed, and peeps at some objects two or three hundred yards off. Having satisfied himself as to the identity of these dark objects, he comes back to his punt, and enters it, kneeling in the stern, with his face to the bow; he then, from under the fodder bed, draws out two stout sticks, shod with iron, and, taking one in each hand, thrusts their points into the ice, and quietly propels himself along. As he approaches the reed rond, by a circuitous route, he keeps himself all the time well hidden behind the screen in the bow of his craft. When within 50yds. of his unsuspicious victims, he lays down his propellers, and rests his gun in such a position that it points a couple of feet over the backs of the ducks, so as to just catch them as they rise on the wing. He then gives a tremendous war whoop, and at the same time pulls the trigger of his gun. Then comes an exciting scene, as he chases the wounded birds, and wrings their necks, some of them having been only slightly hit, and giving a long chase before being captured —or escaping. He then returns to the battle-field, collects the dead, throws them into the boat, reloads his gun, and pipe, and, taking his boat in tow, looks out for a fresh shot.

During any open weather that may occur after Christmas, reed-cutting is commenced, and continued till the work is completed in the early spring. It is, in fact, carried on until the sap begins to rise, and the young shoots are just appearing.

The cutting is done either by men, who wear large, waterproof boots, standing in the water, or from flat-bottomed punts, or reed-boats. A plank is used, which either projects over the bow of the boat, or is laid flat on the stumps of the cut reed, which easily support the weight of a man. In cutting, an upward stroke is made with the sickle (the reed being held in bunches by the left hand), and care is taken to cut the reed as far below water as possible, as a saying prevails, that "an inch of reed below water is worth two above it." This may be accounted for from the fact that the green part below the water turns, when dry, to a rusty black, becomes as hard as horn, and is, consequently, much more durable when placed upon the roof of a house, in the form of thatch, with only these hard "butts" exposed to the weather. When the boat is properly loaded, it is propelled by a long pole, called a "quant," to the landing-place—or, as it is here called, "staithe"— and the reed carefully landed. The reed is then tied into bundles, or sheaves, of such a size that five of them are of the aggregate circumference of 6ft. ; hence the reason of reed for thatching purposes being sold by the fathom.

The method of propagating reed, is to separate the ·root-beds at the cutting time, then drag them to favourable posi- tions, and anchor ,them there by means of stout, wooden stakes. The roots quickly fasten themselves to the bottom, and very soon the reed spikes are found

THE STARLING.

striking upward. The greatest enemy to the young reed is the starling, which is fond of roosting among it before the stalks are sufficiently strong to bear its weight. It sometimes happens that a reed-rond, which apparently presents a good crop, is found, upon being cut, to be almost worthless in the interior, from the damage caused by these and other members of the feathered race.

Besides reed, the Fens grow various other useful plants, which are utilised for many purposes. There is gladdon, a coarse kind of reed, with broad blades and pithy stem; this also is used for the purpose of thatching roofs, but, from its more soft and spongy nature, is not nearly so durable as the lordly, bowing reed. There are also various kinds of sedge and rushes, used for thatching bullock-sheds and outhouses, or as litter for cattle, as well as coarse grass, which, being too rank for cattle provender, is used for bedding. Marsh hay, cut in the summer, is consumed in large quantities by the cattle during the winter. Having exhausted the store of above-ground profitable growths, the natives are, in the summer, often seen going even below the surface for a remunerative article—this is turf, and its lower brother, peat. This peat, or, as it is here called, "hovers," is, when properly dried, a capital and economical substitute for coal. It gives off a blue smoke when burning, and this, as it rises from the cottars' chimneys, wafts a rather pleasant perfume in the air, which is a great improvement on the soot-laden, evil-smelling smoke of the metropolis.

A peat-ground, properly managed, is a rather valuable holding, as may be gathered from the following statistics. The peat blocks, when cut, are about 4in. square (shrinking by drying to about 3¼in.) by from 2ft. to 2½ft. long (the depth of the boggy surface soil). Each square foot, therefore, produces 9 "hovers," each yard 81, each rod 2450; and, consequently, each acre the enormous number of 392,000 hovers. As these are retailed at from 1s. to 1s. 6d. per 100, a good profit must be realised.

In open weather, a great deal of coursing goes on, as the Norfolk hares are said to excel all others in size and speed, the latter probably owing to the openness and flatness of the country. These hares are greatly sought after for turning out at the various coursing meetings held in different parts of England; and their flesh—if we may judge by the placards of the London poulterers, who make "Fine Norfolk Hares" a specialty—is highly esteemed. Fen hares grow to an enormous size, and are noted for their power of jumping, and their endurance over heavy ground.

Multitudes of pewits, plovers, and wild ducks, find their way to the London markets also, and realise good prices, during the hard weather.

I would point out that, during the prevalence of east winds, the Broad district is bitterly cold; and to persons at all weak in the lungs I would certainly say, Go south rather than to these snow-bound regions. It will be seen, by a study of the meteorological tables, that Norfolk is one of the coldest counties in England during January and February, and one of the hottest during July and August. For the robust, winter here is a most enjoyable time, especially for those who can shoot or skate, and also for the angler. February is considered one of the best months for pike; but at this time the scenery is very tame, flat, and colourless.

Flocks of wild ducks and geese are frequent visitors to the Broads during very severe weather, especially on Oulton and Breydon. On the coast, line fishing from the shore, for codling, is a capital amusement. Eighty yards of line, with six or eight hooks attached, baited with lugworms, are thrown out from the shore, during a rising tide, and drawn in and examined every few minutes. Good hauls (as much as a man can carry) are often made in four or five hours.

Now, having glanced at the attractions presented by the district during the four seasons, I will leave the reader to select his own time and amusements; but I am certain that, whatever month he chooses, he will always find something to attract and amuse him in the Land of the Broads, whilst, at the same time, he will be recruiting his health.

CHAPTER XVII.

THE CHARACTERISTICS AND DIALECT OF EAST NORFOLK NATIVES.

Let not ambition mock their useful toil,
Their homely joys and destiny obscure;
Nor grandeur hear, with a disdainful smile,
The short and simple annals of the poor.—GRAY.

R. MARSHALL, the author of "The Rural Economy of Norfolk," writing in 1782, thus describes the natives employed upon the farms:—

"There is an alertness in the servants and labourers of Norfolk which I have not observed in any other district.

"Whilst a boy, he is accustomed to run at the side of his horses while they trot with the harrows. When he becomes a ploughman, he is accustomed to step out at the rate of three or four miles an hour; and if he drive an empty team, he either does it standing upright in the carriage, with a peculiarity of air, and with a seeming pride and satisfaction, or runs by the side of his horses while they are bowling away at a full trot.

"Thus, both his body and mind become active; and if he go to mow, reap, or other employment, his habit of activity accompanies him, and is obvious even in his air, his manner, and his gait. That the Norfolk labourers despatch more work than those of any other county is an undoubted fact, and in this way I think it may be fully accounted for.

"On the contrary, a Kentish ploughman, accustomed from his infancy to walk, whether at harrow, plough, or cart, about a mile and a half or two miles an hour, preserves the same sluggish step, even in his holidays, and is the same slow, dull, heavy animal in everything he does."

These ideas of the Norfolk farm-hand are, perhaps, rather too rosy for him at the present time, although he still bears a very high character for honesty, sobriety, and hard work. One hundred years have brought about vast changes in the habits and daily life of an agricultural labourer. When Mr. Marshall wrote his work the labourer was a constant boarder with his master; he was, frequently, born on the farm, worked on the farm all his life, and on the farm died. Often children born on a farm never left it from cradle to grave. They were, to a certain extent, bondsmen, just as the slaves upon a West Indian sugar plantation, but although, unlike them, they were free to leave when they pleased, seldom changed their masters. Those were happy days, both for masters and men, foreign competition, both in corn and labour, being then unknown.

R

Wages in those days were in curious contrast to those paid in the present day. Thus :—

Yearly wages of	a teamerman ..	..	£8 to £10.
,,	,, ordinary farm-hand	..	£4 to £6.
,,	,, a boy ..	.. ..	£2.
,,	,, a woman-servant	..	£3 to £3 3s.
,,	,, a girl ..	.. ..	30s. to 40s. ;

and their board and lodging in all cases. Day labourers received 1s. 1d. per day in summer, and 1s. per day in winter, together with an allowance of beer, which was, doubtless, as small as the pecuniary payment.

These were the halcyon days of Hodge. Increased wages have brought him no parallel joys, for, in proportion, his money has less purchasing power now than a century ago. He is now upon his own responsibility, hiring himself to whomsoever stands in need of his services, and is liable to dismissal at a week's notice. Compare the present rate of wages with those of 1782, and it will be seen that the poor fellow's rate of remuneration has not kept pace with the times. The following is the present wage list, with which Hodge has to feed and clothe himself, wife, and family, and pay rent :—

Teamerman ..	..	12s. to 13s. per week.
Ordinary labourer	..	10s. to 12s. ,,
Boy	..	2s. to 4s. ,,
Woman-servant ..	..	£6 to £8 per year ⎫ and
Girl	..	£3 to £6 ,, ⎭ board.

In consequence of these low wages, which barely serve to keep body and soul together, nearly all the able-bodied men either seek work in the large English towns, emigrate to distant colonies, or, as is the case with the majority, become fishermen. The farmers' loss is thus the country's gain, for the North Sea fishery is of world-wide celebrity as a school for seamen. It must not be understood, from the above remarks, that the Norfolk farm-servants are a horde of feeble, old, or crippled men; far from it, though the present representatives are not to be compared to those of former days. Five out of six of those who emigrate "alight on their feet," as they express it— that is, meet with the success their enterprise deserves; indeed, some of them have, in a few years, gathered together, by frugality and perseverance, a comfortable competency.

Those who have the hardihood to seek their living upon the sea are much better off than their land brethren, but, at the same time, run great risks from the gales which always occur in the North Sea during the herring harvest, that is, from August to Christmas. Every season sees some of the poor fellows mourned for in their native villages. Sometimes, indeed, a great wail goes up from these bereft villagers; as, for instance, during the October gale of 1883, when no less than 210 lives were lost, and a fund for the maintenance of the widows and orphans was opened at the London Mansion House.

The fisherman's life is a hard one, and only the strong can withstand the toil and exposure consequent upon its pursuit. A peculiarity to be noted,

R 2

is that those men who, at the beginning of the fishing season, come from the plough to join the fleet, and are usually, from their sparse living, thin, after being aboard a smack for a few weeks, get so much heavier and stouter that they can hardly be recognised as the same individuals. This results from the increased appetite created by the briny atmosphere, and their consequent ability to consume an unlimited supply of fish and pork—the staple food. The strength and spirits increase in a like ratio, and at the "making-up" time, at Christmas, when the season's earnings are doled out, these men are, to all intents, superior in body and mind to poor, droning Hodge, who has remained ashore during these five active months of the fisherman's life.

The pay of these fishermen is proportioned to the takes of fish and the prices realised. Thus, when the accounts are made up at the end of the season, the nett profits are divided into so many shares, according to pre-arrangement. For skipper, nine hands, and a boy, the sharing out would be something on this plan: The sum would be divided into eighteen equal shares; three of these would be apportioned for the vessel, three for the nets, two for the skipper, one-and-a-half for the mate, one for each of the hands, and the odd half for the boy. These are not the exact proportions, but will serve to show the manner in which the profits are allotted. It will thus be seen, that it is to the interest of each member of the crew to contribute to the success of the voyage by every means in his power. Of course, luck has to a great extent to do with the success or non-success of the fishing, as at times, toil as the men may, they get but a poor return for their labour, while on other occasions they meet with many good takes of fish in a season. A good season is often sufficient to give each man from £30 to £60 as his portion.

The great breweries (especially Allsopp's) and the various railways employ large numbers of East Norfolk men, who are found to be very civil, industrious, and tractable.   The latter trait is a great consideration where large bodies of men are employed, and the overseers, knowing this, prefer these men to those of almost any other county, as they have much less trouble with them.

The natives are exceedingly superstitious, even in these days of enlightenment; but doubtless much of this is due to ignorance, which the Board Schools will probably assist in dissipating.   Here are a few of these superstitions :—

(1.) If a crow croaks over a house, someone will die there within twelve months.

(2.) Nobody ever thinks of buying or selling, or commencing any new undertaking, on a Friday.

(3.) When going to market, to sell corn or oxen, if you meet a cross-eyed man or woman you had better return, as your dealing will not prosper.

(4.) Poppies brought into a house cause the occupants headaches and fainting.

(5.) Primroses carried into a house bear ill-luck with them.

(6.) If a bough of yew be brought into a house at Christmas, one of the inmates will die ere another Noel comes round.

(7.) If a red bee flies in at the open window, a male visitor will pay a visit; if a white one, a lady will call.

(8.) St. Mark's night (April 5th) is considered to be a favourable time for spells to be cast, and for sights (uncanny) to be seen. If one has the courage to go alone to the porch of the village church on St. Mark's night, he will see pass before him, at midnight, the shadowy forms of those who are to die before the next Easter. Some also say, that those in the village who are to have a serious illness during the same period will be seen.

(9.) If an unmarried girl, or young woman (maw-ther), goes into the garden at twelve o'clock on St. Mark's night, and uses the following spell, her future husband will appear, with a scythe in his hand. She must sow some hemp-seed, and as she sows must keep repeating these lines:—

> Hemp-seed I sow—
> Hemp-seed, come grow!
> He that is my true love,
> Come after me and mow.

Then the ghostly lover mows—or would do so if he ever appeared.

(10.) Here is another charm: The maiden sits before a mirror in her bedroom, in which must only be one

candle, shedding a dim light.   At twelve o'clock
she says :—

> Come, lover—come, lad,
> And make my heart glad ;
> For my husband I'll have you,
> For good or for bad.

Then the future spouse looks over the maiden's
shoulder into the glass.   Several fatal jokes have
been the outcome of these ghostly incantations.

Goblins and fairies are, of course, firmly believed
in, and many legends are told about "White Ladies,"
"Shuck Dogs," and "Shrieking Women."   Some of
these are very quaint, and show by their style that
they are of ancient origin.

Witchcraft is still, to a great extent, believed in,
and the look of an "evil eye" still causes a spell to
be placed upon the unfortunate person displeasing
the owner of the said malevolent optic.   Several cases
of this kind have come under the writer's immediate
notice, one of which he took the trouble to thoroughly
investigate.   The person upon whom the spell was
supposed to be cast was a farm labourer, of about
fifty-five years of age.   This man on a certain occasion drove his team to North Walsham, and in going
into the town nearly ran over an old man, near the
bend of a road.   The old man glared at him, shook
his stick, and muttered something, which K—— (the
teamster) could not catch.   That was enough; the
spell had been cast, and, sure enough, the next day
it worked.   K——, while at work in a field, took out

his ancient watch to see the time; it was eleven (the hour when, on the previous day, he nearly ran over the old man). He put the watch away, and immediately after felt giddy and ill, and remembered no more till he found himself in bed at home, whither he had been carried by his comrades. He soon recovered; but on the following day, when the fatal hour of eleven arrived, was again struck down, and taken home, where he soon regained his usual health. He dreaded going to work the third day, but went, and watched nervously the approach of eleven. His anxiety as the hour approached was very great, so much so, that when the time actually came he was powerless from apprehension, and soon after fainted away. I mentioned the case to a medical friend of mine, who saw the man, and pronounced it a case of epilepsy; he gave the man some physic, and a phial of dark liquid (a "black draught"), which he was to take at 10.55 the next morning, after making the sign of the Cross over it. He took it, and never since has he been troubled with the "evil eye," although he firmly believes in it, and will do so, I have no doubt, in spite of all argument, to his dying day.

We now return to consider the past and present state of the Norfolk peasant. With a change of style in farming, and in everything else, he also has changed. Men and customs are entirely altered from those obtaining in the days of our grandfathers: then the stubble was left, after cutting with the reaping-hook, 18in. and even 2ft. high. Now the machine reaper crops it off close to the ground, and so abridges the days of harvest from six or seven weeks to just half that time. Our grandsires did all farm work by hand, and required a large number of men; now everything is done by machine—threshing, winnowing, turnip-hoeing and cutting, sowing, hay-making, corn-cutting and binding, corn and straw-stacking, breaking oilcake, and a score more things, are all done by machine, to the exclusion of a great deal of manual labour.

Still, the natives are far from being a discontented people, be they fenmen, fishermen, or farm-men; and as with the advent of the Board Schools the light of education has dawned upon them, all those under the age of about thirty years are grounded in at least the three " R's."

Many of the words in use among the people are very old; indeed, some of them are pure Saxon. A perusal of the following list may, perhaps, be of interest to those who are curious in the matter of English etymology :—

GLOSSARY OF NORFOLK WORDS.

BECK.—A rivulet.

BESTOW.—To stow away.

BIN.—A manger, or cow-crib.

BISH-A-BARNABEE.—The ladybird.

'BOR.—A contraction of neighbour; as, " How are you, 'bor ? "

BROAD.—A freshwater lake; the broadening of a river, in distinction from narrow waters or rivers.

BUDDLE.—The corn marigold (*Chrysanthemum segetum*).

BUDS.—Yearling cattle.

CADDER.—A jackdaw.

CANKER.—A caterpillar.

CANKER-WEED.—Common ragwort (*Senecio Jacobæa*).

CAST.—Yield of corn.

CAUSEY.—A causeway.

CLOTE.—The coltsfoot plant (*Tussilago farfara*).

COB.—A seagull.

COCKEY.—The grate over a sewer.

COCKS'-HEADS.—The ribwort grass (*Plantago lanceolata*).

COLDER.—The *débris* of straw after threshing.

CROOM.—Anything hooked; as a turnip croom, a stick handle.

CROWD (TO).—To wheel in a barrow.

DANNOCKS.—Hedging gloves.

DEEK.—A hedgebank at the foot of which is the holl or ditch.

DICKEY.—A donkey.

DINDLES.—Common sow thistle (*Sonchus oleraceus*).

DINGLE.—To hang down.

DODMAN.—A snail.

DOLE.—To portion out, to divide.

DOLE-STONE.—A landmark or boundary stone.

DOSS (TO).—To toss with the horns, or gore.

Dow.—The ringdove.

Dwyle.—A dishcloth.

Dydle.—To bail out, to empty.

Fall Gate.—A gate across a public road.

Fey (to), or Feigh.—To cleanse out ; as a well or tub.

Fourses.—The four o'clock meal.

Gain.—Handy, convenient, docile.   Ungain.—The reverse.

Gladdon.—Common cat's-tail (*Typha latifolia*).

Goose Tansey.—The silver weed (*Potentilla anserina*).

Gotch.—A jug or pitcher.

Grissons.—The stairs or staircase.

Hain.—To raise—either the rent, or the stack, or building.

Hake.—A pothook.

Heck.—A half door.

Helve.—The handle of any implement.

Hilder.—The elder tree.

Hobbidy.—A lad, a boy-man.

Hobby.—A hack or common horse.

Holl.—A ditch at the side of a field.

Hulver.—The holly tree.

Jiffle.—To fidget.

Jimmers.—Door hinges.

Journey.—Half-a-day's work at plough or carting.

Kedgey.—Lively, sprightly.

Keeping-room.—The parlour or sitting-room.

Killer.—A small tub.

KINDLING.—Firewood.

KNACKER.—A horse-collar maker.

LAID.—Just frozen. Slightly frozen water is said to be "laid."

LARGESSE.—A gift, a reward.

LASHY.—Cold wet weather is said to be "lashy."

LOKE.—A narrow lane.

LOPE.—To take long strides in walking.

MARDLE.—Gossip.

MAVISH.—The thrush.

MAWTHER.—An unmarried girl.

MUCK.—Any kind of manure.

MUCK-WEED.—The goose-foot (*Chenopodium album.*)

MUMPS.—Mummers.

NEEDLE-WEED.—Shepherd's needle (*Scandix pecten-Veneris*).

NOCKLE.—A maul or mallet.

NOGG.—Strong beer.

NOONINGS.—The mid-day meal, dinner.

OLLAND.—Unbroken meadow land, "old land."

OWL'S CROWN.—Wood cudweed (*Gnaphalium sylvaticum*).

PACKWAY.—A bridle path.

PAD, OR PED.—A wicker hamper.

PALK.—Wreckage.

PAR YARD.—Cattle yard; straw yard.

PAXWAX.—Gristle.

PICKPURSE.—Common spurrey (*Spergula arvensis*).

PIGHTLE.—A small field; a croft.

PISHMIRE.—The ant.

PLANCHER.—The chamber floor.

POKE.—A sack or bag.

POLLEN, OR HEN POLLEN.—The hen roost.

PULK.—A puddle.

PUSH.—A boil.

QUICKS.—Couch grass (*Triticum repens*).

RANNY.—The little field mouse.

RED-WEED.—Round-headed poppy (*Papaver Rhœas*).

RINGE.—A row of potatoes, corn, &c.

ROKE.—Mist; fog.

ROWEN.—Aftermath; second grass crop.

SCOTCHES.—Notches.

SEAL, OR SEEL.—Time, or season — as hayseel, or
haytime; barkseel, or time of tree-barking.
"What seal of day is it?" That is, "What
is the time?"

SHACK.—To turn cattle out to graze after the corn
has been carted. To wander and feed at will;
thus, a tramp is called a "shack."

SHANNEY.—Mad.

SHUCK.—The shell of peas; or to shell anything.

SHUG.—To shake or scatter.

SKEP.—A beehive, a lidless basket.

SKINK.—To serve out anything; as beer, &c.

SKRIGGLE.—To squirm like an eel.

SLADE.—A sledge.

SLAKE.—Idle; at leisure.

SLUSS.—Dirty water, or mire.

SPIRKET.—A pothook.

SPOULT.—Breaking off short; brittle. Applied to wood.

SQUINDER.—To burn inwardly, as charcoal, &c.

STARK.—Stiff, or tight.

STULP.—A post of any kind.

STUGGY.—Strongly built; well knit.

SUCKLING.—White clover (*Trifolium repens*).

SWIDGE.—A puddle.

TEAM.—Five horses: two for morning work, two for afternoon work, and one taking a daily turn of rest, or grazing.

TEAMERMAN.—A waggoner. The caretaker of horses on a farm.

TEATHE.—Manure.

THACK.—To thatch; thackster, a thatcher.

THAPES.—Gooseberries.

VANCE-ROOF.—A garret.

WINTER-WEED.—Ivy-leaved speedwell (*Veronica hederi-folia*).

WISP.—A seton or rowel.

WRET-WEED.—Sun spurge (*Euphorbia helioscopia*).

WRIT.—A wart.

In thirty-nine out of the forty English counties people speak, but in the fortieth they sing: the singing county is Suffolk. Norfolk people have not the peculiar singing speech of the Suffolk natives; their dialect, however, is full of rising inflections, which make it a very difficult one for persons to imitate successfully. They pronounce the *a* dreadfully long in all words—in fact, as we pronounce it in "fate," but with the addition of an *e* before the long *a*. *H* is pronounced more like ēatch than the town aitch;

o like the *o* in move; *r* has the sound of air; *v* is usually given the same sound as Sam Weller would have given it, namely, *we*; *y* has a broad sound, something like woi. From their peculiar manner of pronouncing certain words, Norfolk men may always be detected. If you shake hands with a Norfolk man, he will at once ask: "How air yu?" or "How du yu du?" The *o* in such words as two, to, do, you, is invariably changed into *u*. In certain words no difference of pronunciation can be observed: thus, hare, hair, or hear, are all hayr; bear, beer, and bare, are alike bayr. The final *g* is usually absent, and thus we have runnen, cumen, jump'n, fight'n, for running, coming, jumping, and fighting. In one particular Norfolk natives certainly have the laugh at Londoners, and that is, in the use of the ill-treated letter *h*. They seldom misplace it, and, as an aspirate, it receives its due force of sound. Another feather in the caps of the Norfolkese, is that their vocabulary does not contain the number of slang words usually met with in counties containing a number of large towns. They seldom pronounce the *h* after *t*. Thus, they say, tree, trew, and trow, for three, through, and throw.

Speaking of a vocabulary, it may be noted that from 800 to 1000 words constitute the whole of the Norfolk natives' stock of English words; in fact, in ordinary conversation they have a way, when at a loss for a word, of coining one instanter; such words are usually comprehended by their listeners, and thus get them over an awkward pause in their narrative. They have curious ways of constructing some of their sentences—ways that are not accidental, but habitual with them. Thus, they would, instead of saying, "You go to the shop," put it in this form: "Do *you* go to the shop"; and the reply would not be: "No; you go," but "No; go you." The verbs rarely have the *s* added to the plural; thus, our native would say: "That dog *run* fast," or, "If he *come* now he will be in time."

It is a difficult thing to give an absolutely correct idea of the dialect of a county in print, as the modulation and inflection of the voice, which give character to the speech, are entirely wanting. Here, however, is a slight attempt to show those who are unacquainted with the dialect what it is like. Two old neighbours meet on a cold winter's morning, and address each other thus:

A. "Well, Nārber Ceiley, and how d'ye fare to feel this sort o' wāther."

B. "Sādla, 'bor, sādla; what wi' wāther and worrits I'm a'most dāde."

A. "Whoi, wat's amiss wi'ye?"

B. "Evrathing, 'bor; I hain't much time to golder;* but howsomdever, I'll tell yow. First, my mawther,† Abégel, trod on har frock, and hulled ‡ herself downstairs last nite, and dropped the candle, in coarse, and set fire to harself, and in a jif she flew all of a fire, and afore I could trow my old fustin coat onter

---

* Gossip.   † A young girl.   ‡ Threw.

har, all the hayr was burnt orf har hāde, lavin' it is bald as a lāard bladder. Then, in the night, my ould dickey* got over th' deek,† and fall inter the holl‡ in Cubitt's pightle,§ and thair she lay till th' mornin'."

A. "Dar seā! they du seā misfort'ns naver come single."

B. "Ay, but thet ain't all. Thet boy Tum o' mine's gorn and got married unbeknown to me, and kem a mārching his gal home yesterday at nune-time as bold as brāss. I could hardla believe my saven sensus, but the gal out with har marriage lines, and in course that pruved it. But tell yow me, 'bor, what make yow so livela?"

A. "Well, y'see, th' trūth is, my ould ooman's gorn op ta Lunnon fer a month, so I'm a gāy young bacheltor agin, 'bor—de'y'see? Eh?" &c., &c.

The names of Norfolk rivers are, many of them, Euskardian or Iberian in their derivation; thus, we have from these sources the Bure, Glaven, Exe, Ant, Nene, Nar, Thurne, Waveney, Wensum, Yare, Thet or Chet, Ouse, and others.

The names of most of the villages are of British derivation, except those bordering on the East coast, which are frequently Danish. In fact, the East coast natives are descendants of the old Danish sea-kings, who landed upon the coast, and there settled. The type of their features is certainly Danish—straight

---

* Donkey.   † Bank.   ‡ Ditch.   § A small field.

noses, open, frank countenances, blue or grey eyes, fair skin, ruddy complexion, and straw-coloured hair. Their language is also interspersed with semi-Danish words, and the accent and pronunciation are, by reason of their Danish extraction, unlike those of any other English dialect.

Most of the Danish sea-kings and their followers had particular cognomens, by which they were known irrespective of their family names, such as " Sea-wolf," " Foam Borne," " The Dragon," &c. ; and this custom has been handed down to the present generation, as nearly every man has a *sobriquet*, or nickname. The martial or sublime of the Danish names has, however, descended to the ridiculous, as a sample of a few nicknames will show. Thus, in one village you may meet " Cadderback " Ceiley, " Punks " Wiseman, " Tight-skin " Hewson, " Tea " Helsdon, " Two-skulled " Thomsen, " Bumble " Peggs, " Splayfoot " Wilson, " Whale " Thatcher, " Pretty-mouth " Mason, " Bluenose " Wayland, " Prickleback " Long, and so on. Most of these names are given to their recipients when boys, usually from some physical peculiarity, and are retained by them to the grave. When these men go to sea, or enter into the employment of any firm (such as a brewery), these nicknames take the place of their baptismal names, and by them, and frequently by them alone, they are known. It is necessary, therefore, if you wish to find a man, say aboard a smack, to know his extra appellation, and instead of asking for William So-and-so, to simply inquire for "Leatherlungs," &c., as the case may be, as the family name is probably unknown to the rest of the crew.

The dress of the natives is not of any particular peculiarity, except in one or two points. The long-sleeved waistcoat is worn by most of them. It is of somewhat peculiar make, being very long in the body, so as to come well over the hips. The front is of velveteen, with plenty of buttons, and the back and sleeves (which reach quite to the wrist) are of jean. The turnover of the cuffs is also of velveteen when the wearer is at all a beau. The long smock, with its elaborate breast work, so well known in many parts of England, is almost absent here, but its place is taken by the slop, which is in make exactly like the French blouse, but is white, or nearly so, in colour. It is a simple, square-cut gar-ment, with a hole in the top for the head to come through, and baggy sleeves, fastened at the wrist with a button. This is a very sensible garment for field work. Buskins are usually worn in wet weather, and stout hobnail boots encase the feet. The head has a billy-cock hat, of a flexible felt, which may be worn in a number of ways, according to the fancy of the owner. Sometimes the hat is worn *à la* brigand, with one side of the brim cocked up, and the other down ; sometimes with the back of the brim curled up, and the front thrust out like a peak, *à la* Mephisto-pheles; and in many other ways. In wet weather it is turned down all round, and looks like the roof-

S 2

thatch on a round stack, but answers its purpose admirably as a shelter from the rain. It is a hat for all weathers. Contrast it with the fine-weather, glossy silk hat of the town man, the supposed mark of respectability, and I am afraid, for utility and comfort, the latter will only be second.

The amphibious portion of the semi-nautical population affect a kind of half sailor rig. A Guernsey (Jersey it is called in London) covers the upper man, thick blue-black cloth trousers encase his lower extremities, and half Wellington or deck boots cover his feet. When at field work, he dons the slop and the billycock, and his dress is complete.

It matters not how the men are dressed, or where they are seen, the seafaring man, who works part of his time on the farm, can be detected at a glance from the purely agricultural labourer. Let half-a-dozen of them walk a short distance, and the difference in their gait and carriage is seen at once. The labourer, being used to walking over ploughed and soft land, takes a long, slow stride, with his shoulders forward, and his arms swinging like pendulums by his side. The fisherman-labourer takes shorter steps, rolls in his gait, and turns his elbows out from his sides, and usually turns the backs of his hands to the front. He is usually the smarter man of the two, as seeing about him brightens his ideas, gives him a better flow of language, and makes him more intelligent, in every way, to his fellow workman who vegetates in one spot all his life.

There is one peculiar article of dress that may be noted, and that is the collar—the Sunday collar, if you please, as during the week a coloured handkerchief, wound round the neck like a rope, takes its place. It is fastened by a button in front, then passed *backwards* round the neck, the strings again brought to the front, and there tied.

A CURIOUS COLLAR.

Should a button fastening an ordinary collar come off, a man (a town man) is helpless; but in this one, if a string gives way, a piece of twine or part of a bootlace is spliced on, and all is well again.

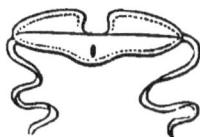

Funerals are conducted here in a very simple, but nevertheless impressive, manner. After being used to our larger metropolitan cemeteries, with their numerous throngs of gaping spectators, many of whom are simply drawn to the grave-side from idle curiosity, and who stare at the mourners and their grief as at a raree show, it is a very solemn and touching sight to witness a country funeral. Let us stand aside by yon epitaph and inscription-begirt column, and witness the burial of a farm-bailiff's little daughter. Near the flint-built wall the tiny grave is dug—not the deep, dark chasm we town-dwellers are used to gaze down into with fear, lest the crumbling sides give way, and precipitate one to the bottom with a broken limb, but a neatly-dug resting-place, not more than 5ft. in depth, for here but one body rests in each grave. The sexton has finished his task of digging, and,

wiping his hot face (for it is summer time), unrolls his
upturned sleeves, dons his coat again, and enters the
church, from the tower of which is presently heard
the dismal and solemn tolling of the passing bell. A
few persons, both men and women, attired in their
darkest clothes (as they have not all black ones), now
begin to cluster near the grave, to await the coming
of the funeral *cortége*. Their conversation is in a
subdued key; but presently there is a stir among
them, for in the distance, some half-mile off, a confused
assemblage of persons is seen slowly wending its
way along the footpath across the fields. Gradually
they draw nearer and nearer, and as they approach
take shape as an orderly procession, partly white
and partly black in colour. As they draw nearer
to the churchyard, a flutter of white linen is seen
in the porch, and the parson, with bare head, and
book in hand, advances to the gate to meet
the procession. First come the schoolfellows of the
dead child, each with an offering of wild and
garden flowers. Then the friends of the family,
immediately followed by four girls of twelve or
fourteen years of age, each sustaining the corner of
a large white cloth, in the centre of which lies the
coffin, nearly hidden by flowers. Following closely,
in pairs, are the father and mother, sisters and
brothers, and other relatives of the little one, whose
voice will never again be heard singing in the
green fields, or in the old thatched church, the
choir of which she constantly attended. A host of

villagers bring up the rear, the solemnity of the
occasion being apparent in their very gait and
whispered words, as they gather at the grave-side.
The voice of the parson breaks the stillness of the
air, for all is now silent save the song of the birds,
who carol sweetly, as if the uprising of the little soul
in its heavenward flight were a thing of joy to them.
The harvestmen, building their corn stack in the adjoining field, pause in their labour, and reverently
doff their hats, as they await, with down-bent heads,
the conclusion of the ceremony. Many a tear from
the eyes of the brave fishermen and farm-men standing
within the sacred acre bedews the soil, and, when
the dull thud of the "earth to earth" resounds on the
coffin-lid, a shudder of awe seems to run through
the gathered villagers. At length the service is
finished, and the broken-hearted father consoles his
half-fainting wife and sobbing children, as they slowly
wend their way homeward, leaving the throng, after
a last look at the little white coffin, to disperse quietly
to their respective homes, and the sexton to finish
his task at his leisure.

Hearses being unknown in these villages, all adults
are carried to their last resting-place upon a cart—
that is, if the distance be more than about a third of
a mile. If less, a bier is requisitioned, and four or
six bearers carry the coffin. A simple band of black
round the hat and sleeve is the only mourning worn.
If the deceased be a little girl, a narrow slip of white
material is worn at the back of the men's hat-bands,

as a symbol of the spotless innocence of the departed
little one.

For the grandees of the district, muffled peals are
frequently rung, which have a very curious and striking effect when heard for the first time. The muffling
is effected by tying pieces of sacking, or carpet, on
one side of the clapper of each bell. The bells are
then rung in sequence, and give forth their full sound;
but on being struck by the other, or muffled, side of
the clapper, a very subdued sound is produced, giving
the effect of the note being produced at a great distance,
in comparison to the first or full notes. The effect
of the soft pedal of a pianoforte gives something of
the idea of the muffled peal, but does not subdue or
blur the tone nearly enough.

As this chapter is getting like Witherington in the
ballad of "Chevy Chase," that is, into the "doleful
dumps," we will change the subject, and turn from the
dead to the living. As living suggests food, we will see
in what respect that which is consumed here differs
from that in other parts of the realm. First comes
the space-filling, all-satisfying Norfolk dumpling, which
is the simplest possible article of manufacture in the
pudding line. Flour, yeast, water, and a pinch of
salt, properly compounded, and popped in the pot
for neither more nor less than twenty minutes, suffice
to produce a pudding fit for a king—or a ploughman.
It is strange how few Londoners can make these
dumplings properly; they are either too large or too
small, too heavy, too little cooked, or too little

"something," which just spoils them. The Norfolk women have the necessary knack of making them, and know to a ·nicety, by a kind of instinct, the exact size to make them ; for, as they roll them in their hands into a globular form, they usually nip a little piece off, or add a small piece, to keep them to the orthodox dimensions.

Pork and apple pie is another favourite, and has a crust neither thicker nor thinner than the sole of the goodman's shoe, which is tantamount to saying that there is something substantial to bite at. The pork and apples are put into the dish, in alternate layers, until the dish is full, when the cover of dough is placed over, and the whole baked in a huge brick oven. This dish sometimes overcomes weak or bilious stomachs. Pumpkin and apple pie (alternate layers of each) is another favourite, and is eaten with plenty of pepper, which is sprinkled over each layer. Pumpkin and raisin pie, with pepper seasoning, is another dish of the same class.

Sausages (always pork) are liked baked in a batter, in which they appear like ships in a troubled sea. This is called "toad-in-the-hole," and is very good, although somewhat rich. *Experto crede.*

Frumerty, or furmety, is new wheat boiled in milk until it bursts and assimilates with the milk. It is then eaten with sugar, and, I should think, would form one of the most nutritious things a person (or children) could possibly consume. When left to cool, it sets in a beautiful thick jelly.

The grand time for feasting is at pig-killing time, and then numbers of queer dishes are concocted from the interior and exterior of the porker. Chitterling and apple pie is a great favourite. "Scraps" is another; this is made by saving all the little bits of fat, from all parts of the animal, and frying them till most of the grease has run out. When of a delicate brown, they are eaten with a little salt, and much gusto, to the wonder of the town looker-on, who sits by wondering how the eaters can keep them down.

In the way of drink, the natives are not at all particular, their summer tipple being very thin, "small beer," of which they consume large quantities, especially in the harvest field. The labourers are usually allowed a certain amount of porter during harvest time. This is given at 11 A.M., when they have their "lavenses,' and at 4 P.M., when they have their "fourses."

Mead is another drink, and is made by those of the cottagers who keep bees. It is a very sweet, and, when good, intoxicating drink. It is made in a very simple manner, as will be seen from the following recipe: In 10 gallons of water well mix the whites of five or six eggs, and add 15lb. of honey. Boil this mixture for not more than an hour, and add (according to taste) some spice—cinnamon, mace, ginger, cloves, &c. Pour the liquor into a large wooden tub, and when nearly cool add enough yeast to set it working. When fermentation has ceased, put it into a barrel, which tightly bung. After keeping in a cellar for six months, it may be bottled for use. This quantity will make about five dozen bottles. This quality is seldom made by the villagers, and had not need be, or the list of "drunk and disorderly" charges would be increased. About 5lb. of honey to 10 gallons of water is nearer the proportion to produce cottage mead. Mead was the old Scandinavian drink.

Purl is a winter early morning drink. It is made of ale, with a *soupçon* of rum or other spirits in it; a little spice is also added, and the whole then placed in a warmer over the fire. It is kept continually stirred, with a bunch of dried wormwood, until sufficiently warm and bitter. The natives are very fond of this tonic. On one occasion, two of my friends expressed their wish to try some. We accordingly adjourned to a tavern near Norwich, and ordered a glass each. It was made and brought in. "Good health!" was nodded by each to other, and a sip taken. No more! Each looked at the other with a look, as much as to say "I'm poisoned," on his face. After enjoying the scene for some time, I found breath enough to ask them what they thought of it. One, a Cambridge student, fresh from his studies, said: "It is not quite the drink of the gods—nectar; but if ever the devil takes a quiet glass, this is his tipple!!" Number Two, a medical student, gave it as his opinion that it was "the finest and most irresistible emetic he had ever tasted." Two millers just then came in; the purl was handed to them, and was out of sight and finished, with a smack of the lips, before one could cry "Jack Robinson." So much for taste. It no doubt creates a good appetite in those who can take it, for, as one of the millers said, "A glass of purl before breakfast will make a man eat bricks."

In a tavern, of which I have forgotten the locality, is the following puzzle :—

More	beer	score	clerk
For	my	my	his
Do	trust	pay	sent
I	I	must	has
Shall	if	I	brewer
What	and	and	my.

To decipher, it is necessary to commence with the last word in the right-hand column, and read upward; then, by reading the other columns in the same way, the verse will be discovered.

Many old ditties of a bacchanalian character are still extant, and there are also a great number of sea songs, which are sung over and over again, and handed down from father to son. Ballads of all kinds are the favourite songs for Saturday night— which is the regular singing night in all the inns. These are interspersed with step dancing and yarns (oh, so tough !). The dancing is usually performed upon the bar table, which is placed in the centre of the room, so that all may have a fair view. Often two dancers will appear on the same table, and dance "the longest and strongest" for a quart of ale; he who gives in first loses. They clatter away, with their hobnailed pumps, till the perspiration trickles down their faces, and every now and then a mug of ale is handed to each of them for a "cooler," which has to be drunk without a pause in their exercise. If one slackens his step, loud exclamations of dissent are immediately raised by the partisans of his opponent. This "dance of asses" goes on till one of them fails from sheer exhaustion, and the other slips off the table on to a settle, amid the shouts of his applauding friends. To while away the monotony of this business, someone usually obliges with a song, and, being in an inn, and inclined, we will hear one of these—a drinking song :—

THE PYE ON THE PEAR-TREE.

The pye sits on the pear-tree top,
        [*Singer holds up a glass of ale.*
The pear-tree top, the pear-tree top;
I hold you a crown she is coming down,
She *is* coming down, she IS coming down;
        [*Brings it slowly down.*
I hold you a crown she is come down,
She *is* come down, she IS come down;
        [*Hands it to his neighbour.*
So lift up your elbow, and hold up your chin,
And let your next nei'bor just joggle it in.
        [*He joggles the drinker, so that he may*
        not drink the proffered draught.

Sometimes the songs, instead of being of a bacchanalian order, are quite learnedly historic, if perhaps a little boastful; but, perhaps, county pride is, after all, the prerogative of an Englishman. Here is one of these loyal lays :—

THE MEN OF NORFOLK.

Come, sing a lay of Norfolk's sons,
    And troll their fame in verse and song,
Recounting doughty deeds they've done,
    On sea and land, with courage strong.
' We'll sing our strain both bold and clear,
    Where'er we roam, on cliff or lea;
So loud our voices let us raise,
    That foes may hear across the sea.

CHORUS.

For the lads who speed the plough, Hurrah!
    And for those who toil on the sea;
If war should come, to the tap of the drum
    They would march and merry be.
To England's aid, in rank arrayed,
    They are first in the battle's roar,*
For on land or sea, or where'er they be,
    They are ever to the fore—
                        Brave boys!
    Our lads are to the fore!

Long ages past fierce Romans came,†
    With mighty hosts, upon our shore;
Then Norfolk's men rose, in their might,
    And marshland men prepared for war;
A battle fought, and victory gained;
    Full many a thousand foemen fell.‡

---

* General Wyndham, a Norfolk man, led the troops to the assault of the Redan, in the Crimean War; and the Norfolk regiments were conspicuous for their bravery.

† Julius Cæsar landed in Britain B.C. 55.

‡ Boadicea, widow of Prasutagus, King of the Iceni (or ancient inhabitants of Norfolk), and whose stronghold was at Kenninghall, roused to revenge by the outrages of the Romans upon herself and daughters, marched upon Camalodunum (Colchester), and slaughtered the garrison, and then upon Londinium (London), which she took and reduced to ashes, besides slaughtering 70,000 Romans and their allies. The remains of her encampment still exist at Kenninghall.

Boa'-dicea! * may thy name
In English hearts for ever dwell.

Chorus :—For the lads who speed the plough, &c.

Long years rolled by: the Normans crossed,
And in our island made a stand;
The fenmen stout resistance made,
And fought the foe with bow and brand.
St. Benet's Abbey long maintained
Unequal strife with mail-clad men,
Till treachery the gate unbarred:
The Normans conquered only then.†

Chorus :—For the lads who speed the plough, &c.

To Norfolk's brave old warrior we
Must give remembrance; for I trow
That Frenchmen, in Good Henry's reign,‡
Were certainly our direst foe.
Sir John Fastolfe,§ at Agincourt,
Against Alençon ran full tilt,
And prisoner home the Frenchman brought,
Whose ransom Caister Castle built.‖

Chorus :—For the lads who speed the plough, &c.

---

* Boadicea was defeated soon after, and her followers slain. She saved herself only by flight, but, fearing to fall into the hands of the enemy, poisoned herself A.D. 61.

† See the story of the taking of St. Benet's Abbey, at page 126.

‡ King Henry V.

§ Sir John Fastolfe, or Fostalfe, born 1377, at Yarmouth; died 1459, and is buried in St. Nicholas' Church, Yarmouth. He must not be confounded with the braggadocio Sir John Falstaff, of Shakespeare's dramas.

‖ It is said that the Duke d'Alençon was taken prisoner by Sir John and brought to England, where, as a ransom, he built Caister Castle, as a residence for his captor. I cannot see how this could be, as Alençon died by the hand of the English king on the field of battle.

In good Queen Bess's lengthened reign,
The fleet called the Armada came,
Whose.Spanish captains, all so bold,
Had threatened us with sword and flame.
But Britain's seamen, undismayed,
Arose their country to defend,
While Yarmouth's gallant ships and men,*
Helped back to Spain the dons to send.

Chorus :—For the lads who speed the plough, &c.

To Norfolk's hero render song—
At Nelson's † name let shouts be raised!
For deeds of valour such as his
Should by his countrymen be praised.
Trafalgar's crowning glory is
By Englishmen held ever dear :
More so by Norfolk's sturdy sons,
Who lost their hero fighting there.

Chorus :—For the lads who speed the plough, &c.

N.B.—*This song, set to music, may be had in sheet form, price* 1s.,
from the Author.

---

* Yarmouth is said to have sent many vessels, manned by the hardy
Norfolk fishermen, to help her Majesty against her Spanish foes.

† Nelson was born at Burnham Thorpe, a hamlet in the north of
Norfolk.

Words by E. R. SUFFLING.

Music by WYNDEYER CLARKE.

The Men of Norfolk.

Allegro moderato.

Come, sing a lay of Norfolk's sons, And troll their fame in verse and song, Re-

T

count-ing doughty deeds they've done, On sea and land, with cou-rage strong.

We'll

sing our strain both bold and clear Wher-e'er we roam, on cliff or lea, So loud our voi - ces let us raise, That

CHORUS

foes may hear a - cross the sea, That foes may hear a - cros the sea. For the

lads who speed the plough, hurrah! And for those who toil on the sea; - - If war should come, To the

staccato

tap of the drum They would march and mer - ry be. - - To Eng - land's aid, in

cres.

f

f

rank ar-ray'd, They are first in the bat - tle's roar, - - For on land or sea, or where'er they be, They are ad lib.

ev - er   to the fore, Brave boys! Our lads are to   the   fore. . .

colla voce

tempo

ff

p

Ped.   *

CHAPTER XVIII.

THE FISH OF THE BROADS, AND HOW TO CATCH THEM.

Now, away to the Broad,
With our tackle all stored:
Here's a day that is worth a day's wishing.
See that all things be right,
For 'twould be a spite
To want tools when a man goes a-fishing.
—COTTON (*localised*).

AS I do not lay claim to being either an Izaak Walton, Cotton, or Pennell, I shall not attempt, in this chapter, to write learnedly, like those noted anglers, upon the various methods of taking fish, but shall simply give a glance at the fish themselves, and offer a few notes and suggestions on angling which will, I think, be sufficient for the general tourist and casual piscator.

The species of fish which are to be found in the Broads and rivers are but few, though what is lacking in variety is certainly made up for in number. Trout, gudgeon, dace, and other well-known river fish, appear to be very scarce in these waters; but the shoals of perch, roach, rudd, bream, and eels, are simply astounding.

Netting and poaching the fish was carried on to such an alarming extent a few years since, that the Broads threatened in a few years to become depopulated of their finny inhabitants. Tons and tons of fish, which could not be sold, were simply used for manure—and capital manure it was found to be ; but what a waste of good food ! Some ten or twelve years since, several gentlemen, by bringing the matter before Parliament, were enabled to get a Bill passed which has had the effect of nearly stopping this wanton destruction. The Broads are now fast regaining their normal number of fish, though these appear to run small, a natural result of so many thousands of the larger and older ones being destroyed. Every year, however, adds to the size, weight, and number of fish, and in a few years more, with careful watching, the waters will be as well stocked as in days of yore.

As the roach, of all the freshwater fish, requires the most delicate skill to capture, we will see, first, how he is to be lured to his doom silently and quickly.

The *Roach (Leuciscus rutilus)* is, in form, too well known to need description. When this fish is in good condition, the head is one-fifth of the entire length, and the depth, at the juncture of the dorsal fin, two-fifths of the length of the body (that is, minus head and tail). The spawning season is about the latter end of May, or, in late seasons, the beginning of June. The roach is a very prolific fish;

in the ovary of one weighing 1½lb., no less than 125,000 eggs were counted. As a table fish, though not so fine as many others inhabiting fresh water, it is, when properly cooked, toothsome enough. It is in finest flavour in October, its flesh being then firmer than at any other period. The roach does not attain to any great size, usually running from 7in. or 8in. to 1ft., though specimens have been taken 15in. in length, and weighing 2½lb.

The best months for taking the roach are July, August, September, and—for the enthusiast—October. A fairly long but light rod will be required, with a thin running line, to which should be attached 5yds. or 6yds. of gut, and—for ordinary sized fish—a No. 10 or No. 11 hook; for large fish, a hook one size larger may be used. As the roach bites very delicately, a very small, quill float will suffice, with just enough shot above the hook to sink the line and leave the float partly on its side. The water should neither be too turbid nor too rough, or the shy nibbles of these fish will not be readily detected. The best bait for these waters appears to be paste, which may be made of simple dough, amongst which has been finely and intimately mixed a small proportion of cotton wool, which will make it adhere more firmly to the hook. Some prefer to colour the paste with a little ver-milion; but this gives it a "wormy" appearance, and roach are not such great lovers of worms as perch. Still, it would not be a bad idea to take a small quantity of each, and try which is the more killing.

What will lure one day will be found of little avail on another occasion. Gentles, in their white state, are often very efficacious; they may be kept until they assume a red hue (which is the chrysalis state), when, at certain times, they will be eagerly taken. The objection to the red gentlemen is that, their outer case being hard and brittle, difficulty is experienced in keeping them on the hook.

Now, if you wish to have a good day's sport, it is imperative that the swim be ground-baited for some distance round, either the night before, or very early on the morning of, the day selected for angling. A good ground-bait is made thus: Take a number of lobworms, and chop them up into pieces one-quarter or one-third of an inch in length; now mix them thoroughly in sand or light clay, so that plenty of it adheres. Add a very small quantity of boiled rice or barley, and make the whole into balls as large as a boy's fist. Throw these balls into the water where you intend to fish, twenty-four hours beforehand, if practicable. Another ground-bait is made by mixing well-soaked breadcrumbs and bran together, and adding a handful of brewers' grains; this, when well worked together, may be rendered heavy by the addition of a little clay or loam. Make into large balls, and cast into the proposed swim.

Roach are very gregarious fish, and on the following morning will be found to have congregated in large numbers about the ground-bait. Having carefully plumbed the depth, allow the bait upon your hook just to clear the bottom by an inch or two. If fishing from a boat, be careful not to make a noise with your feet, or drop anything, as wood, being a conductor of sound, conveys the slightest noise to the fish. If you must talk, do so in a low tone. Be careful to have a landing-net handy, as even a medium-sized fish will be sure to break your delicate tackle if not properly landed. If a large fish (say, one of 2lb. weight), the top joint of the rod would break under the strain if no net were employed. It sometimes happens that, when a roach is being landed, a pike will make a grab at it, and, if he gets it in his mouth, then good-bye line and float, farewell top joint and best part of rod, and adieu sport at this particular spot for some time to come!

The yellow or dung fly is sometimes a useful bait, and should be tried. Roach will sometimes rise at this, if it be gently dangled along the surface of the water. They will rise near it, closer and closer, till, with a loud "flop," they are hooked and landed.

The angler must himself supplement these few notes by trials of the various baits which may suggest themselves, one of the chief pleasures of angling being found in the various schemes and dodges resorted to.

The sense of smell appears to be highly developed in the roach, and such things as saffron, balsam of tolu, aniseed, assafœtida, and other strong-smelling drugs, are at times used with success.

Roach will usually be found at the junction of a

Broad with a river, as they wait there for the food to drift down to them.

The *Bream* (*Abramis brama*), whose bellows-like shape is well known to all anglers, runs much larger than the roach; its ordinary weight is from 2lb. to 3lb., though 12lb. and 14lb. fish have at times been taken. It is, however, a very uncommon thing in England to take one exceeding 5lb. Bream are very gregarious; so that, when once among them, a heavy bag may be

THE BREAM.

soon made. They spawn during May, and may be angled for from June to October. Bream being a strong and weighty fish, a rod stiffer than that used for roach, and a strong silk line, must be used; and it will also be as well to have a larger hook (No. 9 or No. 10). A large float is not necessary, as these fish bite in a very timid manner; but great attention must be paid, and the fish struck promptly. Now comes the tug of war, for they fight in a very game manner; if the place is tolerably clear plenty of line may be given, and the fish played. The landing-net will again be in requisition.

In the winter, bream, when caught, will stand an astonishing amount of cold. On the Continent, they are kept for hours, and transported long distances, by simply wrapping them in snow, and inserting a piece of bread steeped in brandy in their mouths. When thus treated, they will recover after being out of the water for hours. Bream love to get into deep holes, and therefore silence and caution must be observed when angling for them. When caught, do not be too eager to clutch them, for, next to eels, they are the slimiest of all fresh-water fish, and will daub one's clothes over to an alarming extent unless great care be taken.

Various baits may be tried—wasp grubs, greaves, dew worms, red paste, &c.; but a bait seldom refused is the common and easily-procured earthworm.

The bite of the bream may easily be mistaken for the little nibble or bob of the minnow; so that, unless it be responded to by an instantaneous strike, very few fish will be landed.

Bream love the deep holes in the rivers or Broads—the former for choice, as they like running water better than still.

The strike is simply a quick movement from the wrist, with just force enough to dart the barb of the hook into the mouth of the fish, and not, as some imagine, with such power as to jerk its head from its body. The

bait should be only a few inches from the bottom.
Ground-bait of barley-meal and chopped worms, or
mashed potatoes, with shreds of beef, and a few gentles,
may be used with success. Work these ingredients, or
any others that may suggest themselves to you, into
lumps, which drop into the holes or other haunts of the
fish, who will then congregate in large numbers. The
early morning and the evening will be found the best
times to take bream. The heaviest fish frequently bite

THE CARP.

in the most timid manner, so do not forget the motto,
" Strike while the iron's hot "—or the bream bites. As
to its gastronomic qualities—well, tastes differ. The
French are fond of this fish, while an English writer
says " they are a combination of bones and nastiness."

The *Carp* (*Cyprinus carpio*) is a handsome fish, and
the very antithesis of the bream, from an epicurean point
of view. Its flesh is esteemed such a delicacy that
ponds are, in many places, made especially for keeping
them until fit for table. They are very long lived, often
exceeding the century. This has been proved many

times, by attaching metal rings to their tails when young, and then keeping them in ponds. By these means, some have been proved to be 150 years old. Carp grow to a very large size; they have been taken weighing from 15lb. to 18lb., and on the Continent even more. For some unknown reason, they are not so numerous in the Broads as other fish, which is very strange, seeing that they are excessively prolific. A carp 1lb. in weight, being opened, was found to contain 295,000 eggs; one of 5lb., 460,000; and a large one, of 10lb., upwards of 700,000 ! The ovary of this latter fish actually weighed more than the whole of the remaining portion!! Carp spawn in May, and should be angled for from June to October, and even later. They are very tenacious of life, and may be kept, in a net filled with moss or grass, for a week or more, with an occasional wetting. I cannot give the novice much hope of catching many of these beautiful fish, for they are exceedingly wary, and shy of anything uncanny in the form of a baited hook ; still, they are to be caught by the exercise of patience, if the right kind of bait be used, and quietness be observed.

The rod should be strong and pliable, and the tackle as fine as possible compatible with strength. The line should be a running one, thin but strong, and long enough for big rushes, which these fish often make ; a No. 8 or No. 9 hook is the best to use. If you have a bamboo rod, so much the better, this being both light and supple. Keep the shots on your line as far from the bait as possible, and use a small quill float. The size of this last article depends upon the depth of water, and consequent weight of shot employed.

Scores of different kinds of bait are recommended; among others, a bluebottle fly, pastes of various colours, grains of boiled corn, a boiled green pea, &c.; but, after you have tried all, you will find a well-scoured red worm to be the most seductive. Some anglers flavour the paste baits with honey or treacle; but these fancy kinds rarely succeed. Evening is the best time to angle for carp, quite into the twilight; and even after dark (by the feel) good bags are made. An old angler, when asked what was the best bait for carp, replied, " Patience ; " and without this it is useless to try to catch them.

As we have seen, for bream you should strike on the instant of detecting the bite; but with a carp this would be a foolish and useless proceeding. When you notice a bite, let the fish take the bait a little distance, and then strike . gently ; when hooked, let him have as much line as he wants, with an occasional quiet check; presently, his vigorous efforts to escape will tire him, when you may carefully land him, without much fear of a broken line or rod.

For ground-bait, use shred beef, oatmeal and water, with a little treacle or honey added. Another sort, though not quite so pleasant to prepare, is made by chopping up a number of worms and gentles, and mixing them with some well-soaked breadcrumb; then add a small portion of clay or earth, and sink at the required spot.

The following curious idea is prevalent concerning frogs and carp, but I am not in a position to vouch for its correctness. It is said "that frogs will mount a carp's back, to which it will cling with its hind legs, while it thrusts its fore legs into the corners of the fish's eyes, and thus rides it, like an Old Man of the Sea, till it wastes, and wastes, and dies"!!

The *Rudd*, or *Pink-eye* (*Leuciscus erythrophthalmus*), may, in the season, be caught nearly as quickly

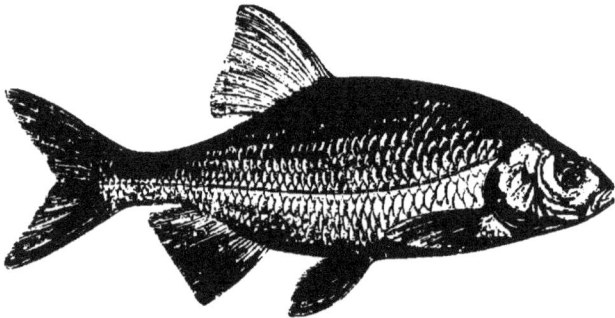

THE RUDD.

as its Latin name can be pronounced. It may be angled for in much the same manner as the roach. Rudd are gregarious, and, when once you get among them, in a deep hole with a gravelly bottom (as on Hickling Broad), you may, with care, nearly empty the spot before the fish become alarmed at their diminishing numbers.

Great diversity of opinion exists respecting this fish. Walton infers that it is a cross between the roach and bream ; other writers class it as a pure-bred fish,

of a quite distinct species; while others, again, maintain that it is a hybrid of the roach and carp. In
France, where it is called the roche-carpe, it attains
a greater size than in England, and is esteemed a
great delicacy.

In the Broads, rudd may be met with in shoals.
The average weight of these fish is from ½lb. to ¾lb.
Barley meal and brewers' grains, or a few gentles,
mixed with soaked bread, will draw them together.
The grub of the "daddy long legs," called the "leather
jacket," used as a fly, should be tried, as also the
wasp grub, or "soldier." These grubs should not be
allowed to get into a too forward state of development,
or they will become brittle, and difficult to keep on
the hook. Three or four pellets of brewers' grains
have been tried with great success, even when the
fish were a little off their feed. When they are on
their feed they will bite at almost anything, especially
when it is raining.

The *Pike* (*Esox lucius*), and young fish of the same
tribe, are known by various names, such as luce, jack,
pickerel, &c., and are veritable fresh-water dragons,
consuming all fish which come in their path, except
the perch, which is armed with a *chevaux-de-frise*
on its back, which would be awkward for the pike's
gullet! Neither does he tackle the diminutive stickle-
back, as he, too, is well armed. As to size, I am
almost afraid to state to what dimensions these fellows
will grow, certainly to 30lb., and even more, though
in this district very few are taken larger than 20lb.

U

At Whittlesea Mere, one was caught, in 1820, weighing about 52lb., and stories are in circulation of monsters, in the deep mountain lochs of Scotland, Wales, and Ireland, of 60lb. and 70lb. weight. But who has seen them? What do you think of this for a pike? I think it more like a whale; but here it is: "In 1498, a person caught at Kaiserlauten, near Mannheim, a pike which was 19ft. long, and weighed 350lb. Its skeleton was for a long time kept at Mannheim. Round its neck was a brazen ring, capable of enlargement by springs. On this ring the Emperor Frederick

THE PIKE.

Barbarossa caused the date to be engraved A.D. 1235 —267 years before its capture."

The pike certainly attains a patriarchal age and gigantic size, but we cannot quite believe all we read without the occasional aid of the salt-cellar. The stories of its voracity are legion, fish, flesh, and fowl, falling a prey to its insatiable appetite. Water-hens, coots, ducks, and all kinds of fish (even his own species), are swallowed whole by this ravenous water-wolf. A list of strange meals eaten by the pike lies by me as I write, from which I extract the following: A swan's head and neck, a mule's lip, a girl's foot, a man's hand, some young kittens, and a large piece of bacon. Pike spawn for the first time when three years old. About the end of March they come out of the deep water in which they lie during the winter, enter the shoal waters of the dykes, and commence to spawn, which operation lasts about a couple of months. When twelve months old, the pike is about 9in. long; at two years, 12in. to 14in.; and at three years attains a length of about 18in. or 19in. After this age it continues to grow, no doubt, to a great size, but certainly not to 19ft., as the German one is reported to have done.

Watermen have a curious way of snaring the pike during hot summer days. During July and August these fish love to lie near the surface of the water, basking in the sun. To snare them, our friend the fisherman proceeds thus: He takes a stout ash stick, or straight sapling, 10ft. or 12ft. in length, from the thin end of which is suspended a noose of copper wire; this wire is previously heated in burning hay, to make it pliable. He then walks along the sides of a river or dyke until, peeping cautiously over the margin, he discovers a basking pike; then, expeditiously and cautiously, he drops the noose over the pike's head, gives a jerk, and the deed is done.

This mode of capture is, however, never resorted to by gentlemen who follow angling for pastime, and not for a living. The legitimate modes are known as trolling, spinning, and live-baiting. These methods

I will endeavour to describe without entering into the minutiæ, which would occupy too much space.

A cloudy sky, a nice gentle breeze, and a day not too warm, is the best time for pike fishing. A rod 12ft. in length is about the handiest, though some prefer one a couple of feet longer; a certain degree of stiffness and strength is indispensable. The line must be a long one—not less than 50yds. or 60yds. of waterproof trolling line, neatly wound on a winch at the butt of the rod. The hook for trolling is the ordinary double-headed one for pike, and upon the shank is a little cylinder of lead, a couple of inches long; the shank of the hook ends in an eye, through which the gimp trace is fastened, the other end being in turn secured to the line. One or more swivels are usually attached to the trace, but may be dispensed with.

A small roach makes a good bait (dead gorge bait), and is placed upon the hook thus: Take your roach, and, with a pair of scissors, cut off the tail close to the flesh, and one of its side fins, which will cause it to have an eccentric rotary motion in the water. Now get out your baiting-needle, and fix the loop of your trace to the little hook at the end of the needle; then thrust the needle, gimp and all, down the throat of the roach, and out at the tail; draw the needle quite through, and detach, at the same time drawing the gimp through till only the end with the loop hangs from the mouth of the bait. Attach the hook, and draw the shank into the stomach, till only the barbs of the hooks protrude from the mouth. It only remains for the line to be attached to the gimp, and you are ready for the first cast.

The most likely places for pike are in pools, by the side of beds of weeds, rushes, or reeds, or even in the rivers themselves; but, in the latter case, always fish within 2ft. or 3ft. of the bank. Cast your bait lightly, and let it sink; then draw it slowly, with a swimming motion, from side to side, and in all conceivable directions. When the "knock," or "run," as the bite of the pike is called, occurs, there will be no mistaking it; the fish will simply clutch the bait in his jaws, and swim off with it to his haunt. Let him go; do not ask him to stay with you—in fact, pay out your line slowly, so as not to check him. Now comes the patience test: for eight or ten minutes, not less nor more, you must simply wait, though you may be bubbling over with suppressed excitement. At the end of that time, you may reel up any loose line, till you feel the fish, then give a sharp tug; for the rest, you must play him according to the special circumstances of the case. Exercise patience, and in his rushes give him an occasional turn, until by-and-by, when your quarry begins to tire, you may quietly wind him in, and thus secure your first "luce." In order to save time, have three or four hooks ready baited at hand; they can be kept in a tin box filled with moist bran.

Spinning is performed with a live-bait, a roach or fair-sized dace for choice; let them rather incline to a small than to a large size. What is termed a flight of hooks—a most frightful-looking implement —is generally used. One hook is fastened through the lip of the live-bait, and another through the flesh, near the tail, leaving a set of three hooks, secured in the form of a triangle, to depend from the back of the fish quite freely. Some authorities advocate the use of two sets of these triangles of hooks, while others aver that less fish are missed when but one set is employed. To use this flight, when properly baited, sufficient line should be run off the reel upon the bank to allow of the flight being cast to any given spot. Then, with a swaying motion of the rod (which requires some practice), a cast may be made. If, after a short period, no response is received from Mr. Pike, reel up the line, draw the bait out of the water, and repeat the cast. If you get a " knock," as it is termed (a bite), from the fish, strike very hard at once, and play him, giving and taking in line according to his rushes, until he turns on his side exhausted, when you may gently draw him to the side of the bank or boat, and gaff or net him in. See that your line is strong, your hooks very sharp, and that your reel runs freely.

There are various kinds of artificial spinners which, in turbid water, are very killing, viz.: The artificial live-bait, the Norfolk spoon-bait (with red tassel), and Hearder's plano-convex. Pike will also, at times, rise at a large, coloured fly; but as very little fly-fishing is indulged in in Norfolk, I cannot say if this bait is generally successful, although I am informed that it is.

Live-baiting, or Snap-fishing, is largely practised here, as much simpler tackle is required. The apparatus consists of a small hook, on gimp, from which depends an ordinary triangle of hooks; above this, at a distance of 10in. or 12in., is a leaden plummet, of elongated form, and a swivel. A small but lively roach is used for bait ; this is secured to the small hook, which is passed through the skin of the back, near the fin. A float will be required, so that the bait may not go deeper than mid-water, where it should be allowed to swim about in all directions. When a bite occurs, do not be in a hurry to strike. When you do strike, do so boldly and vigorously. When once hooked, play the pike as you would in spinning or trolling. A frog is at all times a tempting bait ; but should you be unable to procure any other bait than perch, if you cut off the spinous back fins before using, you will find that a hungry pike will not turn up his nose at it. There are many other baits which may be tried, such as a mouse, small bird, or eel cut into lengths, each on particular days proving efficacious.

September, October, and February, are the best months for pike-fishing, though November also is accounted to be good. Some pike-fishers favour a breezy, frosty morning; but September will be found the finest month for the pleasure-seeker in these waters. See that you do not place your fingers too near the mouth of a pike, for the purpose of removing the hooks, until he is quite dead, as his teeth are set in rows like those of an alligator, and are as sharp as needles.

Lastly, remember that patience and skill are the two chief desiderata required (in trolling especially) of the true follower of the immortal Izaak Walton.

The *Tench* (*Tinca vulgaris*) is a handsome, plump-looking fish, with small scales and a very shiny coat. It is fond of weeds and muddy places, and, being shy, is not often seen, except during hot weather, when

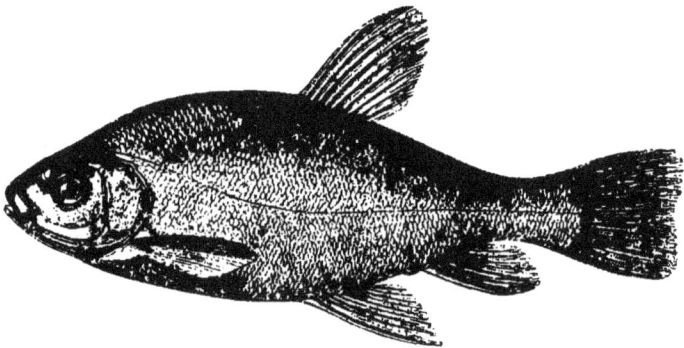

THE TENCH.

it loves to bask in the sun in some quiet nook. Stagnant, or nearly still water, suits this fish better than that of rivers. Tench intended for market are kept in ponds, and fattened on meal; being extremely tenacious of · life, they are frequently brought to market alive in wet moss; so that, if not sold, they may be returned to the water, to await some other epicure's pleasure.

Their spawning time is the month of June. Like many other freshwater fish, they are very prolific, as

many as 297,000 eggs having been obtained from
a 4lb. fish. If a few tench be left undisturbed for
two or three years, their progeny will stock quite
a large pond. Tench attain a large size, and weigh as
much as 7lb. or 8lb. Not many years since, a monster, 33in. long, and weighing 11½lb., was captured.
During the cold weather, these fish bury themselves
in the mud. The best time to angle for them is from
May to September; and even as late as November,
if the weather be open, good bags may be made.

A triangle of small hooks is usually employed to
capture this fish, as he is a very delicate biter; in
fact, he rather sucks at the bait than bites at it. You
must give him time; and, even when he takes the
float quite under water, do not be in a hurry to
strike, but wait till it re-appears: then, if there are
indications of his attentions observable, strike. If
you hook him, he usually takes to the mud at the
bottom, though you must endeavour, by keeping a
strain on the line, to prevent his doing so. Check
all his dives and rushes, until he becomes exhausted;
then draw him coolly to the side, and land him by
deftly inserting the landing-net under him.

A muggy, drizzly day is the best time to take this
fish; you cannot be either too early or too late for
him, as he does not usually bite freely during the
middle portion of the day.

Some anglers make good bags by baiting with
large dew-worms; and in France, during hot weather,
the small white garden slug is found useful.

I think, however, that in this district the angler cannot do better than use the common red garden worm, varied occasionally with a piece of parboiled potato. The bait should actually touch the ground, whether in a river or pool.

Beef, cooked and chopped fine, mixed with bran or wheatmeal, is a useful ground-bait. Some add a little sugar or honey to this, and moisten it with a very little milk—just enough to make it adhere. Another ground-bait is composed of bran, worked up with bullock's blood and a few chopped worms.

The *Eel* (*Anguillidæ*), whose serpentine form is too well known to require any description here, is found—well, where is he not found? He may be taken in Broad, pool, river, or ditch ; in clear or muddy water, and in any weather. In the way of food, he has no dislikes, and will eat anything that comes in his way. Nothing is too delicate or too distasteful for him. He is found in most unlooked-for places ; in fact, during the dewy nights of late summer, he will go for long crawls in the wet grass of the surrounding fields, and will visit neighbouring ponds having no connection with the stream he frequents.

There are three varieties of the eel, namely, the Sharp-nosed, the Broad-nosed, and the Snig; the last is sometimes classed with the first-named. The sharp-nosed eel attains the largest size ; in the Medway, eels of this variety have been taken of enormous size, some of them weighing from 20lb. to

25lb. each, and being nearly 6ft. in length. The greatest size to which they attain in this district is about 3ft., and the greatest weight, 10lb. to 12lb. The broad-nosed eel very seldom exceeds 4lb. in weight; and the snig, though esteemed the finest for the table, is even smaller still.

The eel is a long-lived fish. Many instances are on record of its attaining threescore years and ten, and even much more.

During the winter, eels lie torpid in the mud, and do not take food of any kind; like the bear, they live on their own fat, as they are found to be much thinner in the spring than in the autumn.

In angling for them, a strong, stiff rod, a strong line, and a rather large hook, will be required. It is found expedient to have a swivel or two on the lower end of the line, so as to prevent it from "kinking" with the evolutions of the eel.

The hook should be upon gimp, as the eel's teeth quickly cut through the thickest gut or silk line. Garden worms are the best bait. If, when you draw the fish to the surface, you let its tail just dangle upon the bottom of the punt, or the earth, it will not wriggle about so much. It is best to put your foot upon it as quickly as possible. The head may then, by a longitudinal cut, be divided, when the hook will drop out. A cut across the back, severing the spinal cord, kills an eel instantly.

Another way of taking eels is by spearing. This is done with a kind of trident, notched at the edges, and placed upon a long pole. This implement is variously called a dart, pick, glave, or spear. The method is easily acquired. It simply consists of prodding the mud with the tines of the spear, and occasionally bringing it to the surface to see if an eel has been transfixed. Sometimes two or three are impaled at once. The novice must be careful not to overbalance himself, or dig the spear so deep into the mud that he cannot withdraw it before the boat is carried away by the current. This sport, if kept up for three or four consecutive hours, will be found rather tiring. After dark is the best time to select for spearing; and August and September are the best months.

Another method of taking eels, called "bobbing," is performed thus: Dig a large quantity of garden worms —the more the better. Get a long, thin, packing needle, and a hank of coarse worsted. Proceed to thread the needle with worsted, and then thread the worsted with worms lengthwise. When you have got a large bunch, go to the river after dark, and having attached a strong cord to the bunch, heave it overboard. (During the day, you will, of course, have noted the most likely spots.) Wait a few minutes, and then draw up your "bob" quietly, when, if you have selected a favourable spot, the eels will be found with their teeth entangled in the worsted. Shake them off, put them in a bucket of water, and continue taking fresh casts as long as the eels bite.

Night-lines for eels are permissible, and may only contain one baited hook. It is optional how many

of these lines you put out—that depends on the fisherman's patience; they should be baited with worms or
slugs. Roach, dace, or minnows, if procurable, will
prove very enticing; they should be used in the same
manner as when trolling for pike.

The *Perch* (*Perca fluviatilis*) is a handsome and
game fish, and easily recognisable by the novice in
the gentle art. His greenish-olive back, golden sides,
with their tiger-like stripes, and spiny dorsal fin,
render him very conspicuous. The perch casts its

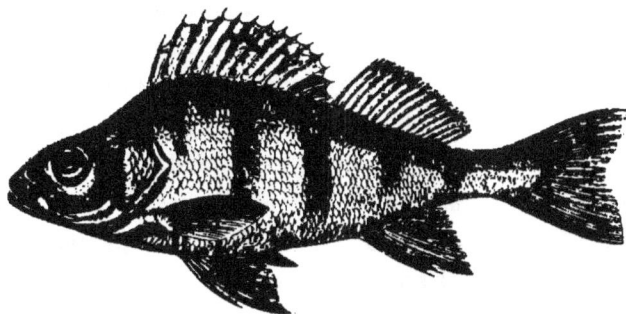

THE PERCH.

spawn in April, during which month it may be seen·
floating in long strings on the water. The number
of ova contained in a single fish is marvellous. Many
years since, a Swiss naturalist, Picot, took the trouble
to count the eggs in a fish weighing about 16oz. or
18oz., and found the number to be upwards of
990,000. Fancy this for a single family!

A 4lb. perch is reckoned a large one in the Broad
district, though heavier ones are occasionally taken.
A fish weighing a pound—a very nice size—will try

one's tackle severely; and mark this, that if you are
unfortunate enough to lose a perch—that is, if it
should get back among its companions—a stampede
will follow, and then good-bye to your sport in that
particular spot, for all the fish will take their departure
in alarm. The largest authentic capture in England
I ever heard of, was that of a 9lb. fish, taken from
the Serpentine, Hyde Park, London, some years since;
but in the Church of Lulea, in Lapland, the head of
a perch of enormous size is preserved. It is nearly
12in. long: and as the head of a perch is rather
less than two-sevenths of the entire length, this
particular fish must have been about 43in. or 44in.
in length, and would probably weigh from 28lb. to
30lb.! There would seem to be a mistake somewhere;
or possibly it may have been the head of a giant
perch (*Lucia perca*), brought from the Caspian Sea,
where they are often caught over a yard long.

The perch is a capital fish for the table after the
middle of July, when it assumes its bright colouring.
From May to July it is out of season, of a dull, leaden
colour, and with an unpleasant flavour. The angling
season commences in August, and the sport may be
prosecuted as long as the weather keeps open enough
to enable one to angle without fear of being frozen
to the spot. The most useful rod is one about 12ft.
or 14ft. in length, with a fairly strong top joint; the
tackle should also be strong. A silk line, with a
length of gut at the end, and a rather large hook
(No. 5 or 6), on gimp, will answer well. In perch-

fishing, two, or even more, hooks may be used; in fact, the most approved way seems to be by "paternoster" fishing. The paternoster is a gut line, about 1yd. long, from which two, three, or four hooks depend, at equal distances. A small leaden plummet should be suspended at the end of the flight, so as to keep all taut, and prevent the fouling of the hooks.

The method of using this apparatus is to cast it into a likely pool, and let it sink until the bullet touches the bottom; then draw it up a few inches, and move it gently from side to side, to you and from you, and in every direction, until a bite is felt; then wait for a second or two, and, if another tug be felt, strike, when with very little trouble the fish may be landed.

The perch is at times rather capricious in his taste, so that it will be found a good plan to try a different bait on each hook, till his particular taste is discovered, when it will be wise to bait all the hooks with his particular choice till he is tired of it—then give him a change. Perch may also be taken by trolling with a very small roach, in the same manner as recommended for pike, but with smaller tackle.

The bait used may be either worms, very small roach, or minnows. Live shrimps, when procurable, are often used as a bait with great success. If live-bait be used, the hook should either be run through the lip or the skin of the back; when found to be dead, replace by a live one, as the more lively the bait the more attractive will it be.

When simply angling with a single hook, a cork float will be necessary; but the smaller it is, the better. The size of float must be regulated by the depth of water to be fished.

Perch will take a number of baits, so you may try a small frog, which should be hooked by the skin of the thigh, and allowed to swim about in mid stream; both red and white gentles, garden slugs, &c., also prove successful; but for these waters nothing is equal to the red garden worm. These worms are best found after a shower of rain, when they come out of their holes. A method of procuring worms, which I find easier than digging, is to throw a couple of pails of water on the mould; after waiting a short time, take a spade, thrust the blade into the ground as far as possible, and wriggle it from side to side, flatways, for a space of a couple of minutes; then, upon looking on the ground, you will perceive the worms appearing on the surface. They should then be picked up, placed in a can filled with moss, and sprinkled with new milk. Next day they will be ready for use, but are better if kept two or three days, changing the moss occasionally. Perch love a hard, gravelly bottom, and are seldom found in a muddy locality. In the Bure, especially near Acle Bridge, several trout, of from 3lb. to 4lb. weight, have been taken with a spoon-bait during the past twelve months. Would it not be a good idea for some angler who is used to fly-fishing to try his skill with a few casts between Acle Bridge and Thurne Mouth?

General Remarks.—The Broads vary greatly in depth. Hickling is from 3ft. to 5ft. nearly everywhere except in the channel, which is marked out by posts. Barton Broad is in many parts very shallow, and, I believe, nowhere exceeds 8ft. or 9ft. In Wroxham you have deep water, in some parts 12ft. and 14ft. Fritton Decoy has still deeper water; there are spots in it known to the brethren of the angle, 16ft. or 18ft. deep. There is very little current in any of the Broads. The rivers, near their mouths, are, during the run of the tide, rather swift, and vary greatly in depth; perhaps 9ft. to 10ft. would be about the average. The angler will, therefore, see that little can be done without the use of a leaden plummet.

The following is a list of angling necessaries, which may be added to by the expert:

A couple of rods, one long and light, the other shorter and firmer; or a fairly long rod, with two or three top joints, of various thicknesses.

Reels for running tackle.

Baiting needles of various sizes, and a packing needle.

Lines—gut, silk, and trolling.

Hooks, on gut and gimp, of various sizes. Swivels, &c.

Traces. Paternosters, eel-line. Spoon-baits, &c.

Floats—quill, cork, and luminous.

Disgorger, clearing ring, and drag (for lost lines).

Landing-net, jointed to fold.

Bait-tin and gentle-box.

Plummets, split shot, pliers, cobbler's wax, and the other little sundries which complete an angler's outfit.

X

Although not strictly within the scope of this work, I may, *en passant*, mention sea-fishing. Plaice, and flat fish of all kinds, are taken from the jetties at Yarmouth; and, by taking a boat, good sport may be had chopsticking for mackerel, whiting, and haddock, large quantities of these fish being caught here by this popular method. *Soles* and *Flounders* are taken by laying long lines about a quarter of a mile from the shore; the bait used is the common lugworm, dug from the sand at low water, or mussels. From October to March good hauls of *Codling* and *Cod* are made by casting from the shore, or by laying long cod lines, baited as for soles in the summer. Although the beach at Yarmouth is shelving and sandy, very little seining seems to be done, albeit it is essentially a summer method, and at times very profitable. In two nights, with a crew of four, I have brought in over 400 pairs of soles, the largest being 22in. long. I must own, however, that it is hard work rather than pleasure.

Mackerel in the season, may be caught from a boat, with rod and line. Bait with a piece of scarlet cloth, or a piece of fresh fish of any kind. They will sometimes take the spoon-bait, if allowed to trail after the boat.

Whiting will take the lugworm or fresh fish as a bait. Have a sinker a foot beneath the hook, and let this plummet just touch the bottom. Slack tide is the best time—that is, at the top of the flood, or low ebb.

I tried a curious plan for catching *Whelks* off Happisburgh last summer. I procured an old iron tyre off a
cart-wheel, and a piece of herring-net. The net I
fastened round the tyre, so as to form a kind of bag-
net, and in the bottom of this I fastened a heap of
fish offal. To the edge of the tyre, at equal distances,
I next tied four strong cords, meeting at a point above
the centre; to this I attached twenty fathoms of line
and a leather buoy. I now took my whole apparatus
out half-a-mile to sea, and hove it overboard. It was
left for four days, and then I took a boat and went
off, and after a time found the buoy, took it aboard,
and hauled on the line till the boat was right over it,
and then drew up my net. The contents were peculiar:
about a peck of whelks, two crabs, two soles, and
a copper oilcan !

And now I will conclude this chapter by remarking
that, although I do not put myself forward as an
authority in angling matters, yet, if the instructions
I have given are duly carried out, not even the merest
tyro will come home empty-handed. It is almost
impossible to give instructions that will prove effectual
at all times, and under all circumstances, but I have
endeavoured to give a general idea of the methods
of angling for the various kinds of fish which are to
be found in the "Land of the Broads."

X 2

TABLE OF FISH OF THE BROAD DISTRICT.

	NAME OF FISH.	BEST TIME FOR ANGLING.	BEST PLACES.	SIZE OF HOOK.	BAITS, &c.
1	Carp	Mar. to Oct.	Still Water; Ponds	10, 11	Dainty Morsels required: Green Pea, piece of Cherry, &c.
2	Bream	Mar. to Sept.	Deep, slow Rivers	9 to 11	Greaves; Lobworms.
3	Dace	Any time	Rivers and Broads	12, 13	Pastes; Rice Grains.
4	Eels	Any time	Everywhere	8 to 10	Lobworm; piece of Fish; Anything.
5	Miller's Thumb	April to Oct.	Dykes and Shallows	13	Ditto; Rice Grains.
6	Minnow	Mar. to Sept.	Broads and Shallows	13	Ditto; Paste.
7	Perch	Feb. to Nov.	Deep Holes in Broads	8, 9	Lobworm; Fly; Minnow.
8	Pike	Aug. to Feb.	Weedy Rivers and Broads	4 to 6	Roach and Dace (Live-bait).
9	Pope	April to Oct.	Still Pools	10, 11	Paste.
10	Roach	July to April	Rivers and Broads	11 to 13	Pastes; Gentles; Lobworm.
11	Rudd	April to Sept.	Broads	9 to 11	Lobworm; Gentles.
12	Smelt	Aug. to Jan.	Estuaries: Breydon	11 to 13	Ditto; piece of Eel; Nets.
13	Stone Loach	May to Sept.	Still Pools	13	Worms or Gentles.
14	Tench	May to Sept.	Muddy Rivers	10 to 12	Delicate Morsels, according to fancy.
15	Trout	Mar. to Aug.	Deep, fast Rivers	7 to 9	Fly; Spoon-bait.

TABLE FOR ASCERTAINING THE APPROXIMATE WEIGHT OF A FISH BY ITS LENGTH.

By J. T. BURGESS.

Length in Inches.	PIKE.	CARP.	ROACH.	RUDD.	PERCH.	TENCH.	TROUT.
	lb. oz.	lb. oz.	lb. oz.	lb. oz.	lb. oz.	lb. oz.	lb. oz.
9	..	0 8	0 8	0 9	0 12	0 7	0 5
10	..	0 11	0 13	0 10	0 13	0 10	0 6
11	..	0 15	1 2	0 13	0 15	0 14	0 9
12	..	1 2	1 4	1 1	1 0	1 1	0 11
13	..	1 8	1 8	1 6	1 4	1 6	0 14
14	..	1 14	1 14	1 12	1 10	1 12	1 2
15	1 0	2 4	2 5	2 3	1 14	2 2	1 6
16	1 4	2 11	2 14	2 12	2 5	2 10	1 10
17	1 8	3 4	3 7	3 6	2 13	3 2	2 0
18	1 13	3 14	4 1	4 0	3 5	3 12	2 6
19	2 2	4 9	4 12	4 10	3 15	4 6	2 12
20	2 7	5 5¼	5 9	5 7	4 9	5 2	3 4
25	4 14	10 7	..	..	8 15	10 0	6 5
30	8 6	..	..	..	..	..	10 15
35	13 4						
40	20 0						

The above weights are representative of fish in good condition : a fish after spawning would naturally weigh less.

CHAPTER XIX.

A TABLE OF DISTANCES FROM GREAT YARMOUTH BRIDGE.

RIVER YARE—   Miles.

Cross Stake	$3\frac{1}{4}$
Berney Arms	$4\frac{1}{4}$
Reedham Town	$8\frac{1}{2}$
Hardley Cross	10
Cantley Red House	13
Buckenham Ferry	$15\frac{1}{2}$
Rockland Dyke	$16\frac{1}{2}$
Coldham Hall	18
Surlingham Ferry	20
Bramerton	$22\frac{1}{2}$
Postwick Grove	23
Whitlingham	24
Carrow Bridge, Norwich	$26\frac{1}{4}$

RIVER WAVENEY—

Burgh Dyke or Cage	$4\frac{3}{4}$
St. Olave's Bridge	$9\frac{1}{2}$
Mouth of New Cut	$9\frac{3}{4}$

RIVER WAVENEY—*continued.* Miles.

Somerleyton Bridge	12¼
Mouth of Oulton Dyke	15
Entrance Oulton Broad	16½
Mutford Bridge	17¼
Lowestoft Harbour	19
Carlton Share Mill	16¼
Seven-Mile Corner	17¾
Six-Mile Corner	18¾
Norlingham Staithe	20
Aldeby Staithe	20½
Beccles Mill	21
Sayer's Grove	22
Beccles Bridge	23
Nine Poplars	24¼
Dawson's Boat House	24¾
Barsham's Boat House	25¾
Ellingham	37
Bungay	40
Length of New Cut	2½

RIVER BURE—

One-Mile, or Lone House	1
Two-Mile House	1¾
Three-Mile House	2¾
Four-Mile House	4
Five-Mile House, or Runham Ferry	5
Runham Ferry	5½
Six-Mile House	6¼
Seven-Mile House	7¾

RIVER BURE—*continued.* Miles.

Stokesby Ferry.	9½
Acle Bridge	12
Thurne Mouth	15
St. Benet's Abbey	16½
Mouth of Ant	17
Horning Ferry	20½
Entrance Wroxham Broad	25
Wroxham Bridge	26½
Coltishall Bridge	33½
Aylsham Bridge	44

YARMOUTH BRIDGE to

Potter Heigham Bridge	17½
Martham Broad	20½
Hickling Staithe	23
Entrance Horsey Mere	21½
Mouth of Barton Broad	21
Stalham Staithe	23½
Wayford Bridge	24½

WROXHAM BRIDGE to

Belaugh	4
Coltishall Bridge	7
Aylsham Bridge	18

THURNE MOUTH to

Potter Heigham Bridge	3¼
Kendal Dyke	4¾
Horsey Mere	7½

THURNE MOUTH to   Miles.

     Hickling Staithe . . . . $8\frac{1}{2}$

     Martham Broad   . . . . . $6\frac{1}{2}$

FROM ANT MOUTH to

     Entrance Barton Broad . . . . . $4\frac{1}{2}$

     Entrance Stalham Broad 6

     Stalham Staithe . .   . . . $6\frac{3}{4}$

     Wayford Bridge 8

     Briggate Mill 11

     North Walsham Flour Mill . . . 14

     Bradford (source of Ant) . . . . $18\frac{1}{2}$

CHAPTER XX.

TABLE OF TIDES.

H. M.

High Water is   43 later at Lowestoft than at Yarmouth

,,   3.0   at Cantley   ,,   ,, [Bar.

,,   3.45   at Coldham Hall ,,   ,,

,,   4.0   at Oulton   ,,   ,,

,,   4.0   at Horning   ,,   ,,

	Spring.	Neap.
The rise at Yarmouth is	6ft.	... 4½ft.
,, Lowestoft	6½	... 5¼
,, Cantley	2½	... 1½
,, Oulton	2	... 1¼
,, Horning	1	... ½

The direction of the wind and the quantity of drainage water cause the tides to fluctuate greatly.

After a heavy rainfall the rush of water in a river, helped by a strong wind, will to a great extent neutralise the rise of the tide for a great distance; so that, at places where the rise and fall of the tide usually makes a difference of, say 1ft. in height, no perceptible change occurs.

CHAPTER XXI.

CARRIERS FROM NORWICH.

THIS list of Carriers from Norwich to places which, in most cases, are inaccessible by rail, will, no doubt, be of service to those wishing to reach a given point. It will be noticed, that these carriers only make the journey once or twice a week. Traps, however, may be hired, by those who can afford the expense, at the rate (usually) of 1s. per mile. The only other means of reaching these places, if the journey by water is considered too tedious, is to walk.

Acle, 11 miles, Hales (Carrier), 3.30 p.m., Wed. and Sat.; starting from Waggon and Horses, Tombland. Lambert, 4 p.m., Wed. and Sat.; Capon's Stables, Rose Lane. Dove, 3.30 p.m., Wed. and Sat.; Lion, Castle Meadow.

Aylsham, 11 miles, Stapleton (Carrier), 4.30 daily; starting from Duke's Palace Inn. Olley, 2 p.m., Tues. and Fri.; White Horse, Haymarket. Horner, 4.30 p.m., Wed. and Sat.; York Tavern, Castle Hill. Fiddey, 10 a.m., Mon. and Thur.; Duke's Head, Duke Street.

Barton Turf, 13 miles, Lubbock (Carrier), 4 p.m., Wed, and Sat.; starting from Waggon and Horses, Tombland.

Beccles, 18 miles, Flegg (Carrier), 4 p.m., Wed. and Sat.; starting from Star, Haymarket.

Blickling, 14 miles, Fiddey (Carrier), 10 a.m., Mon. and Thurs. ; starting from Duke's Head, Duke Street.

Brundall, 5 miles, Hayes (Carrier), 4 p.m., Wed. and Sat. ; starting from York Tavern, Castle Hill.

Burgh (Yarmouth), 15 miles, Dove (Carrier), 3.30 p.m., Wed. and Sat.; starting from Lion, Castle Meadow.

Buxton, 9 miles, Gostling (Carrier), 4 p.m., Mon., Wed. and Sat.; starting from Bell, Orford Hill. Brown, 4 p.m., Mon., Wed. and Sat. ; Elephant, Magdalene Street.

Cantley, 10 miles, England (Carrier), 3 p.m., Sat.; starting from Bell, Orford Hill.

Coltishall, 7 miles, Thurston (Carrier), 4.30 p.m., Mon., Wed., Fri. and Sat.; starting from George Inn, Haymarket.

Dilham, 12 miles, Barber (Carrier), 3 p.m., Wed. and Sat. ; starting from White Horse, Haymarket.

Fritton, 11 miles, Leech (Carrier), 4 p.m., Wed. and Sat. ; starting from Trowel and Hammer, St. Stephen's.

Gunton, 16 miles, Bloom (Carrier), 3.30 p.m., Wed. and Sat.; starting from Waggon and Horses, Tombland.

Happisburgh, 20 miles, Blackburne (Carrier), 4 p.m., Wed. and Sat.; starting from White Horse, Magdalene Street.

Hautbois, 8 miles, Eke (Carrier), 4 p.m., Wed. and Sat. ; starting from Queen Caroline, St. Martin's.

Hickling, 16 miles, Goose (Carrier), 3 p.m., Sat. ; starting from White Lion, Palace Plain. Leatherdale, 4.45 p.m., Mon., Wed. and Sat. ; Royal Hotel.

Horning, 9 miles, Thurgate (Carrier), 4 p.m., Mon., Wed. and Sat.; starting from Waggon and Horses, Tombland.

Hoveton, 9 miles, Thurgate (Carrier), 4 p.m., Mon., Wed. and Sat.; starting from Waggon and Horses, Tombland.

Ingham, 15 miles, Blackburne (Carrier), 4 p.m., Mon. and Wed.; starting from White Horse, Magdalene Street.

Irstead, 11 miles, Leatherdale (Carrier), 4.45 p.m., Mon., Wed. and Sat.; starting from Royal Hotel.

Ludham, 13 miles, Thurgate (Carrier), 4 p.m., Mon., Wed. and Sat.; starting from Waggon and Horses, Tombland.

Martham, 17 miles, Hales (Carrier), 3.30 p.m., Wed. and Sat.; starting from Waggon and Horses, Tombland. Dove, 3.30 p.m., Wed. and Sat.; Lion, Castle Meadow.

Ormsby, 16 miles, Dove (Carrier), 3.30 p.m., Wed. and Sat.; starting from Lion, Castle Meadow.

Oulton, 14 miles, Laxton (Carrier), 4.30 p.m., Mon., Wed. and Sat.; starting from Duke's Head, Duke Street.

Oxnead, 8 miles, Smith (Carrier), 4.30 p.m., Mon., Wed. and Sat.; starting from Waggon and Horses, Tombland.

Potter Heigham, 16 miles, Thurgate (Carrier), 4 p.m., Mon., Wed. and Sat.; starting from Waggon and Horses, Tombland. Dove, 3.30 p.m., Wed. and Sat.; Lion, Castle Meadow.

Ranworth, 8 miles, Chapman (Carrier), 4 p.m., Wed. and Sat.; starting from White Lion, Palace Plain.

South Walsham, 10 miles, Chapman (Carrier), 4 p.m., Wed. and Sat.; starting from White Lion; Palace Plain.

Stalham, 14 miles, Leatherdale (Carrier), 4.45 p.m., Mon., Wed. and Sat.; starting from Royal Hotel.

Stimpson, 4 p.m., Sat.; Waggon and Horses, Tombland.

Surlingham, 6 miles, Aldis (Carrier), 4 p.m., Wed. and Sat.; starting from King's Arms, Ber Street.

Worstead, 14 miles, Abigail, 12 noon, Wed. and Sat.; starting from Duke's Palace Inn. Burrell, 5 p.m., Sat.; White Horse, Magdalene Street.

Wroxham, 6 miles, Leatherdale (Carrier), 4.45 p.m., Mon., Wed. and Sat.; starting from Royal Hotel. Burrell, 5 p.m., Sat.; White Horse, Magdalene Street.

INDEX.

Acle Town and Bridge, 120
Acreage of Norfolk, 8
Agreement for hiring yacht, 16
Aldeby, 38
Angling referred to in Bible, 59
Ant, river, 150
Ashby, 193
Aylsham, 145

Bacton Abbey, 191
Barton Broad, 157
Bastwick, 195
Beccles, 38
Beeston Hall, 158
Belaugh Broad, 140
Billockby, 117
Blickling Hall, 146
Bloaters, 230
Boom towers, Norwich, 64
Borrow, George, Author of
    " Romany Rye," 33
Bowls, game of, 167
Bramerton, 60
Brasses in churches, 5
Breakdown, 187
Breydon Water, 26
Briggate, 181
Broad district in autumn, 225
    District in spring, 210
    District in summer, 218
    District in winter, 231
Brundall, 60
Buckenham Ferry, 55
Bungay, 46
Bure, river, 49
Burgh Castle, 27

Burgh St. Peter, 37
Buxton, 144
Buzzer, 223

Caister Castle, 115
Calthorpe Broad, 198
Canoeing, hints on, 98
Cantley, 54
Carlton Colville, 34
Carriers from Norwich, 315
Carrow Bridge, 64
Characteristics of natives, 240
Chedgrave, 53
Chet or Ket, river, 53
Churches, 4, 66
Claxton, 55
Climate, 3
Clippesby, 118
Coldham, 58
Coltishall, 141
Commissariat Depots, 205
Cost of a trip, 15
Coursing, 238
Cromer, 187
Crow boys' war song, 223
Curious sign, 195

Dancing, natives, 268
Derivation of names, 257
Destroying a lighthouse, 169
Devil's Ditch, 178
Dialect, 254
Dilham Bridge, 179
    Broad, 181
Dishes, local, 265
Distances from Yarmouth, 310

Dress for tourists, 20
Of natives, 259
Drink, what, to take, 20
Dumplings, Norfolk, 264
Dunburgh Hill, 44

East winds, 238
Eccles steeple, 174
Eels, 57, 150, 198
Bobbing for, 300
Ellingham, 45
Epitaphs, 6, 122, 132, 165, 171, 172, 173, 180, 183, 190

Farm labourers, 241
Wages, 242
Fenman's life described, 210
Implements, 214
Eloquence, 215
Filby Broad, 114
Fisherman's life, 243
Fishing requisites, 305
Fishley, 122
Fish poachers, 30, 228
When in season, 308
Fleet Dyke, 127
Fogs in the Fens, 42
Fossil remains, 170
Fritton Church, 28
Decoy, 32

Galille porches, 43
Geldestone, 44
Giants, 202
Gillingham, 43
Glossary of Norfolk words, 249
Gunton Hall, 190
Gulls, breeding season of, 136

Haisbro' Sands, 165
Happisburgh, 163
Hardley Cross, 52
Harvest time, 213
Hautbois, Great, 142
Little, 144
Hearses, 263
Heckingham, 53
Heigham Sound, 195
Heron, the, 199

Herring fishing fleet, 229
Herringfleet Hills, 32
Hickling Broad, 196
Priory, 198
Honing, 179
Horning, 132
Horstead, 141
Hoveton Great Broad, 133
Little Broad, 135

Ice boats, hints on, 111
Impedimenta for a voyage, 21
Ingham Priory, 162
Inscriptions on bells, 129
Insurance of yachts, 17
Irstead, 155

Kingfishers, 143
Knapton, 190
Ket, or Chet, river, 53

Lake Lothing, 34
Lammas, 144
Langley Abbey, 54
Lighthouses, 168
Lilies, where found, 219
"Lily" steam launch, 25
Litester's Cross, 185
Loddon, 52
Lothbrock, story of, 50
Lowestoft, 35
Ludham, 194
Bridge, 150
Luminous floats, 221

Machine farming, 249
Man with two tongues, 183
Marram banks, 173
Martham Broad, 201
Mead—a drink, 266
"Men of Norfolk"—patriotic song, 270
Mile houses, 112
Monkey House, 61
Morning dip, 221
Muck Fleet, 113
Mud pattens, 27
Muffled peals, 264
Mundesley, 190
Mundham St. Peter, 53
Mushrooms, 228

New Cut, 50
Nicknames, 258
Norman architecture, 38, 43
Norwich, ancient houses in, 95
  Bellringers, 75
  Bishop's Palace, 73
  Cathedral, 71
  Cattle, 70
    Market, 91
  Churches:
    St. Andrew's, 79
    St. Clement's, 79
    St. Edmund's, 80
    St. Etheldred's, 80
    St. George's, 80
    St. Giles', 81
    St. Gregory's, 81
    St. John's, Maddermarket, 83
    St. John's, Timberhill, 83
    St. Jude's, 88
    St. Lawrence's, 84
    St. Martin's-at-Oak, 85
    St. Martin's-at-Thorne, 85
    St. Michael's, 86
    St. Michael's-at-Plea, 87
    St. Michael's-at-Thorne, 87
    St. Michael's-de-Coslaney, 86
    St. Peter Mancroft, 76
    St. Peter-per-Mountergate, 78
    St. Saviour's, 88
    St. Simon's, 88
    St. Stephen's, 88
    St. Swithin's, 89
  Circular windmills, 90
  Corn Exchange, 92
  Cringleford, 90
  Curiously-named yards, 96
  Eaton, 90
  Foolish climbing feat, 72
  Foundation of city, 70
  Gateways, 74
  Libraries, 92
  Mammoth bones, 91
  Market place, 92
  Museum, 92
  Rambles round, 89
Norwich, St. Andrew's Hall, 93
Nowhere, village of, 122

Oby, 193
Ormsby Broad, 116
Oulton Broad, 33
Oxnead, 144

Peat, or hovers, 237
Perch, 301
  Large, 302
Pews, high-backed, 67
Pig-killing, 266
Pike, 216
  Large, 48, 61, 290
  Snaring, 291
  To angle for, 289
Pleasure Hill, 196
Population, 80
Porson, 181
Postwick Grove, 60
Potter Heigham, 191
Prehistoric, 7
Purl—a drink, 267
Puzzle, 268
"Pye on Pear-tree"—song, 269

Quant, 125
Queen Anne Boleyn, 147

Rabbits, 4, 202
Rainfall, 3
Ranworth Broad, 129
Raspberries, 220
Reed-cutting, 212, 235
Reedham, 50
Rise of tides, 174
River "devils," 31
Rockland Broad, 56
"Roger" blasts, 137
Rollesby Broad, 115
Round towers, 5
Runham Swim Ferry, 113
Ruston Common, 179

St. Benet's Abbey, 126
St. Olave's Bridge, 27
Salhouse Broad, 134
Scratby, 117

Y

Sea encroachments, 186
  Fishing, 306
Sexton for fifty years, 184
Sherringham, 191
Shipwreck described, 165
Shooting, 109
  Free in parts, 227
  From punt described, 233
Silly Suffolk, 48
Skating, 110, 231
Sleeping accommodation, 14
Somerleyton, 32
Source of Waveney, 47
South Walsham Broad, 127
Spoon-bait, 294
Stained glass, 45, 156, 159
Stalham Broad, 160
Startings, 236
Stokesby, 118
Strumpshaw, 58
Summerton, 202
Superstitions, 245
Surlingham Broad, 50
Swallows, 226

Tench, angling for, 296
Thorpe, 63
Thurne Mouth, 125
  Village, 193
Tide table, 314
Tonnage Bridge, 178
Trout, 119, 304
Tumuli, 8
Types of natives, 9

Victualling for a cruise, 18

Walcott, 171

Waterproofing boots, 156
Water telescope, 129
Waveney, river, 49
Wayford Bridge, 177
Weight of fish, 309
Wensum, river, 63
Whelks, 307
Wherry cargo, 123
  Flags, 124
  Inn, Oulton, 33
  Pleasure, 12
Whiteslea, 195
Whitlingham, 62
Wild flowers, 218
Wildfowl, 213, 239
  Decoy, 28
Witchcraft, 247
Witton, 184
Womack Broad, 138
Woodbastwick Broad, 134
Worstead, 181

Yare, river, 49
Yarmouth, 100
  Bridges, 101
  Dutch whipping-tops, 107
  Jetty, 105
  Market Place, 101
  Nelson Column, 104
  North Gate, 102
  Piers, 104
  Quay, 103
  Sailors' Home, 105
  St. Nicholas Church, 106
  Star Hotel, 102
  Toll House Jail, 106
  Town Hall, 102
  Trinity Wharf, 104

GREAT EASTERN RAILWAY.

⊸ SEASIDE. ⊱

TOURIST, FORTNIGHTLY, and FRIDAY or SATURDAY to
TUESDAY TICKETS,

(1st, 2nd and 3rd Class) are issued by all Trains from

LIVERPOOL STREET & ST. PANCRAS
TO

YARMOUTH, LOWESTOFT,
CROMER, AND HUNSTANTON,

And from **LIVERPOOL STREET** to

CLACTON-ON-SEA, WALTON-ON-NAZE, DOVERCOURT, HARWICH, FELIXSTOWE, SOUTHWOLD & ALDEBURGH.

For full particulars, see bills.

FISHING and *YACHTING* on the *BROADS.*

GREAT EASTERN RAILWAY.

COMMENCING ON JUNE 1st,

CHEAP EXCURSION TICKETS FOR

FISHING AND YACHTING

Are issued DAILY by any Train as under, available for return by any Train on the day of issue only.

	FARES THERE AND BACK.		
YARMOUTH to	First Class.	Second Class.	Third Class.
Reedham .. ..⎫			
Cantley.. .. ..⎪			
Buckenham.. .. ..⎰ 1s. 8d.	1s. 2d.	1s. 0d.	
Brundall .. ..⎭			
Acle .. .. 1s. 6d.	1s. 0d.	0s. 10d.	
CROMER to			
North Walsham .. .. .. 1s. 3d.	0s. 9d.	0s. 8d.	
Worstead .. ..⎱ 1s. 8d.	1s. 2d.	1s. 0d.	
Wroxham .. ..⎰			
LOWESTOFT to			
Somerleyton .. .. 1s. 6d.	0s. 11d.	0s. 9d.	
Haddiscoe .. ..⎫			
Reedham .. ..⎪			
Cantley.. .. ..⎬ 1s. 8d.	1s. 2d.	1s. 0d.	
Buckenham .. ..⎪			
Brundall .. ..⎭			
NORWICH to			
Brundall .. .. 1s. 3d.	0s. 9d.	0s. 8d.	
Acle .. .. 1s. 6d.	1s. 0d.	0s. 10d.	
Buckenham .. ..⎫			
Cantley.. .. ..⎬ 1s. 8d.	1s. 2d.	1s. 0d.	
Reedham .. ..⎭			
Wroxham .. .. 1s. 6d.	0s. 11d.	0s. 9d.	
Worstead .. ..⎱ 1s. 8d.	1s. 2d.	1s. 0d.	
North Walsham .. .. ..⎰			

London, May, 1887.   WILLIAM BIRT, General Manager.

Y 2

❧ ELIZA · JORDAN, ☙

Bookseller, Stationer, Bookbinder, Newsagent, &c.,

MARKET STREET, BECCLES,

HAS ALWAYS A CAREFULLY-SELECTED STOCK OF THE NEWEST

Goods Suitable for Presents,

COMPRISING

PORTRAIT ALBUMS, SCRAP BOOKS, WRITING DESKS, BLOTTING CASES, BOOK SLIDES, CARD CASES, WORK BOXES, PURSES, WATCH STANDS, and OTHER FANCY GOODS, and

A Variety of the Newest, Cheapest, & Best Toys.

Bibles, Church Services, Prayer Books, and the Hymn Books for Beccles Church and Chapels, and for the Churches of the surrounding Parishes, always in Stock.

DAY BOOKS, CASH BOOKS, LEDGERS, MEMORANDUM BOOKS, NOTE PAPER, ENVELOPES, AND ALL KINDS OF STATIONERY.

ORDERS FOR PLAIN AND ORNAMENTAL PRINTING, DIE STAMPING, &c., PROMPTLY EXECUTED.

London and Local Daily and Weekly Newspapers, Periodicals, Magazines, &c., punctually delivered to all parts of the Town FREE OF CHARGE for delivery.

WOOLS and SILKS In all COLOURS for EMBROIDERY, CANVAS, and CREWEL WORK, &c.

Patterns for Tracing and Braiding. Crochet and Knitting Cottons.

AGENT for P. & P. CAMPBELL, THE PERTH DYE WORKS.

DEPÔT for the BRITISH & FOREIGN BIBLE SOCIETY.

Anything not in Stock procured as quickly as possible.

PARCELS FROM LONDON DAILY.

Advertisements Inserted in all London and Local Newspapers.

AGENT FOR: *"Ipswich Journal," "Daily Press," "Norfolk News," "People's Weekly Journal," "Lowestoft Press,"* &c., &c.

C. CLEMENTS,

◁ PRINTER, ▷

Bookbinder, Bookseller,

STATIONER, &C.,

MARKET-PLACE,

NORTH WALSHAM,

AND

AYLSHAM.

A CLEARANCE SALE.

J. MALING,

MARKET HILL, DISS,

BEGS TO ANNOUNCE

That at MIDSUMMER he intends Removing to LARGER PREMISES in

CROWN STREET.

A GENERAL SALE is now going on at MARKET HILL, and will be continued for a time at CROWN STREET.

THE STOCK

CONSISTS OF

Pianos, Harmoniums, American Organs,

SHEET AND BOOK MUSIC,

GENERAL STATIONERY, BOOKS,

Fancy and Useful Articles, Sewing Machines,

AND MANY OTHER THINGS.

ALL OFFERED AT CLEARANCE PRICES.

For Particulars, see Circulars.

ℭATALOGUE of
New & Practical
BOOKS

Published by

L. UPCOTT GILL, 170, Strand, London.

CONTENTS.

Angling 20, 22
Bazaars 21
Bees 7
Bicycles and Tri-
cycles 21
Bird Stuffing 19
Boats........... 17, 18
Boats and Yachts
17, 18, 20
Bookbinding 17
Books 13
Butterflies......... 19
Cage Birds........ 9, 10
Carpentry 18
Coffee Stalls 17
Coins 7
Conjuring 21
Cookery 17
Decorations 14
Degrees 13
Dogs.............. 3, 4

Eggs............... 8
Exhibition........ 4
Farming 4, 5, 19
Ferrets 5
Gardening 11
Goats 4
Guinea Pigs 6
Handwriting........ 13
Holiday Guides 14
Horses.............. 5
Indian Outfits 17
Journalism 14
Lace 16
Legal Profession.... 13
Metal Working 18
Mice 5
Music 6
Natural History 19
Needlework 16, 17
Painting.......... 6, 7
Pheasants 10

Photography 21
Pianofortes 19
Picture Frames 17
Pigeons 10
Pigs 5
Pottery 7
Poultry 8
Printing 18
Rabbits 5
Repoussé 17
Shooting........... 21
Shorthand 13, 14
Sick Nursing........ 16
Skating 20
Theatricals 21
Toymaking 18
Trapping 20
Tuning 19
Turning 18
Wood Carving 18

No. 2.—1887.

✠ CATALOGUE ✠

— OF —

PRACTICAL HANDBOOKS.

ANIMALS.

"We strongly recommend a perusal of it to all who have to do with young dogs, whether for sport or as companions."—*Farmers' Gazette.*

BREAKING AND TRAINING DOGS: Being Concise Directions for the proper Education of Dogs, both for the Field and for Companions. Second Edition. By "PATHFINDER." With Chapters by HUGH DALZIEL on Work of Special Breeds; Trail or Drag Hounds; Training Bloodhounds; Defenders and Watch Dogs; Sheep Dogs — Stock Tenders; Life Savers — Water Dogs; Vermin Destroyers; House Manners; Behaviour Out of Doors. Illustrated. *In cloth gilt, price 6s. 6d.*

BRITISH DOGS: Their Varieties, History, Characteristics, Breeding, Management, and Exhibition. By HUGH DALZIEL, Author of "The Diseases of Dogs," "The Diseases of Horses," &c., assisted by Eminent Fanciers. NEW EDITION, Revised and Enlarged. Illustrated with First-class COLOURED PLATES and full-page Engravings of Dogs of the Day. This will be the fullest and most recent work on the various breeds of dogs kept in England, and, as its Author is one of the first living authorities on the subject, its accuracy can be relied upon. *In Monthly Parts, price 7d.*

"As a rule, no authors are more egotistic than those who write on subjects connected with sport, but Mr. Dalziel is a brilliant exception. . . . . Mr. Dalziel's summary of the points of a Greyhound is admirable, and young coursers would do well to learn it by heart. . . . . The chapter on Breeding is one of the most interesting in the book."—*Saturday Review.*

THE GREYHOUND. A Monograph on the History, Points, Breeding, Rearing, Training, and Running of the Greyhound. With Coloured Frontispiece. *In cloth gilt, price 2s. 6d.*

"Will enable anybody who keeps a dog to deal with cases of ordinary indisposition
or injury."—*The Scotsman.*

DISEASES OF DOGS: Their Pathology, Diagnosis, and Treat-
ment ; to which is added a complete Dictionary of Canine Materia
Medica ; Modes of Administering Medicines; Treatment in cases of
Poisoning, and the Value of Disinfectants.   For the use of Amateurs.
By HUGH DALZIEL, Author of "British Dogs," &c. New, Revised,
and greatly Enlarged Edition.   *In paper, price* 1s.; *in cloth gilt,* 2s.

"The editor has left little room for improvement."—*Live Stock Journal.*

KENNEL DIARY.   A Register for Owners, Breeders, and Ex-
hibitors of Dogs, wherein they can keep full particulars of their
Studs in a convenient and comprehensive manner.   It contains, in
addition to a complete Gestation Table for the Year : 1, Index
Diary ; 2, Owner's Diary ; 3, Breeder's Diary ; 4, Diary of Pups ;
5, Stud Diary ; 6, Exhibition Diary ; 7, General Diary ; 8, Pedigree
Diary ; 9, Receipts ; 10, Expenditure ; 11, General Balance Sheet.
In cloth, with Pockets for Certificates, 3s. 6d.

"Just what are wanted, for a set of these books will save a vast amount of
labour and trouble."—*The Stock-keeper.*

EXHIBITION ACCOUNT BOOKS.   For use at all Dog Shows.
In Four Books, comprising: I. Minute Book ; II. Cash Book ;
III. Entries Book ; IV. Ledger.   With Full Directions, and Illustrative Examples for Working them.   N.B.—The Set of Four
Books is kept in Three Series : No. 1, for Show of 500 Entries, 5s.
the Set ; No. 2, for 1000 Entries, 7s. 6d. the Set ; and No. 3, for
1500 Entries, 12s. 6d. the Set.   Larger sizes in proportion.   The
books can be had separate. ' MINUTE BOOK—No 1, 1s. ; No. 2,
1s. 3d. ; No. 3, 2s. CASH BOOK—No. 1, 2s. ; No. 2, 2s. 6d. ;
No. 3, 4s. ENTRIES BOOK—No. 1, 2s. ; No. 2, 2s. 6d. ; No. 3, 4s.
Ledger—No. 1, 2s. ; No. 2, 2s. 6d. ; No. 3, 4s.

"A mass of interesting material."—*The Field.*

PRACTICAL DAIRY FARMING.   A Short Treatise on the
Profitable Management of a Dairy Farm.   Illustrated.   By G.
SEAWARD WITCOMBE.   *In paper, price* 1s. 6d.

"The best book we know on the subject."—*Chambers's Journal.*

BOOK OF THE GOAT.   Containing Full Particulars of the
various Breeds of Goats, and their Profitable Management.   With
many Plates.   By H. STEPHEN HOLMES PEGLER.   Third Edition,
Revised, Enlarged, and with additional Illustrations and Coloured
Frontispiece.   *In cloth gilt, price* 4s. 6d.

"We can conceive of no better book for anyone commencing to keep these valuable
animals."—*Fanciers' Gazette*

GOAT-KEEPING FOR AMATEURS : Being the Practical
Management of Goats for Milking Purposes.   Abridged from "The
Book of the Goat," by H. S. HOLMES PEGLER.   Illustrated.   *In
paper, price* 1s.

DISEASES OF HORSES: Their Pathology, Diagnosis, and Treatment ; to which is added a complete Dictionary of Equine Materia Medica. For the use of Amateurs. By HUGH DALZIEL. *In paper, price* 1s. 6d.

BOOK OF THE PIG. Containing the Selection, Breeding, Feeding, and Management of the Pig ; the Treatment of its Diseases ; the Curing and Preserving of Hams, Bacon, and other Pork Foods ; and other information appertaining to Pork Farming. By Professor JAMES LONG. Fully Illustrated with Portraits of Prize Pigs, by HARRISON WEIR and other Artists, Plans of Model Piggeries, &c. *In cloth gilt, price* 15s.

PIG-KEEPING FOR AMATEURS. A Practical Guide to the Profitable Management of Pigs. By G. GILBERT (" Gurth "). *In paper, price* 1s.

RABBITS FOR PRIZES AND PROFIT. Containing Full Directions for the Proper Management of Fancy Rabbits in Health and Disease, for Pets or the Market, and Descriptions of every known Variety, with Instructions for Breeding good specimens. Illustrated. By the late CHARLES RAYSON. Revised by the Editor of " The Book of the Rabbit." *In cloth gilt, price* 2s. 6d. May also be had in Two Parts, as follow :

GENERAL MANAGEMENT OF RABBITS. Including Hutches, Breeding, Feeding, Diseases and their Treatment, Rabbit Coverts, &c. Fully illustrated. (*Forming Part I. of* " *Rabbits for Prizes and Profit.*") *In paper, price* 1s.

EXHIBITION RABBITS : Being Descriptions of all Varieties of Fancy Rabbits, their Points of Excellence, and how to obtain them. Illustrated. (*Forming Part II. of* " *Rabbits for Prizes and Profit.*") *In paper, price* 1s.

FERRETS AND FERRETING. Containing Instructions for the Breeding, Management, and Working of Ferrets. *In paper, price* 6d.

FANCY MICE : Their Varieties, Management, and Breeding, Re-issue, with Criticisms and Notes by DR. CARTER BLAKE. Illustrated. *In paper, price* 6d.

"Of great interest and practical value."—*Nottingham Daily Express.*

THE GUINEA PIG, for Food, Fur, and Fancy. Illustrated with Coloured Frontispiece and Engravings. An exhaustive book on the Varieties of the Guinea Pig, or Cavy, and their Management for Pleasure or Profit. By C. CUMBERLAND, F.Z.S. *In cloth gilt, price* 2s. 6d.

ART AND VIRTU.

"Can be heartily commended to students who wish to lay a solid foundation for good and artistic playing."—*Musical Standard.*

PRACTICAL VIOLIN SCHOOL for Home Students. A Practical Book of Instructions and Exercises in Violin Playing, for the use of Amateurs, Self-learners, Teachers, and others. By J. M. FLEMING, Author of "Old Violins and their Makers." 1 *vol., demy* 4to, *cloth gilt, price* 7s. 6d.

"We can cordially commend this work to the attention of teachers as well as students." —*The Graphic.*

EASY LEGATO STUDIES FOR THE VIOLIN, for Home Students. A Supplement to "The Practical Violin School for Home Students." By J. M. FLEMING. *In demy* 4to, *cloth gilt, price* 3s. 6d.

THE ESSENTIALS OF PERSPECTIVE. With numerous Illustrations drawn by the Author. By L. W. MILLER, Principal of the School of Industrial Art of the Pennsylvania Museum, Philadelphia. This book is such a manual as has long been desired for the guidance of art students and for self-instruction. It contains as much information about the science of Perspective as the artist or draughtsman ever has occasion to make use of, except under the most unusual conditions. The point of view throughout is that of the artist rather than the merely scientific theory of the art. The instructions are clearly set forth, free from all unessential or merely theoretical discussion, and the principles are vividly enforced by a large number of attractive drawings by the author, which illustrate every phase of his teachings. *Price* 6s. 6d.

MIRROR PAINTING IN THE ITALIAN STYLE. A Practical Manual of Instruction for Amateurs. This highly decorative art has become very popular, but the execution is not always worthy of the design, in consequence of want of knowledge on the part of the artist; this book will supply the deficiency. By Mrs. SHARP-AYRES. *Price* 1s.

ALL ABOUT PAINTING ON CHINA. With Twelve Descriptive Lessons. The object of this little book is to teach, by easy, Progressive Lessons, all that a beginner requires to know about China Painting. By Mrs. CONYERS MORRELL. Second Edition. *In paper, price* 9d.

"Spared no pains to give useful information as to the various processes of decorative painting."—*Academy.*

DECORATIVE PAINTING. A Practical Handbook on Paint ing and Etching upon Textiles, Pottery, Porcelain, Paper, Vellum, Leather, Glass, Wood, Stone, Metals, and Plaster, for the Decoration of our Homes. By B. C. SAWARD. *In the new "Renaissance" binding, price* 7*s.* 6*d.*

"Practical, satisfactory in its treatment, and very interesting."—*The Queen.*

ARTISTIC AMUSEMENTS: Being Instructions in Colouring Photographs, Imitation Stained Glass, Decalcomanie, Queen Shell Work, Painting on China, Japanese Lacquer Work, Stencilling, Paint· ing Magic Lantern Slides, Menu and Guest Cards, Spatter Work, Picture and Scrap Screens, Frosted Silver Work, Picture Cleaning and Restoring, Illuminating, and Symbolical Colouring. Illustrated. *In cloth gilt, price* 2*s.* 6*d.*

A GUIDE TO ENGLISH PATTERN COINS in Gold, Silver, Copper, and Pewter, from Edward I. to Victoria, with their Value. By the REV. G. F. CROWTHER, M.A., Member of the Numismatic Society of London. Illustrated. *In silver cloth, with gilt facsimiles of Coins, price* 5*s.*

"Such a book as this has never before been placed within the reach of the ordinary collector. . . . . A model of careful and accurate work."—*The Queen.*

A GUIDE TO THE COINS OF GREAT BRITAIN AND IRELAND, in Gold, Silver, and Copper, from the Earliest Period to the Present Time, with their Value. By the late Colonel W. STEWART THORBURN. Of immense value to collectors and dealers. Plates in Gold, Silver, and Copper, and Gold and Silver Coins in raised facsimile. *In gold cloth, with silver facsimiles of Coins, price* 6*s.* 6*d.* _____ [*Re-issue in the Press.*

"The collector will find the work invaluable."—*Broad Arrow.*

ENGLISH POTTERY AND PORCELAIN. A Manual for Collectors : Being a Concise Account of the Development of the Potter's Art in England. Profusely Illustrated with Marks, Monograms, and Engravings of Characteristic Specimens. New Edition. *In cloth gilt, price* 3*s.* 6*d.*

BEES AND BIRDS.

"This is a very interesting book. . . . The illustrations are admirable."—*The Saturday Review.*

BEES AND BEE-KEEPING : Scientific and Practical. By F. R. CHESHIRE, F.L.S., F.R.M.S., Lecturer on Apiculture at South Kensington. Vol. I., SCIENTIFIC. A complete Treatise on the Anatomy and Physiology of the Hive Bee. *In cloth gilt, price* 7*s.* 6*d.* VOL. II., PRACTICAL MANAGEMENT OF BEES. *In Monthly Parts, price* 7*d.*

"We cannot too strongly advise all poultry-keepers to get a copy of this book, for it is the cheapest shilling's worth we have seen for a long time."—*Farm and Home.*

POULTRY AILMENTS AND THEIR TREATMENT. A Book for the Use of all Poultry-keepers, describing the Causes, Symptoms, and Cure of Diseases affecting Domestic Fowl. By D. J. THOMPSON GRAY. *In paper boards, price* 1s.

"We can recommend the books as admirably adapted for the purposes for which they are intended."—*The Field.*

EXHIBITION ACCOUNT BOOKS. For use at all Poultry, Pigeon, Rabbit, and Cage-Bird Shows. In Four Books, comprising : I. Minute Book ; II. Cash Book ; III. Entries Book ; IV. Ledger. With Full Directions and Illustrative Examples for Working them. N.B.—The Set of Four Books is kept in Three Series : No. 1, for Show of 500 Entries, 5s. the Set ; No. 2, for 1000 Entries, 7s. 6d. the Set ; and No. 3, for 1500 Entries, 12s. 6d. the Set. Larger sizes in proportion. The books can be had separate. MINUTE BOOK—No. 1, 1s. ; No. 2, 1s. 3d.; No. 3, 2s. CASH BOOK—No. 1, 2s.; No. 2, 2s. 6d.; No. 3, 4s. ENTRIES BOOK—No. 1, 2s.; No. 2, 2s. 6d. ; No. 3, 4s. LEDGER—No. 1, 2s.; No. 2, 2s. 6d.; No. 3, 4s.

"Every breeder should provide himself with this useful little record."—*Poultry.*

THE SITTING HEN RECORD. Forming a Convenient Record of all Eggs Set, and supplying in a handy and concise form Labels which can be readily attached to or above the Nest-boxes, showing at a glance the Number of Eggs under the Hen, the Variety, and when they should be brought off. *Price*—50 *Forms*, 6d.; 100 *Forms*, 1s.

FERTILITY OF EGGS CERTIFICATE. These are Forms of Guarantee given by the Sellers to the Buyers of Eggs for Hatching, undertaking to refund value of any unfertile eggs, or to replace them with good ones. *In books, with counterfoils, price* 1s.

"Should be in the hands of all breeders of poultry."—*The Stock-keeper.*

POULTRY FOR PRIZES AND PROFIT. Contains : Breeding Poultry for Prizes, Exhibition Poultry, and Management of the Poultry Yard. Handsomely Illustrated. New Edition, Revised and Enlarged. By Professor JAMES LONG. *In cloth gilt, price* 3s. 6d.

"A very desirable little work."—*The Queen.*

DUCKS AND GEESE : Their Characteristics, Points, and Management. The only book on the subject of Domestic Waterfowl and their Proper Treatment. By Various Breeders. Splendidly Illustrated. *In paper, price* 1s. 6d.

PRACTICAL HANDBOOKS.]　　　**[All Books sent Carriage Free.**

FOREIGN CAGE BIRDS. Containing Full Directions for Successfully Breeding, Rearing, and Managing the various Beautiful Cage Birds imported into this country. Beautifully Illustrated. By C. W. Gedney. *In cloth gilt, in two vols., price* 8s. 6d.; *in extra cloth gilt, gilt edges, in one vol., price* 9s. 6d.

Parrots, Parrakeets, Cockatoos, Lories, and Macaws: Their Varieties, Breeding, and Management. Illustrated. *(Forming Vol. I. of " Foreign Cage Birds.") In cloth gilt, price* 3s. 6d.

Waxbills, Finches, Weavers, Orioles, and other Small Foreign Aviary Birds: Their Varieties, Breeding, and Management. Beautifully Illustrated. *(Forming Vol. II. of " Foreign Cage Birds.") In cloth gilt, price* 5s.

CANARY BOOK. Containing Full Directions for the Breeding Rearing, and Management of all Varieties of Canaries and Canary Mules, the Promotion and Management of Canary Societies and Exhibitions, and all other matters connected with this Fancy. By Robert L. Wallace. Second Edition, Enlarged and Revised, with many new Illustrations of Prize Birds, Cages, &c. *In cloth gilt, price* 5s. May also be had in two Sections as follow:

General Management of Canaries. Including Cages and Cage-making, Breeding, Managing, Mule Breeding, Diseases and their Treatment, Moulting, Rats and Mice, &c. Illustrated. Second Edition, Revised and Greatly Enlarged. *(Forming Section I. of the " Canary Book.") In cloth, price* 2s. 6d.

Exhibition Canaries. Containing Full Particulars of all the different Varieties, their Points of Excellence, Preparing Birds for Exhibition, Formation and Management of Canary Societies and Exhibitions. Illustrated. Second Edition, Revised and Enlarged. *(Forming Section II. of the " Canary Book.") In cloth, price* 2s. 6d.

DISEASES OF CAGE BIRDS: Their Cause, Symptoms, and Treatment. A Handbook which should be in the hands of everyone who keeps a Bird, as successful Treatment of Ailments depends on knowing what to do, and *doing it promptly.* By Dr. W. T. Greene, F.Z.S. *In paper, price* 1s.

BRITISH CAGE BIRDS. Containing Full Directions for Successfully Breeding, Rearing, and Managing the various British Birds that can be kept in Confinement. Illustrated with COLOURED PLATES and numerous finely-cut Wood Engravings. By R. L. Wallace. *In cloth gilt, price* 10s. 6d.

"Here is all that can be desired; the directions how to feed and how to keep foreign birds in health are given by the greatest authority living."—*Public Opinion.*

THE SPEAKING PARROTS. A Scientific Manual on the Art of Keeping and Breeding the principal Talking Parrots in Confinement. By Dr. KARL RUSS, Author of " The Foreign Aviary Birds," "Manual for Bird Fanciers," &c. Illustrated with COLOURED PLATES. *In cloth gilt, price 6s. 6d.*

"Is worthy of a hearty welcome from all breeders and keepers of foreign birds." —*Live Stock Journal.*

AMATEUR'S AVIARY OF FOREIGN BIRDS; or, How to Keep and Breed Foreign Birds with Pleasure and Profit in England. Illustrated. By W. T. GREENE, M.D., M.A., F.Z.S., F.S.S., &c., Author of "Parrots in Captivity," &c. *In cloth gilt, price 3s. 6d.*

"A prettier present for anyone who is fond of these household pets it would be difficult to find."—*Stock-keeper.*

BIRDS I HAVE KEPT IN YEARS GONE BY: With Original Anecdotes, and Full Directions for Keeping them Successfully. By W. T. GREENE, M.A., M.D., F.Z.S., &c., Author of "Parrots in Captivity," "The Amateur's Aviary"; Editor of "Notes on Cage Birds," &c., &c. With COLOURED PLATES. *In cloth gilt, price 5s.*

"No fancier, in our judgment, should be without a copy of the work."—*The Stockkeeper.*

FANCY PIGEONS. Containing Full Directions for the Breeding and Management of Fancy Pigeons, and Descriptions of every known Variety, together with all other information of interest or use to Pigeon Fanciers. Third Edition, bringing the subject down to the present time. 18 COLOURED PLATES, and 22 other full-page Illustrations. By J. C. LYELL. *In cloth gilt, price* 10s. 6d.

AVIARY PHEASANTS FOR AMATEURS. A Practical Handbook on the Breeding, Rearing, and General Management of Fancy Pheasants in Confinement. By GEO. HORNE. Illustrated with Diagrams of the necessary Pens, Aviaries, &c., and a COLOURED FRONTISPIECE, and many full-page Engravings of the chief Varieties of Pheasants, drawn from life by A. F. LYDON. *Price 3s. 6d.*

GARDENING.

" This important undertaking."—*Daily Telegraph.*
" The most complete work of its kind."—*Daily News.*
" The fullest information is given, and the illustrations, which are exceedingly
numerous, are first rate."—*The World.*

DICTIONARY OF GARDENING. A Practical Encyclopædia of Horticulture, for Amateurs and Professionals. Illustrated with upwards of 2000 Engravings. Edited by G. NICHOLSON, Curator of the Royal Botanic Gardens, Kew ; assisted by Prof. Trail, M.D , Rev. P. W. Myles, M.A., B. W. Hemsley, A.L.S., W. Watson, J. Garrett, and other Specialists. Vol. I., A to E, 552pp., 743 Illustrations ; Vol. II., F to O, 544pp. and 811 Illustrations ; and Vol. III., P to S, 537pp. and 564 Illustrations. *Now ready, price* 15s. *each ; also in Monthly Parts, price* 1s.

" Lovers of these beautiful flowers will welcome this edition."—*Paper and
Printing Trades Journal.*

LILY OF THE VALLEY : All About It, and How to Grow It; Forced Indoors and Out of Doors, in Various Ways. By WILLIAM ROBERTS. *In paper covers, price* 6d.

" Ought to be in the hands of everybody."—*The Queen.*

GREENHOUSE MANAGEMENT FOR AMATEURS. Descriptions of the best Greenhouses and Frames, with Instructions for Building them, particulars of the various methods of Heating, Illustrated Descriptions of the most suitable Plants, with general and special Cultural Directions, and all necessary information for the Guidance of the Amateur. Second Edition, Revised and Enlarged. Magnificently Illustrated. By W. J. MAY. *In cloth gilt, price* 5s.

" Seems particularly useful."—*Athenæum.*

HARDY PERENNIALS AND OLD-FASHIONED GARDEN FLOWERS. Descriptions, alphabetically arranged, of the most desirable Plants for Borders, Rockeries, and Shrubberies, including Foliage as well as Flowering Plants. Profusely Illustrated. By J. WOOD. *In cloth, price* 5s.

" Full of practical remarks, tending to make it a reliable and useful guide to
amateur gardeners."—*The Farmer.*

ARBORICULTURE FOR AMATEURS : Being Instructions for the Planting and Cultivation of Trees for Ornament or Use, and Selections and Descriptions of those suited to Special Requirements as to Soil, Situation, &c. By WILLIAM H. ABLETT, Author of " English Trees and Tree Planting," &c. *In cloth gilt, price* 2s. 6d.

" It is just the sort of book one would refer to in emergency."—*The Florist and
Pomologist.*

GARDEN PESTS AND THEIR ERADICATION. Containing Practical Instructions for the Amateur to overcome the Enemies of the Garden. With numerous Illustrations. *In paper, price* 1s.

"The joint work of a competent botanist . . . . and a successful cultivator with the experience of a quarter of a century."—*Gardener's Chronicle.*

ORCHIDS FOR AMATEURS. Containing Descriptions of Orchids suited to the requirements of the Amateur, with full Instructions for their successful Cultivation. With numerous beautiful Illustrations. By JAMES BRITTEN, F.L.S., and W. H. GOWER. *In cloth gilt, price 7s. 6d.*

"One of the best and most trustworthy books on bulb culture that have been put before the public."—*Gardener's Chronicle.*

BULBS AND BULB CULTURE: Being Descriptions, both Historical and Botanical, of the principal Bulbs and Bulbous Plants grown in this Country, and their chief Varieties ; with Full and Practical Instructions for their Successful Cultivation both In and Out of Doors. Illustrated. By D. T. FISH. *In cloth gilt, in one vol., 465 pp., price 5s.*

"Full, practical, ... and contains many valuable hints."—*Garden.*

ROSE BUDDING. Containing Full Instructions for the Successful Performance of this interesting Operation. Illustrated. Amateurs will find the information here given of great assistance. By D. T. FISH. *In paper, price 6d.*

"One of the few gardening books that will suit everybody."—*Gardener's Magazine.*

PRUNING, GRAFTING, AND BUDDING FRUIT TREES. Illustrated with Ninety-three Diagrams. A book which can be followed with advantage by amateur fruit growers. By D. T. FISH. *In paper, price 1s.*

"Before entering on the cultivation of cucumbers, melons, marrows, or gourds, we would recommend to their perusal Mr. May's handbook."—*Dublin Evening Mail.*

CUCUMBER CULTURE FOR AMATEURS. Including also Melons, Vegetable Marrows, and Gourds. Illustrated. By W. J. MAY. *In paper, price 1s.*

"Plain and practical."—*The Queen.*

VINE CULTURE FOR AMATEURS : Being Plain Directions for the Successful Growing of Grapes with the Means and Appliances usually at the command of Amateurs. Illustrated. Grapes are so generally grown in villa greenhouses, that this book cannot fail to be of great service to many persons. By W. J. MAY. *In paper, price 1s.*

"None more simple and practically useful."—*The British Mail.*

VEGETABLE CULTURE FOR AMATEURS. Concise Directions for the Cultivation of Vegetables so as to insure Good Crops in Small Gardens, with Lists of the Best Varieties of each Sort. By W. J. MAY. *In paper, price 1s.*

"This excellent little book gives every direction necessary."—Daily Bristol Times and Mirror.

ⓂUSHROOM CULTURE FOR AMATEURS. With Full Directions for Successful Growth in Houses, Sheds, Cellars, and Pots, on Shelves, and Out of Doors. Illustrated. By W. J. May, Author of "Vine Culture for Amateurs," "Vegetable Culture for Amateurs," "Cucumber Culture for Amateurs." *In paper, price* 1s.

"Labour greatly assisted by a perusal of this work."—North British Agriculturist.

ⓅROFITABLE MARKET GARDENING. Adapted for the use of all Growers and Gardeners. By William Earley, Author of "High-class Kitchen Gardening," &c. *In cloth, price* 2s.

GENERAL LITERATURE.

"Is a complete storehouse of educational information."—The Graphic.

Ⓐ GUIDE TO DEGREES in Arts, Science, Literature, Law Music, and Divinity, in the United Kingdom, the Colonies, the Continent, and the United States. By E. Wooton, Author of "A Guide to the Medical Profession," &c. *In cloth, price* 15s.

"Anyone who, before entering on either branch of the profession, desires information to determine which branch it shall be, will find a great deal here that will assist him."—The Law Student's Journal.

Ⓐ GUIDE TO THE LEGAL PROFESSION. A Practical Treatise on the various Methods of Entering either Branch of the Legal Profession ; also a Course of Study for each of the Examinations, and selected Papers of Questions ; forming a Complete Guide to every Department of Legal Preparation. By J. H. Slater, Barrister-at-Law, of the Middle Temple. *Price* 7s. 6d.

"Is certain to be very much appreciated."—The Derby Mercury.

ⓈHORTHAND SYSTEMS; WHICH IS THE BEST? Being a Discussion, by various English Authors and Experts, on the Merits and Demerits of Taylor's, Gurney's, Pitman's, Everett's, Janes', Pocknell's, Peachey's, Guest's, Williams', Odell's, and Redfern's Systems, with Illustrative Examples. Edited by Thomas Anderson, Author of "History of Shorthand," &c. This is a book which ought to be carefully read by every person who is about to take up the study of shorthand. *In paper, price* 1s.

"An amusing little book."—Public Opinion.

ⒸHARACTER INDICATED BY HANDWRITING. With Illustrations in Support of the Theories advanced taken from Autograph Letters of Statesmen, Lawyers, Soldiers, Ecclesiastics, Authors, Poets, Musicians, Actors, and other persons. Second Edition, Revised and Enlarged. By R. Baughan. *In cloth gilt, price* 2s. 6d.

"A very practical and sensible little book."—*Spectator.*

PRACTICAL JOURNALISM: How to Enter Thereon and Succeed. A Manual for Beginners and Amateurs. A book for all who think of "writing for the Press." By JOHN DAWSON. *In cloth gilt, price* 2s. 6d.

"A most excellent and useful handbook."—*Public Opinion.*

THE LIBRARY MANUAL. A Guide to the Formation of a Library and the Valuation of Rare and Standard Books. By J. H. SLATER, Barrister-at-Law, Author of "A Guide to the Legal Profession." Second Edition. *In cloth*, 112pp., *price* 2s. 6d.

"A very entertaining and able little book."—*Literary World.*

LESSONS IN SHORTHAND, ON GURNEY'S SYSTEM (IM-PROVED): Being Instruction in the Art of Shorthand Writing as used in the Service of the two Houses of Parliament. By R. E. MILLER, of Dublin University; formerly Parliamentary Reporter; Fellow of the Shorthand Society. *In paper, price* 1s.

"Much valuable and practical information."—*Sylvia's Home Journal.*

CHURCH FESTIVAL DECORATIONS. Comprising Directions and Designs for the Suitable Decoration of Churches for Christmas, Easter, Whitsuntide, and Harvest. Illustrated. A useful book for the Clergy and their Lay Assistants. *In paper, price* 1s.

GUIDES TO PLACES.

"A capital guide to the angler, the yachtsman, or the artist."—*Scotsman.*

THE LAND OF THE BROADS. By E. R. SUFFLING. ILLUSTRATED EDITION.—The most Complete Guide to the whole of the District—embracing the Broads and their Waterways of Norfolk and Suffolk—that has yet been published, as it contains more practical and reliable information than is to be found elsewhere respecting Yachting, Fishing, Places of Interest, Archæological Remains, Natural Features of the Country, the Birds and Fishes found there, the Customs of the Natives, and other points concerning which Tourists desire to know. A good Map of the Broads, Rivers, Chief Roads, and Places named, *printed in four* colours, accompanies the work. *Price* 2s. 6d.

CHEAP EDITION.—A Cheap Edition of a reliable Guide to the Norfolk Broads, which would meet the requirements of the general Public, having been called for, the *First* Edition of the above Book has been issued in this form, but it has been embellished with some Plates of Characteristic Sketches taken on the spot by the well-known artist of Fishing and Waterside Subjects, Mr. J. TEMPLE. A good and *clear* Map, in black and white, is also given. In Illustrated Cover, printed in colours, *price* 1s.

Reliable and accurate ; . . . an admirable companion to tourists and cyclists."—*The Tourist and Traveller.*

⟨T⟩HE TOURIST'S ROUTE MAP OF ENGLAND AND WALES. Second Edition, thoroughly Revised. Shows clearly all the Main, and most of the Cross Roads, and the Distances between the Chief Towns, as well as the Mileage from London. In addition to this, Routes of *Thirty of the most Interesting Tours* are printed in red. The Map is mounted on linen, so as not to tear, and is inclosed in a strong cloth case ; it is thus in a convenient form for the pocket, and will not suffer from ordinary fair wear and tear, as is the case with most maps. This is, without doubt, the fullest, most accurate, handiest, and cheapest tourist's map in the market. *In cloth, price* 1s. 2d.

"The information it gives is of a decidedly practical and reliable nature."—*The Spectator.*

⟨S⟩EASIDE WATERING PLACES. A Description of 179 Holiday Resorts on the Coasts of England and Wales, the Channel Islands, and the Isle of Man, including the gayest and most quiet places, giving full particulars of them and their attractions, and all other information likely to assist persons in selecting places in which to spend their Holidays according to their individual tastes, with BUSINESS DIRECTORY OF TRADESMEN, arranged in order of the town. Fifth Edition, with Maps and Illustrations. *In cloth, price* 2s. 6d.

"We can confidently recommend this book."—*The Literary World.*

⟨T⟩OUR IN THE STATES AND CANADA. Out and Home in Six Weeks. By Thomas Greenwood. Illustrated. *In cloth gilt, price* 2s. 6d.

"One of the most useful handbooks to the River yet published."—*The Graphic.*

⟨T⟩HE UPPER THAMES: FROM RICHMOND TO OX-FORD. A Guide for Boating Men, Anglers, Picnic Parties, and all Pleasure-seekers on the River. Arranged on an entirely New Plan. Illustrated. *In paper, price* 1s.; *in cloth, with elastic band ana Pocket,* 2s.

"It is a model ' guide,' and supplies a want."—*The Field.*

⟨W⟩INTER HAVENS IN THE SUNNY SOUTH. A Complete Handbook to the Riviera, with a Notice of the New Station, Alassio. Splendidly Illustrated. By Rosa Baughan, Author of " The Northern Watering Places of France." *In cloth gilt, price* 2s. 6d.

"We have pleasure in recommending this work."—*Cook's Excursionist.*

⟨N⟩ORTHERN WATERING PLACES OF FRANCE. A Guide for English People to the Holiday Resorts on the Coasts of the French Netherlands, Picardy, Normandy, and Brittany. By Rosa Baughan, Author of " Winter Havens in the Sunny South," &c. *In paper, price* 2s.

HOUSEHOLD.

"This very complete and rather luxurious volume is a thorough encyclopædia artistic, plain, and fancy needlework. . . . After being submitted to the severe test of feminine criticism, the Dictionary emerges triumphant. . . . The volume as a whole deserves no small commendation."—*The Standard.*

"This volume, one of the handsomest of its kind, is illustrated in the best sense of the term. . . . It is useful and concise—in fact, it is exactly what it professes to be. . . . This book has endured the severest test at our command with rare success."—*The Athenæum.*

⊙HE DICTIONARY OF NEEDLEWORK. An Encyclopædia of Artistic, Plain, and Fancy Needlework; Plain, practical, complete, and magnificently Illustrated. By S. F. A. CAULFEILD and B. C. SAWARD. Accepted by H.M. the Queen, H.R.H. the Princess of Wales, H.R.H. the Duchess of Edinburgh, H.R.H. the Duchess of Connaught, and H.R.H. the Duchess of Albany. Dedicated by special permission to H.R.H. Princess Louise, Marchioness of Lorne. *In demy 4to, 528pp.,* 829 *illustrations, extra cloth gilt, plain edges, cushioned bevelled boards, price* 21*s.; with COLOURED PLATES, elegant satin brocade cloth binding and coloured edges,* 31*s.* 6*d,*

" We have seldom seen a book of this class better got up."—*Bell's Weekly Messenger.*

⊙ONITON LACE BOOK. Containing Full and Practical Instructions for Making Honiton Lace. With numerous Illustrations. *In cloth gilt, price* 3*s.* 6*d.*

" Will prove a valuable acquisition to the student of art needlework."—*The English-woman's Review.*

⊙RTISTIC FANCY WORK SERIES. A Series of Illustrated Manuals on Artistic and Popular Fancy Work of various kinds. Each number is complete in itself, and issued at the uniform *price* of 6*d.* Now ready—(1) MACRAMÉ LACE (Second Edition); (2) PATCHWORK; (3) TATTING; (4) CREWEL WORK ; (5) APPLIQUE.

" It cannot fail to be useful and appreciated."—*Weldon's Ladies' Journal.*

⊙HURCH EMBROIDERY : Its Early History and Manner of Working ; Materials Used and Stitches Employed ; Raised and Flat Couching, Appliqué, &c., &c., including Church Work over Cardboard. Illustrated. A practical handbook for Church Workers. *In paper, price* 1*s.*

" A copy ought to be in every nursery."—*Society.*

⊙ICK NURSING AT HOME : Being Plain Directions and Hints for the Proper Nursing of Sick Persons, and the Home Treatment of Diseases and Accidents in case of Sudden Emergencies. By S. F. A. CAULFEILD. *In paper, price* 1*s.* ; *in cloth, price* 1*s.* 6*d.*

"A most valuable guide."—*The Queen.*

PRACTICAL HINTS ON COFFEE STALL MANAGE-MENT, and other Temperance Work for the Laity. *In paper, price 1s.*

"Is admirably suited to its purpose."—*The Broad Arrow.*

COOKERY FOR AMATEURS; or, French Dishes for English Homes of all Classes. Includes Simple Cookery, Middle-class Cookery, Superior Cookery, Cookery for Invalids, and Breakfast and Luncheon Cookery. By Madame Valérie. Second Edition. *In paper, price 1s.*

"Is thoroughly healthy in tone, and practical."—*Saturday Review.*

INDIAN OUTFITS AND ESTABLISHMENTS. A Practical Guide for Persons about to Reside in India; detailing the Articles which should be taken out, and the Requirements of Home Life and Management there. By an Anglo-Indian. *In cloth, price 2s. 6d.*

MECHANICS.

"A handy manual for the study of an interesting and important art."—*The Graphic.*

BOOKBINDING FOR AMATEURS: Being Descriptions of the various Tools and Appliances Required, and Minute Instructions for their Effective Use. By W. J. E. Crane. Illustrated with 156 Engravings. *In cloth gilt, price 2s. 6d.*

"It is thoroughly practical, is well illustrated, and contains the information that beginners require."—*Saturday Review.*

REPOUSSÉ WORK FOR AMATEURS: Being the Art of Ornamenting Thin Metal with Raised Figures. By L. L. Haslope. Illustrated. *In cloth gilt, price 2s. 6d.*

"A capital manual. . . . All is clearly and concisely explained."—*The Graphic.*

PRACTICAL BOAT BUILDING FOR AMATEURS. Containing Full Instructions for Designing and Building Punts, Skiffs, Canoes, Sailing Boats, &c. Fully Illustrated with Working Diagrams. By Adrian Neison, C.E. New Edition, Revised and Enlarged, by Dixon Kemp, Author of "Yacht Designing," "A Manual of Yacht and Boat Sailing," &c. *In cloth gilt, price 2s. 6d.*

"The book is thoroughly exhaustive."—*The Building World.*

PICTURE FRAME MAKING FOR AMATEURS. Being Practical Instructions in the Making of various kinds of Frames for Paintings, Drawings, Photographs, and Engravings. Illustrated. By the Author of "Carpentry and Joinery," &c. Cheap Edition, *in paper, price 1s.*

" Concise and comprehensive."—The Figaro.

PRINTING FOR AMATEURS. A Practical Guide to the Art of Printing ; containing Descriptions of Presses and Materials, together with Details of the Processes Employed, to which is added a Glossary of Technical Terms. Illustrated. By P. E. RAYNOR. *In paper, price* 1s.

" Will be found of great interest."—Illustrated Carpenter and Builder.

WOOD CARVING FOR AMATEURS. Containing Descriptions of all the requisite Tools, and Full Instructions for their Use in producing different varieties of Carvings. Illustrated. A book of very complete instructions for the amateur wood carver. *In paper, price* 1s.

" The best of the book consists of practical instructions."—Iron.

CARPENTRY AND JOINERY FOR AMATEURS. Contains Full Descriptions of the various Tools Required in the above Arts, together with Practical Instructions for their Use. By the Author of " Turning for Amateurs," &c. *In cloth gilt, price* 2s. 6d.

" We can safely commend the volume."—The Graphic.

MODEL YACHTS AND BOATS : Their Designing, Making, and Sailing. Illustrated with 118 Designs and Working Diagrams. A splendid book for boys and others interested in making and rigging toy boats for sailing. It is the best book on the subject now published. By J. DU V. GROSVENOR. *In leatherette, price* 5s.

" Every possible information is given."—The Reliquary.

WORKING IN SHEET METAL : Being Practical Instructions for Making and Mending Small Articles in Tin, Copper, Iron, Zinc, and Brass. Illustrated. Third Edition. By the Author of " Turning for Amateurs," &c. *In paper, price* 6d.

" Gives the amateur copious descriptions of tools and methods of working."—The Builder.

TURNING FOR AMATEURS : Being Descriptions of the Lathe and its Attachments and Tools, with Minute Instructions for their Effective Use on Wood, Metal, Ivory, and other Materials. New Edition, Revised and Enlarged. By JAMES LUKIN, B.A., Author of " The Lathe and its Uses," &c. Illustrated with 144 Engravings. *In cloth gilt, price* 2s. 6d.

" A capital book for boys."—Dispatch.

TOYMAKING FOR AMATEURS. Containing Instructions for the Home Construction of Simple Wooden Toys, and of others that are Moved or Driven by Weights, Clockwork, Steam, Electricity, &c. Illustrated. By JAMES LUKIN, B.A., Author of " Turning for Amateurs," &c. *In cloth gilt, price* 4s.

"A very useful little book."—*Sylvia's Home Journal.*

TUNING AND REPAIRING PIANOFORTES. The Amateur's Guide to the Practical Management of a Piano without the intervention of a Professional. By CHARLES BABBINGTON. *In paper, price 6d.*

"A valuable handbook for ready reference."—*Journal of Forestry.*

PRACTICAL ARCHITECTURE. As applied to Farm Buildings of every description (Cow, Cattle, and Calf Houses, Stables, Piggeries, Sheep Shelter Sheds, Root and other Stores, Poultry Houses), Dairies, and Country Houses and Cottages. Profusely Illustrated with Diagrams and Plans. By ROBERT SCOTT BURN. *In cloth gilt, price 5s.*

NATURAL HISTORY.

"Throughout the volume is essentially practical."—*Daily Telegraph.*

PRACTICAL TAXIDERMY. A Manual of Instruction to the Amateur in Collecting, Preserving, and Setting-up Natural History Specimens of all kinds. Fully Illustrated with Engravings of Tools, Examples, and Working Diagrams. By MONTAGU BROWNE, F.Z.S., Curator of Leicester Museum. New and Enlarged Edition. *In cloth gill, price 7s. 6d.*

From PROFESSOR RUSKIN.—"I have just opened your proofs, and am entirely delighted by the glance at them. . . . The engraving of the cobra—Mr. Babbage's—is the only true drawing of it I ever saw."

ZOOLOGICAL NOTES on the Structure, Affinities, Habits, and Faculties of Snakes, Marsupials, and Birds ; with Adventures among, and Anecdotes of, them. By ARTHUR NICOLS, F.G.S., F.R.G.S., Author of "Natural History Sketches." *In walnut or sycamore, 8vo, price 7s. 6d.*

"This little volume is full of interest."—*Nature.*

NATURAL HISTORY SKETCHES AMONG THE CARNIVORA—Wild and Domesticated ; with Observations on their Habits and Mental Faculties. By ARTHUR NICOLS, F.G.S., F.R.G.S., Author of "Zoological Notes," "The Puzzle of Life." Illustrated by J. T. NETTLESHIP, C. E. BRITTAN, and T. W. WOOD. *In cloth gilt, price 5s.*

"One of the handiest little helps yet published."—*Excelsior.*

COLLECTING BUTTERFLIES AND MOTHS : Being Directions for Capturing, Killing, and Preserving Lepidoptera and their Larvæ. Illustrated. Reprinted, with Additions, from "Practical Taxidermy." By MONTAGU BROWNE, Author of "Practical Taxidermy." *In paper, price 1s.*

SPORTS AND PASTIMES.

"It is by a thoroughly practical angler. . . . Will form a valuable addition to the angler's library."—*Fishing Gazette.*

PRACTICAL FISHERMAN. Dealing with the Natural History, the Legendary Lore, the Capture of British Freshwater Fish, and Tackle and Tackle Making. Beautifully Illustrated. By J. H. KEENE. *In cloth gilt, gilt edges, price* 10s. 6d.

"An ingenious method . . . and the instructions are brief and clear."—*The Queen.*

SKATING CARDS. A Series of Cards, of convenient size for *Use on the Ice*, containing Clear Instructions and Diagrams for Learning the whole Art of Figure Skating. One of the cards, containing the figure to be learnt, is held in the hand whilst skating, so that the directions are read and acted on simultaneously. *Tinted cards, gilt edges, round corners, inclosed in strong leather pocket book, price* 3s. 6d.*; or in extra calf, satin lined (for presentation), price* 5s. 6d.

"Cleverly written and illustrated."—*Sportsman.*

PRACTICAL TRAPPING: Being some Papers on Traps and Trapping for Vermin, with a Chapter on General Bird Trapping and Snaring. By W. CARNEGIE. *In paper, price* 1s.

"A capital manual. . . . All is clearly and concisely explained."—*The Graphic.*

PRACTICAL BOAT BUILDING AND SAILING. Containing Full Instructions for Designing and Building Punts, Skiffs, Canoes, Sailing Boats, &c. Particulars of the most Suitable Sailing Boats and Yachts for Amateurs, and Instructions for their Proper Handling. Fully Illustrated with Designs and Working Diagrams. By ADRIAN NEISON, C.E., DIXON KEMP, A.I.N.A., and G. CHRISTOPHER DAVIES. *In one vol., cloth gilt, price* 7s. 6d.

"We know of n better companion for the young Yachtsman."—*Sporting Chronicle.*

BOAT SAILING FOR AMATEURS. Containing Particulars of the most Suitable Sailing Boats and Yachts for Amateurs, and Instructions for their Proper Handling, &c. Illustrated with Numerous Diagrams. By G. CHRISTOPHER DAVIES. Second Edition, Revised and Enlarged, and with several New Plans of Yachts. *In cloth gilt, price* 5s.

"Mr. Carnegie gives a great variety of useful information as to game and game preserving. . . . We are glad to repeat that the volume contains much useful information, with many valuable suggestions. . . . . The instructions as ;to pheasant rearing are sound, and nearly exhaustive."—*The Times.*

"It is practical, straightforward, and always lucid. The chapters on poaching and poachers, both human and animal, are particularly to the point, and amusing withal."—*The World.*

PRACTICAL GAME PRESERVING. Containing the fullest Directions for Rearing and Preserving both Winged and Ground Game, and Destroying Vermin ; with other Information of Value to the Game Preserver. Illustrated. By WILLIAM CARNEGIE. *In cloth gilt, demy 8vo, price* 21s.

"A thoroughly practical as well as a very interesting book."—*The Graphic.*

NOTES ON GAME AND GAME SHOOTING. Miscellaneous Observations on Birds and Animals, and on the Sport they afford for the Gun in Great Britain, including Grouse, Partridges, Pheasants, Hares, Rabbits, Quails, Woodcocks, Snipe, and Rooks. By J. J. MANLEY, M.A., Author of "Notes on Fish and Fishing." Illustrated. *In cloth gilt,* 400*pp., price* 7*s.* 6*d.*

"It is as comprehensive as could be desired. . . . We can readily testify to the strict impartiality of the author."—*The Field.*

BICYCLES AND TRICYCLES OF THE YEAR. Descriptions of the New Inventions and Improvements for the Present Season. Designed to assist intending purchasers in the choice of a machine. Illustrated. By HARRY HEWITT GRIFFIN. (Published Annually.) *In paper, price* 1*s.*

"No one interested in conjuring should be without this work."—*Saturday Review.*

SLEIGHT OF HAND. A Practical Manual of Legerdemain for Amateurs and Others. New Edition, Revised and Enlarged. Profusely Illustrated. By EDWIN SACHS. *In cloth gilt, price* 6*s.* 6*d.*

"Most amusing. . . . A better book cannot be purchased."—*Ladies' Journal.*

BAZAARS AND FANCY FAIRS: A Guide to their Organisation and Management, with Details of Various Devices for Extracting Money from the Visitors. *In paper, price* 1*s.*

"Alike valuable to the beginner and the practised photographer."—*Photographic News.*

PRACTICAL PHOTOGRAPHY: Being the Science and Art of Photography, both Wet Collodion and the various Dry Plate Processes. Developed for Amateurs and Beginners. Illustrated. By O. E. WHEELER. *In cloth gilt, price* 4*s.*

"We can heartily commend these six plays."—*Ladies' Journal.*

SIX PLAYS FOR CHILDREN. Written specially for Representation by Children, and Designed to Interest both Actors and Audience. With Instructions for Impromptu Scenery, Costumes, and Effects, and the Airs of the Various Songs. By CHAS. HARRISON, Author of "Amateur Theatricals and Tableaux Vivants." *Price* 1*s.*

"Will be found invaluable."—*Court Journal.*

THEATRICALS AND TABLEAUX VIVANTS FOR AMATEURS. Giving Full Directions as to Stage Arrangements, "Making-up," Costumes, and Acting. With Numerous Illustrations. By CHAS. HARRISON. *In cloth gilt, price* 2*s.* 6*d.*

BOOKS ✛ IN ✛ THE ✛ PRESS.

ANGLING IN SALT WATER. A Book for all Visitors to the
Seaside, showing how to catch Sea Fish from Piers, Jetties, Rocks, and Boats, so
as to obtain true sport. By the use of proper Tackle and Baits, Angling in Salt Water
may be made to yield as much sport as Angling in Fresh Water, which, it must be
admitted, is a very decided advance upon the usual methods. "ANGLING IN SALT
WATER" is written by a thoroughly practical Angler, and is well Illustrated with
Engravings of Tackle, Methods of Fishing, &c. *Price 1s.*

FRUIT CULTURE FOR AMATEURS. A Practical Handbook on
Selecting and Successfully Growing the Best Varieties of our Hardy Fruits, in-
cluding the Apple, Apricot, Cherry, Chestnut, Currant, Fig, Filbert, Gooseberry, Medlar,
Mulberry, Nectarine, Peach, Pear, Plum, Quince, Raspberry, Strawberry, Walnut.
Illustrated. By JOHN GARRETT. *Price 1s.*

HORSE-KEEPING FOR AMATEURS. A Practical Manual on
the Management of Horses, for the guidance of those who keep from one to six
for their personal use. By FOX RUSSELL. *Price 1s.*

THE ST. BERNARD (No. II. of Monographs on British Dogs),
with Coloured Frontispiece and a full-page Engraving. The most complete treatise
on this noble Dog that has yet been published. By HUGH DALZIEL. *Price 3s. 6d.*

ROSES FOR AMATEURS. A Practical Guide to the Selection
and Cultivation of the best Roses, both for exhibition or mere pleasure, by that
large section of the Gardening World, the amateur lover of Roses. Illustrated. By the
Rev. J. HONEYWOOD D'OMBRAIN, Hon. Sec. of the National Rose Society. *Price 1s.*

OLD VIOLIN MASTERS AND THEIR MUSIC, with Examples
and Illustrations. By J. M. FLEMING, Author of "Old Violins and their Makers,"
"The Practical Violin School," and "Easy Legato Studies for the Violin," with which
latter works the present one will be uniform in size and style. *In Monthly Parts, price 7d.*

A CLEAR COMPLEXION.

PIMPLES, Black Specks, Sunburn, Freckles, and unsightly Blotches on the
Face, Neck, Arms, and Hands, can be instantly removed by using Mrs. JAMES'S
HERBAL OINTMENT, made from herbs only, and warranted harmless. It imparts such
a lovely clearness to the skin that astonishes everyone. Of all chemists, 1s. 1½d. A box
(with directions) sent free from observation, post free, on receipt of 15 stamps to—

Mrs. A. JAMES, 268, Caledonian Road, London, N.

LUXURIANT HAIR.

LONG, FLOWING EYELASHES, EYEBROWS, &c., are QUICKLY
PRODUCED by using JAMES'S HERBAL POMADE. It is invaluable for the production of Whiskers, Beards, and Moustachios; it causes the hair to grow on bald places
and scanty partings. Of most chemists, 1s.; or a box of it sent free from observation, post
free, for 15 stamps.

Mrs. A. JAMES, 268, Caledonian Road, London, N.

HAIR DESTROYER.

JAMES'S DEPILATORY Instantly Removes Superfluous Hairs from the
Face, Neck, or Arms, without Injury to the Skin. Of most chemists, 1s.; or sent
with direct ons for use, free from observation, post free, for 15 stamps.

Mrs. A. JAMES, 268, Caledonian Road, London, N.

A Few Recipes for Household Use.

TO MAKE A RICH PLUM CAKE.—Take half-a-pound of butter and half-a-pound of white sifted sugar, beat these with the hand well together to a cream; add four eggs, one at a time, and well beat each one with the butter and sugar; lightly mix in one pound of flour, previously mixed with one teaspoonful of BORWICK'S GOLD MEDAL BAKING POWDER, then lightly mix with the whole half-a-pound of sultanas; bake at once thoroughly, in a quick oven.

TO MAKE A FULL GOOD PLAIN CAKE.—Mix well together one pound of flour, two teaspoonfuls of BORWICK'S GOLD MEDAL BAKING POWDER, a little salt and spice, and a quarter-of-a-pound of sugar; rub in a quarter-of-a-pound of butter, add six ounces of sultanas, two ounces of currants, and one ounce of candied peel; moisten the whole with two eggs, and half-a-teacupful of milk previously beaten together; bake in a quick oven very thoroughly.

BORWICK'S BAKING POWDER

If BORWICK'S is not the best in the world, why has it gained 5 gold medals,

Any housewife will answer: Because it makes the best bread, the lightest pastry, and most tempting cakes and puddings. Tell your grocer you must have BORWICK'S.

TO MAKE BREAD.—To every pound of flour add a *heaped-up teaspoonful* of BORWICK'S GOLD MEDAL BAKING POWDER, with a little salt, and *thoroughly mix* while in a dry state, then pour on gradually about half-a-pint of *cold* water, or milk and water, mixing quickly but thoroughly into a dough of the usual consistence, taking care not to knead it more than is necessary to mix it perfectly; make it into *small* loaves, which must be *immediately* put into a *quick* oven.

PUFF PASTE.—Mix one pound of flour with a teaspoonful of BORWICK'S GOLD MEDAL BAKING POWDER, then cut half-a-pound of butter into slices, roll it in thin sheets on some of your flour, wet up the rest with about a quarter-of-a-pint of water, see that it is about as stiff as your butter, roll it to a thin sheet, cover it with your sheets of butter, double it in a three double; do the same five times; it is then fit for use, or it may stand an hour covered over to keep the air from it.

Tell your Grocers you <u>must</u> have BORWICK'S.

ROWLANDS' TOILET ARTICLES

Have been known for nearly 100 years to be the best which can be obtained : the best articles are, in the long run, always the cheapest.

ROWLANDS' MACASSAR OIL

Is the best and safest preserver and beautifier of the hair, and has a most delicate and fragrant bouquet. It contains no lead or mineral ingredients, and can also be had in

A GOLDEN COLOUR

for fair and golden-haired children, and people whose hair has become grey. Sizes : 3/6, 7/- ; 10/6, equal to four small.

ROWLANDS' KALYDOR

Is a most soothing emollient and refreshing preparation for the face, hands, and arms. It removes all freckles, tan, sunburn, sting of insects, prickly heat, chaps, redness, irritation and roughness of the skin, &c., produces a beautiful and delicate complexion, and renders the

SKIN SOFT, FAIR,

and delicate ; it is warranted free from any greasy or metallic ingredients. Sizes : 4/6 and 8/6. *Half-sized bottles at 2/3.*

ROWLANDS' ODONTO

Is the best, purest, and most fragrant Tooth Powder; it prevents and arrests decay, strengthens the gums, gives a pleasing fragrance to the breath, and renders the

TEETH WHITE AND SOUND.

ROWLANDS' EUKONIA

Is a pure and delicate toilet powder, free from any bismuth or metallic ingredients. Sold in three tints, white, rose, and cream, 2/6 per box. Ask for

ROWLANDS' ARTICLES,

of 20, HATTON GARDEN, LONDON, and avoid cheap, spurious imitations, under the same or similar names.

Why many Persons Permanently Submit

to the vexatious and unsightly appearance

" For every defect of Nature of *Art offers a remedy."*

GREY HAIR

Rather than attempt to Restore it.

1st.—Because the old fashioned and objectionable Hair Dyes dry up and spoil the Hair.
2nd.—Because the majority of "Hair Restorers" bring the users into ridicule by producing only a sickly yellow tint or dirty greenish stain, instead of a proper colour.
The following Testimonials (of many hundreds received) declare the value of

LATREILLE'S HYPERION HAIR RESTORER

As positively restoring grey or white hair to the REALLY NATURAL colour, gloss, softness, luxuriance, and beauty of youth; it so perfectly accomplishes its work and fulfils its promise, that in brilliant sunshine, or under glaring gaslight, the user can alike defy detection in ever having been grey, or used a remedy, while as a nourisher and strengthener of weak hair it has no equal.

Price 3s. 6d., sent in return for Postal Order or Stamps, by the Proprietors,
Latreille & Co., Kennington, London (*Established 25 years at Walworth*), or may be had of Chemists ;
But it is strongly advised that anything else, offered from interested motives, be resolutely refused, as Latreille's Hyperion NEVER DISAPPOINTS. All Chemists can readily procure through wholesale houses, if they have it not themselves in stock.

SPECIMEN TESTIMONIALS.

20, Royal George-street, Stockport,
February 26, 1880.
DEAR SIR,—My hair went white through trouble and sickness, but one bottle of your Hyperion Hair Restorer brought it back to a splendid brown, as nice as it was in my young days. I am now forty years old, and all my friends wonder to see me restored from white to brown. You can make what use you like of this. Yours truly,
(Mrs.) MARIA WORTHINGTON.

132, High-street, Stourbridge, May 16, 1878.
SIR,—I find your Hyperion Hair Restorer is a first-class and really genuine article, and is well worth the money. After using it thrice, my hair began to turn the natural colour, whereas before it was quite grey; it also keeps the hair from falling off, and I shall always recommend it to everyone I know. You are at liberty to publish this if you choose. Yours truly, (Mrs.) M. DAVIS.

Thirsk, Yorks, January 26, 1876.
DEAR SIR,—I use your Hyperion Hair Restorer, and find it everything which has been said in its favour. I am, dear Sir, yours truly, T. COATES.

Porchester, near Fareham, Hants, Oct. 16, 1875.
SIR,—Please send me another bottle of your Hyperion Hair Restorer; it is better than any other restorer I have tried. Yours faithfully,
(Mrs.) C. CHRISTIE.

High-street, Corsham, Wilts,
December 2, 1874.
DEAR SIR,—I enclose stamps for another bottle of your Hyperion Hair Restorer; its clean qualities are sufficient to recommend it anywhere.
Yours respectfully, E. MAYNARD.

St. Heliers, Jersey,
August 1, 1873.
SIR,—Please send me another bottle of your Hyperion Hair Restorer; I bear willing testimony to its being very pleasant to use, both as to cleanliness and absence of disagreeable smell.
Yours truly, F. DE LUSIGNAN.

2, Fir-street, Sydenham,
July 15, 1873.
DEAR SIR,—I am most happy to tell you that I have reason to commend your excellent Hyperion Hair Restorer, as it has already turned the grey hair of a person fifty-seven years old to its natural colour. Yours respectfully,
T. WHATMORE.

83, Dewsbury-road, Leeds,
May 23, 1873.
DEAR SIR,—I want half-a-dozen more bottles of your Hyperion Hair Restorer, some for friends and the remainder for myself ; it is the best restorer of grey hair to its natural colour.
Yours truly, JAMES DAWSON.

。 Be careful to ask for Latreille's Hyperion Hair Restorer, as the manufacturer is also proprietor of Latreille's Excelsior Lotion, which is a separate preparation, of universal repute for 25 years past, as a Producer of Hair.

✠ THE ✠ BOOKS ✠

Mentioned in this Catalogue are kept in stock by the following leading Booksellers:—

Aberdeen, Wyllie and Son.

Barnstaple, H. A. Foyster, 90, High Street.
Bath, W. Gregory and Son, 1, Wood Street.
Belfast, Wm. Mullan and Son.
Birmingham, Midland Educational Co.
Blackburn, R. Denham, King William Street.
Bolton, G. Winterburn.
Bournemouth, F. J. Bright, 10 and 11, Arcade.
Bradford, Matthews and Brooke, Sun Buildings.
Bridgwater, Whitby and Son.
Brighton, Treacher Bros., North Street.
Bristol, W. D. Buckle, 7, Corn Street.
Burnley, J. and A. Lupton.
Bury, W. Wardleworth.

Cambridge, H. W. Wallis.
Cardiff, Scholastic Trading Co.
Carlisle, A. D. Moss, English Street.
Cheltenham, W. Norton, Clarence Street.
Chester, Minshull and Meeson.
Chichester, W. H. Barrett, The Cross.
Cirencester, Bailey and Son.
Clacton-on-Sea, Nunn and Ubsdell, 1, Pier Avenue.
Clevedon, E. J. Wareham.
Coventry, W. W. Curtice and Co., Corn Exchange.
Croydon, Roffey and Clark.

Derby, Bemrose and Son, Irongate.
Devonport, J. Clark.
Dublin, C. Combridge, Grafton Street.

Edinburgh, Douglas and Foulis, 9, Castle Street.
Exeter, H. S. Eland, High Street.

Glasgow, W. and R. Holmes, Dunlop Street.
Great Yarmouth, A. and W. Huke, 12 and 14, Market Row.

Halifax, J. Crossley, 19, Union Street.
Hereford, Jakeman and Carver, High Street.
Hertford, Simpson and Son.
Hinckley, W. Pickering.

Hull, A. Brown and Sons.

Kingston-on-Thames, Phillipson.

Leeds, Walker and Laycock, 37, Brigate.
Leicester, Midland Educational Co., Market Street.
Liverpool, Hales and Freeman, 13, Moorfields.
Llandudno, W. Wardleworth.
Llanelly, W. Davies, Market Street.
Loughborough, H. Wills, 4, Market Place.

Manchester, J. Heywood, Deansgate.
Melton Mowbray, W. Loxley.

Newcastle-on-Tyne, R. J. Porteus and Co., 19, Grainger Street West.
Norwich, Jarrold and Son.
Nottingham, R. Denham, Wheelergate.

Oldham, W. Wardleworth.
Oxford, Slatter and Rose.

Peterborough, W. H. Pentney, 9, Narrow Street.
Plymouth, Doidge.
Portsea, Mr. Gardner.
Portsmouth, Mr. Long.

Reading, A. Farrer and Co., 39, Broad Street.
Rugby, Over.

Scarborough, E. T. W. Dennis.
Sheffield, T. T. Widdison.
Southport, W. Wardleworth.
Spilsby, T. A. Bellamy.
Sunderland, Hills and Co.
Swansea, E. and J. Griffiths.

Taunton, Barnicott and Son.
Torquay, A. Iredale, Cary Place, Fleet Street.
Trowbridge, G. W. Rose, Church Street.

Warwick, Cooke and Son.
Worcester, Deighton and Co., High Street.

York, North of England Trading Co.

✦ RULES FOR ADVERTISING ✦

In "THE BAZAAR."

1. **Charges.**—(*a*) Fourpence for twelve words or less, and one penny for every additional three words, to be sent with the advertisement. Advertisements may be paid for by Stamps, Postal Notes, Money Orders, Cash, or Cheques, as may be most convenient.

    (*b*) A single figure or letter, or a group of figures, undivided by letter, space, stop, or word, counts as one word; compound words count as two words. The name and address, whether published or not, are charged for; but a private number at our office, in place of a published address, may be had FREE OF CHARGE. If a private number be used, the advertiser should give the name of his post town or county, which also will be inserted FREE.

    (*c*) When two or more advertisements are sent at one time, each must be on a separate piece of paper, not smaller than a post card, written on one side only, and the words counted and paid for apart from each other.

    (*d*) *An Advertisement may be Booked for a Monday's, Wednesday's, or Friday's issue, or for a specified date, on payment of a fee of 1d.* Advertisements so Booked must be marked separately in the bottom *right-hand* corner, thus: "Book, Wed., 1d."

2. **Classification.**—Only one *class* of article may be offered in each advertisement, except in the "Unclassified" column.

3. **Dress.**—Articles of dress (with the exception of furs, feathers, artificial flowers, Indian shawls and scarves, lace, naval and military uniforms, and ecclesiastical or academical vestments and hoods) MUST BE NEW, *i.e.*, *never worn beyond the trial occasion*, and specified as such IN the advertisement.

4. **Prohibitions.**—Advertisements of copied music, prescriptions, recipes, loans, false hair, worn wearing apparel (with the above-mentioned exceptions) cannot be inserted. Tobacco and wines may *not* be sold without a licence, but may be exchanged for specified articles.

5. **Stamp for Reply.**—The request for a "stamp for reply," or "first P.O.O.," will not be permitted in any advertisement, unless the advertiser be on the Reference Book.

6. **Identity.**—The advertiser's full name and private address must be at all times given for the Editor's use, even though it is not to be published.

*"THE BAZAAR" may be obtained through all Newsagents, **price 2d.**; but Readers who cannot easily and punctually obtain it should send us the following*

SUBSCRIPTION ORDER.

Please send "**THE BAZAAR**" *every** ....

for † ....*months, commencing from*

.................................*for which I enclose§* ....

Date.................... *Name*..

                            Address..

NOTE.—Terms of Subscription.

	3 Months.	6 Months.	12 Months.
1 issue weekly	2s. 8d.	5s. 4d.	10s. 8d.
2 issues weekly	5s. 4d.	10s. 8d.	21s. 4d.
3 "	8s. 0d.	16s. 0d.	32s. 0d.

P.O.O.'s, money orders, or cheques should be payable to L. Upcott Gill, and crossed "London and Westminster Bank" for security. Stamps can be sent for small sums.

NOTE.—Arrangement.

Each issue is so arranged as to be independent of the others, *e.g.*, serial articles commenced in a Monday's paper are continued in Monday issues only, and so on, with queries, &c. Editorial replies and advertisements are inserted in any issue desired by the subscriber. Thus a subscriber can take which issue is most convenient without losing touch of the subjects that are interesting him.

* *State days required, e.g., Monday, Wednesday, or Friday.* † *State 3, 6, or 12 Months.* *State amount and how sent, whether by P.O.O., or Cheque, &c.*

OFFICE:—170, STRAND, LONDON, W.C.

www.ingramcontent.com/pod-product-compliance
Lightning Source LLC
Chambersburg PA
CBHW030859270326
41929CB00008B/495